Indian Ethos in Shobhaa De's Works

Indian Ethos in Shobhaa De's Works

Shashi Kant Gupta

ATLANTIC
PUBLISHERS & DISTRIBUTORS (P) LTD

Published by
ATLANTIC
PUBLISHERS & DISTRIBUTORS (P) LTD
7/22, Ansari Road, Darya Ganj,
New Delhi-110002
Phones : +91-11-40775252, 23273880, 23275880, 23280451
Fax : +91-11-23285873
Web : www.atlanticbooks.com
E-mail : orders@atlanticbooks.com

Branch Office
5, Nallathambi Street, Wallajah Road,
Chennai-600002
Phones : +91-44-64611085, 32413319
E-mail : chennai@atlanticbooks.com

ISBN 978-81-269-1374-9

Printed in India at Nice Printing Press, A-33/3A, Site-IV, Industrial Area, Sahibabad, Ghaziabad, U.P.

ACKNOWLEDGEMENTS

I express my deep regards to my only and the most venerable Lord, Lord Shiva whose blessings helped me in completing my work. Therefore, I consider him as my eternal *Guru* and to salute Him, I would like to take the help of this couplet:

Itawe jagatmew sansaraarnav setwave

Prabhave sarv vidhyanamum sambhawe guruwe namah:

(Salutation to Shri Guru, who with the collyrium stick of knowledge, opens the eyes of one who is blinded by the darkness of ignorance).

I am highly indebted to my parents (Dr. Kedar Nath Ram Gupta and Smt. Kaushilya Devi), my younger brother Mithlesh Kumar Gupta, and wife Sunita Gupta, whose unstinted support and perennial encouragement stood me in good stead and made every task a pleasure, to practically materialize this book, eventually. I do not have words to express my feelings of gratitude for them. Prof. Bihari Lal Tripathi played a crucial role of torchbearer to impart valuable and virtuous knowledge on me. I am sincerely thankful to him.

I would like to put on record my sincere thanks to Shri Ram Bhusan Singh (a scholar of ten subjects and younger brother of profound Gandhian Acharya Sri Ram Murti Singh who is working for social emancipation at Vaishali, Bihar), who with his long experience and mature wisdom was ever a source of encouragement and helped me at every stage of writing this book.

I am indebted to Prof. O.P. Mathur, Prof. M.K. Chaudhary, Prof. A.K. Triapthi, Prof. N.K. Lal, Prof. R.K. Shukla, Prof. S.N. Pandey, Dr. H. Swarup, Prof. Sushila Singh for their invaluable scholarly help. I am thankful to Prof. C.B. Dwivedi for his words of encouragement and good wishes. I am also highly obliged to Emeritus Prof. N.K. Oberoi of Panjab University, Prof. Nirupa Rani of Andhra University and Late Prof. R.S. Pathak of Sagar University, who readily assisted me whenever I needed their help.

I am thankful to the staff of Jawahar Lal Nehru University Library and Delhi University Library for their help and cooperation. Thanks are also due to the non-teaching members of the Department of English, B.H.U., for their cooperation and small helps that kept things moving.

I put on record my gratitude to Prof. Prabhat Kumar Pandey (Head, Department of English, B.H.U.) for giving me citations and helping me selflessly by lending me his books and extending every kind of support. I have no words to express my feelings.

Last but not least, I express my sincere gratitude and debt to Atlantic Publishers and Distributors (P) Ltd, New Delhi for seeing this book through the press. There are many others to whom I owe a lot, but I am unable to acknowledge my gratitude to them individually. My sincere thanks to all those who have helped me directly or indirectly in completing the book.

Finally, my entire work is dedicated to my parents, without whose blessings, I myself am nothing.

Shashi Kant Gupta, Ph.D.
drshashikantgpt@gmail.com
guptakantshashi@yahoo.co.in

PREFACE

The general impression and critical opinion about Shobhaa De's fiction is that it is soft porno and she has been given epithets like 'Porn queen', 'Pulp Pasha', 'Vatsyayani', etc. It is true that she writes about sexuality and her fiction contains almost every variety of sexual behaviour—heterosexuality, homosexuality, incest, and lesbianism, but she is more than this. She is generally described as a feminist, which she clearly denies. She rejects this label. She does not want to be confined to the gender. Then what is she? She prefers to call herself a humanist. It is but natural that she can be taken as feminist, for she is a woman who writes about women. This book aims at the thematic study of her novels, so as to bring out the human values that underlie her each novel. The study will show that despite apparent glossy life of permissive high society, the novels in the end project traditional Indian values emphasising the importance of the family and marital fidelity. Permissiveness and various kinds of sexual behaviour are simply deviations, which are not approved of by the novelist. Her views in this regard are found in her non-fiction writings and interviews.

The book makes an in-depth thematic study of her novels. Her non-fiction writings are referred to in order to illustrate her views on the themes of her novels. The book is divided into eight chapters.

The first chapter is Introduction, which describes Shobhaa De's life in brief, her literary career, critical opinions about her, her own views on her writing, and the aim of the book, i.e. to prove that she is a feminist-humanist. Despite her rejection of the term 'feminist', she remains one because she is a woman who writes about women. The second chapter deals with her first novel *Socialite Evenings*. The third chapter deals with *Starry Nights*. The fourth chapter deals with *Sisters*. The fifth chapter deals with *Strange Obsession*. The sixth chapter analyses *Sultry Days*. The seventh chapter deals with *Snapshots*. The eighth chapter brings forth the ideas that underlie *Second Thoughts*. The book ends with the conclusion, which establishes the opinion that the novelist is feminist-humanist writer who projects human values, which are necessary for a happy life and healthy society. Most of these values are traditional Indian ones.

The book also contains Appendix I and II which provide a historical survey of woman in Indian culture, the feminist movement, and the Indian women novelist. Besides, an Epilogue is added on the current condition of womankind in India, with an emphasis on practical needs for emancipation of entire nation, through them.

The book ends with a Selected Bibliography. My debt to existing scholarship is acknowledged in the body of the book and bibliography. In the world of scholarship, and that too increasing so fast, it would be presumptuous to claim originality. However, I may modestly say that I have tried to present existing facts in a new light. To what extent I have succeeded is to be decided by others, not by me. Shortcomings and errors, if any, are totally mine.

The response of each reader will be revered for further improvement.

Shashi Kant Gupta, Ph.D.
drshashikantgpt@gmail.com
guptakantshashi@yahoo.co.in

CONTENTS

1
Introduction

Shobhaa De, nee Rajadhyaksha is the third and "lucky"[1] daughter of her family. She was born in January 1948 in the humble, affectionate and supportive parentage of Justice Govind Hari Rajadhyaksha and his benevolent wife Mrs. Indira Govind Rajadhyaksha, of *Saraswat Brahmin* community, in Satara, Maharashtra. At the time of her birth, her father was a special magistrate in Satara, but soon after her birth, he was appointed as an assistant solicitor to the government of India, at the Centre in Delhi and in later phase of his life, he was promoted as the joint secretary in the Ministry of Law with a posting at Mumbai where he presided over the first ever law wing of the Centre to be established in the city.

Owing to her father's transferable service, she received her education in Delhi Public School, Delhi and then graduated from St. Xavier's College, Mumbai, with a second-class B.A. degree in Psychology and Sociology. Her focus was not on studies. She approached her books only a week or two before the exams, as she writes: "Studies did not interest me—that was that. There was a life right outside the classroom that I vastly preferred. And I wanted to make the most of it."[2] In her school days, she attained the state level in Athletics, Basketball and Hockey and set state level record in long jump and sprint events, but her father prohibited her from competing in the National meet in Patiala. On the other hand, she was already working in the field of modelling and "enjoying the independence it brought" to her. She was introduced to this field by Shashi Banker and worked as a model, because it gave her enough money equivalent to that of full-fledged salary and the feeling of independence. However, she was not too serious about modelling.

It was Mr. Nari Hira, a Sindhi businessman who introduced her to the field of writing through her friend Shilpa Shah, who asked her "Can you write?"[3] While Mr. Nari Hira suggests her that she should write for magazines. She commemorates these incidents of her life. "'Can you write?' that changed my life for me, gave me my future vocation,"[4] for "Nari Hira was the right man at the right time in life. He gave me the opportunity to break loose from a life I had outgrown."[5] She says, "I didn't choose modelling, it chose me. I didn't choose writing, writing chose me."[6] She enjoys writing like her independence and with the help of Shilpa and Mr. Nari Hira, she entered into the field of journalism in 1970 with *Stardust,* which shows her credible level of objectivity about society and her experience about film people who are in her eyes devoid of "loyalty, friendship, caring"[7] and are equally heartless. She left *Stardust* in 1980.

Shobhaa De, on account of her dynamic and industrious personality, has been "many things to many people: super model, celebrity, journalist and best-selling author; friend, rival, colleague and confidante."[8] But "despite her commitment to work and the frantic pace of her life, Shobhaa De's first priority in life has always been her family."[9] In fact, her "high voltage career 'happened' in unexpected ways, starting with her unplanned entry as a teenager into the glamorous world of modelling, and moving on to her high-profile years as a magazine editor, columnist, social commentator, TV scriptwriter and author."[10] Yet, "she keenly observed and astutely chronicled the new India—brash, affluent astutely High-society hi-jinks, movie-star follies, celebrity neuroses—none of these escaped her unsparing eye."[11]

Since 1970, when she started her career as a journalist, she founded and edited three popular magazines *Stardust, Society* and *Celebrity* and was Consulting Editor to *Sunday* and

Megacity. As a result of her persistent writing, she has written fifteen books till now, the first seven of them being novels. Her publications are *Socialite Evenings* (1988), *Starry Nights (*1990), *Sisters* (1992), *Strange Obsession* (1992), *Sultry Days* (1994), *Snapshots* (1995), *Second Thoughts* (1996), *Uncertain Liaisons* (Co-edited with Khushwant Singh, 1993), *Shooting from the Hip: Selected Writings* (1994), *Surviving Men* (1997), *Selective Memory* (1998), *Small Betrayals* (1995) and *Speedpost* (2000), Spouses (2004), *Super* India (2008), while *Swabhimaan Kity Party* and *Sukanya* are her TV serials telecast by DD1 and DD2 in 1997, 2001 and 2003-04 respectively. She is also renowned as a freelance writer and columnist for several leading newspapers and magazines and still she is continuing to write, despite her role as a mother of six children.

Indian English literature has a rich and long tradition of women novelists going back to the Nineteenth Century. The first English novel by an Indian woman is *The Hindu Wife: The Enchanted Fruit* (1876). Since then, many women tried their hand on the novel. It went through many changes according to changing socio-cultural conditions such as feminist and humanist movements. A detailed survey of it is given in the appendix. Suffice to say that Shobhaa De is writing in the background of a long tradition. In the 1980's and 1990's, many women novelists have emerged who portray the India of our time. Some of them are NRI's. The Indian English novel by women is growing day by day focusing on the problem of women and their genuine aspirations for economic independence, equality and freedom. Some male novelists like R.K. Narayan and Mulk Raj Anand have also treated the theme of place of women, their dilemmas and difficulties in Indian societies.

She portrays the true picture of modern metropolitan life, family, society, life-style and thoughts in her novels which appears to many of us too harsh, brutish, crude and uncivilized, for why she has been criticized as "Vatsyayani," "Soft porn queen," "Paasha of pulp," "Vamp," "Vamp feminist," "Masaala," "Mirchmasaala," "Pulp fiction,"

"Fuction" and "Merchant of sex", etc. There are a few critics who consider her a writer and her works "not a junk but novel,"[12] which expose "the hollowness of Indian" urban life, family and society, particularly about urban women. In fact, her novels simply represent the true state of city life, which is the mark of human civilization. Through her novels, she raises many questions such as: 'Is this the fruit of progress? Is this the life and place where we must be? Are we correct and following the right direction and track in our life? Is it the meaning of civilization?' But, unfortunately such issues, which are the undercurrents of her fiction have been neglected by many critics.

After the failure of *Celebrity*, the magazine edited and published by Shobhaa De, which led to her financial bankruptcy, isolation and even divorce from her first husband Sudhir, the superstitious streak in De "compelled her to search her titles that begin with 'S,' the first alphabet of her first name."[13] Inspired by the success of *Socialite Evenings* she begins the title of all her writings with 'S.' She is a non-canonical writer with no fixed or particular idea, for she started with feminist concerns (*Socialite Evenings*) and subsequently switched over to the feminist-cum-humanist approach to life.

Shobhaa De is different from her predecessors, as she makes it clear where she writes about herself and her books:

> I was caught between the two—not quite here and not quite there. Perhaps because of the publicity I received, my books were regarded with suspicion and scepticism for being commercially successful. We were still clinging to the virtue of low-key, underplayed, quite conformist writing in English that didn't shake the status quo. Writers, who preceded me particularly women, were either erudite elderly ladies or fierce single woman with a strong message to deliver. I didn't fit in. There was no clear slot for me. It was far easier to dismiss my books and concentrate on the publicity—which, when I think back, was phenomenal by those days' standards, but modest by today's.[14]

Shobhaa De, the mother of "*Hinglish*,"[15] has never been considered a serious writer, because she has been always "misquoted and misunderstood"[16] by critics, reader and society. But, she has never bothered about anything except her "family and writing,"[17] for she has firm faith that she has "never done the unusual"[18] and in the last thirty-eight years "she's built her life word by word, column by column, book by book [and is now recognised as] the word factory."[19] Critics consider her a vamp writer, *masala* writer, pulp writer, but they are wrong, because she is a serious, sensitive, responsible and alert writer as we can evaluate from her comment on herself and her own books:

> I thrive on challenges and change. I like to innovate and attempt new things. I refuse to confirm my critic's version of me—highly distorted one to begin with. I have always gone ahead and written what comes naturally to me. My books have always been one step ahead of the wave. But I make no conscious effort to reinvent myself. If I shift the goal-spots with each new book, it is because I have grown, changed or moved away. Each book has its own specific context and validity.[20]

It is because she could either "ruminate or write."[21] She further says about her novels that each of her books is "with a strong woman protagonist. And it took that one encounter to bring home the fact. I had always been gravitating towards women. I was a woman's woman."[22] In her view, "a writer is a product of his or her immediate environment"[23] as well as "a person who writes regularly, ideally, every single day. That's all it takes to make you one."[24] According to her, "writing is about reaction,"[25] "wave is history"[26] and "the world is desperately youth-oriented"[27] she maintains herself with the *rhyme and rhythm* of time with full faith because she knows it very well that "writing for a living is something very few people take seriously," asserting "Keep writing. It does have its rewards,"[28] but she very emphatically says "No"[29] when she is asked, "whether her books are designed to shock?" Urbashi Barat has tried to know her a little bit when she writes about her, "she is a serious writer with her cleareyed honest appraisal of human relationships and her overriding concern for human values even though she may not realize that this is what emerges in her fiction".[30] About her novels she says:

"The darker side of human nature, the squalor and the evil in society and in human relationships that Shobhaa De explored in her fiction."[31] Thus, we can say her novels are based on some real story, but presented through fictitious characters. About her stories, she (Shobhaa De) says: "Nothing I wrote was made up—somewhat exaggerated perhaps, but not fabricated" and reaffirms it in an interview: "Subject of my books are my own which I pick up from the people around me, my writing is based on ideas. I don't write to harm society. The rotten inside of society may be our subject."[32]

So, we can say that she writes what she sees in society. In other words, we can say she is "a social commentator."[33] She comments on society, she never considers herself a revolutionary, as is clear from her words:

> I'm only a newspaper hack. My printed opinions are hardly likely to change the world, topple government, make heads roll. A mention or two in my column may help some society lady sell a few more salwar-kameezes. It may let a few readers of the paper know that such-and-such person exists and is doing interesting stuff or that I feel strongly about certain issues.[34]

The same thing she suggests in an interview: "Where people could not be reformed by the writings of revered saints and gurus, can my writing reform them?"[35]

Even though, Shobhaa De has been mercilessly criticised by various critics as: "Her name is Shobhaa De (Day), but her subject is night. The writer of colourful novels, she is known as the 'Merchant of Sex.'"[36]

Malvika Sanghvi holds different opinion and says that Shobhaa De is:

> ...a woman who has been a celebrity target for all manners of accusations, for almost three decades, this

> kind of revelation, hardly earth-shaking to others, is uncommon. So tired is Shobhaa of having to deal with what is projected on to her (rich bitch, India's answer to Jackie Collins, pornographer, goddess, successful author, one-time model, social commentator).[37]

Yet Shobhaa De tries her best to give suitable reply to negative and too negative remarks, which are libel on her and her books due to levities against her. She emphatically denies these charges when she writes on *Starry Nights* as partial, whimsical and prejudiced (patriarchal) because; "They [critics and scholars] don't want to find out anything new. All they're looking for is a confirmation of their theories, lopsided as they are."[38] About pornography she writes:

> Abusive, raw, and employing the filthy idiom of the gutters, *Starry Nights* caused major shock waves when it was published. My deliberate use of choice Hindi epithets and the descriptive sex scenes got everybody worked up, which was rather precious. There was nothing in the book that was not known to the public, nothing the fanzines hadn't already written about. Nothing, that wasn't being proclaimed on prominent hoardings dotting the city. Everybody knew just how sordid this life was, but my retelling of it was found obscene and objectionable.[39]

Yet if anybody finds or hopes for "plenty of 'hot' passages"[40] in her books, she frankly tells them that "it was far cheaper to go buy a girlie magazine from pavement hawkers if that's what they were looking for."[41] She emphatically says that she is not a writer of sex alone. Sex is there in her novels and no one can deny it, but according to her, she is not like Khushwant Singh and condemns him for writing *The Company of Woman*:

> I may write something for stronger in future. And no, I'll definitely not write *The Company of Woman*. It gives sex a bad name. My fantasies happen to be far more imaginative. Khushwant should never have written the book—sex, in Khushwant's case, has always been in his

> head. And there it should have remained. I adore Vikram Seth. And I love reading Amy Tan, Kathy Lette, and new women writers with something original to say, like Helen Fielding of *Bridget Jone's Diary*. If they [critics] were looking for dirt, this wasn't their book.[42]

She does not welcome those beings who have no logical insight to understand the undercurrent of her writings especially novels. She simply says to them: "I am teller of stories. If there is a subliminal message in there, somewhere, readers are welcome to it. I do not see myself as a Nineties version of Raja Ram Mohan Roy in a *saree*."[43] She criticises critics for their immature views. According to her, "critics like to put writer in straitjackets because it makes their job easier."[44] And about their critical attack she says: "If they [critics] were looking for dirt this was not their book."[45] Therefore, one can say that Shobhaa De is not a pornographer but a true narrator and painter of society. Is this the life and place where we must be? Is it the meaning of civilization? Are we following right direction and track in our life? Sudhir Kumar considers Shobhaa De "a vamp author"[46] and in S.P. Swain's eyes she is a "vamp-feminist"[47] and "her novels are pulp-fiction,"[48] but Shobhaaa De doesn't consider herself a feminist. She says, "I write with a great deal of empathy towards women. Without waving the feminist flag, I feel very strongly about the woman's situation."[49] This is because her "Feminist thought is 'humanist' thought."[50] "In the 1980's, feminism emerges as a thought system, a point of view to reorganize the world realities, a positivist holistic approach to life, a step towards sanity in human relationship, and perhaps the only mode for preservation of very human existence on this planet."[51] Thus, she is a humanist rather than a feminist.

Even though Shobhaaa De rejects the label of being a 'feminist,' her feminist concerns cannot be denied. In order to have a clear idea about the concept, one must have a first hand knowledge of 'feminist movement' which has been given in the appendix. This is done deliberately because otherwise, the chapter would have become unnecessarily too long and unwieldy.

Shobhaa De says, "I had always been gravitating towards women. I was a woman's woman,"[52] and "writing comes to me as naturally as breathing,"[53] or "I write what is within me without any hesitation, fear or self-consciousness."[54] She says it with her humanistic approach towards life and she herself verifies it when she comments, "As a writer, I am concerned with humanity at large. I hate bringing gender into it. I am not a social reformer."[55] And again "I don't dislike men—I just feel sorry for them."[56] We cannot therefore, say that "Shobhaa De writes from a definite feminine perspective"[57] or "pornography in Shobhaa De's novels becomes a symptom and symbol of the female's defiance of a male regulated sexuality,"[58] because she is not a pornographer. In her writings, she treats men and women on equal terms, that is why she writes about equality as:

> Eventually, every relationship is a power struggle either on an overt or subliminal level. Control over the situation has been a male prerogative over the centuries. Women's destinies have been determined largely in that context alone. It is time they were made aware of their own potential and power. Shakti needs to be harnessed, directed and explored for the furtherance of over all human development. Men will have to come to terms with woman power.[59]

So, it seems that Urbashi Barat is correct up to some extent when she says, "The darker side of human nature, the squalor and the evil in society and inhumane relationships that Shobhaa De explores in her fiction."[60]

Shobhaa De has brought in the economic aspect of power struggle, when she says:

"Eventually, everything boils down to money—that great leveller. There can be no talk of independence for women, without economic self-sufficiency. An independent mind or a free spirit, is meaningless so long as the body and soul are being kept together by somebody else."[61] The above quotation shows that the novelist doesn't give too much importance to money in comparison to human life and human relationship. She criticises money because it some time embitters the sweet homely life. After observing the troubled life of a family particularly the couple she evaluates: "I can see there is trouble in paradise. And it is being caused by a dirty word 'money.' Money is a tricky commodity, because it's a recurrent theme for a bad dream in modern marriages—regardless of class or financial status [due to it] Men...treat their wives like pretty thieves"[62] and question their each and every act. Shobhaa De stresses on the word "trust"[63] instead of "money," because, 'Trust' strengthens and harmonises the human relationships between individual and individual, family and family and one society to another. So, we find Shobhaa De's "Humanism made man the measure of all things,"[64] for:

> The individual is responsible for his life and actions and may at any time creatively change his attitudes or behaviour through awareness and will. The humanist is concerned with the fullest growth of the individual in the areas of love, fulfilment, self-worth and autonomy: maturation is considered a process during which one establishes and follows his own system of values. The concept of the self is a central focal point for most humanistic Psychologists. In the 'personal construct' theory and the 'self-centred' theory... the individual perceives his world according to his own experience. This perception affects his personality and leads him to direct his behaviour to satisfy the needs of the total self in the development of an individual's personality he strive for self-actualisation (to become oneself), self-maintenance (to keep on being oneself), and self-enhancement (to transcend the status quo).[65]

We can find the humanistic-cum-feministic approach in Shobhaa De's practical life as well as in her fiction too. Let us take some examples from her practical life, which she has mentioned in her book *Selective Memory*.

> Money matters have always embarrassed me. Perhaps, 'stumped' is a better word. I hate discussing money,

> though I enjoy making it. I belonged to that self-conscious generation of woman who thought it 'unfeminine' to discuss money. Bullshit. Money is sexless, only suckers are stupid enough to bring gender into it.[66]

> I wrote on regardless—a cheeky, insolent, cynical take on the social scene, often featuring identifiable people. The observations were spot-on but cruel.[67]

> My columns are always written from 'Every person's' point of view.[68]

So, for Shobhaa De "Money was certainly one of the incentives but not the main one."[69] We also have her opinions about herself, marriage, family and home. In her teens, her "sole ambition in life was to get married and have lots of children."[70] She reasserts the same thing when she says, "I guess not. But I sure as hell didn't want to be a doctor, lawyer or engineer. I didn't want to be anything at all, except a happy, carefree young person."[71] About her father's family she writes, "I've actually thanked God for my family's deep and genuine involvement in my life, even when it has led to small arguments and minor fights."[72] She further writes:

> I like the fact that they take me, and what I do so completely for granted. For my part, I try and include them in all aspects of my world. Whenever I meet somebody new, a person who leaves an impact of any sort, I come home and share the experience with the family.[73]

About the influence of her father's family on her, she writes:

> Perhaps it's because I belonged to a large family that I decided to have more than one child myself. When I see my children today, I feel they'll value each other's presence far more in the future, even if they don't recognise that fully right now. I was never lonely as a child. And I've never been lonely as an adult. The family has always been there to lean on, talk to, laugh with, even cry with.[74]

> I didn't invest too much of myself in friendship—the emotional need was simply not there. My life was crowded with family and I preferred it that way. I don't trust people all that easily and good friendships are based on trust. I feel very contained and complete within the family fold. I no longer have the time to nurture new relationships, nor the desire to do so. As I grow older and more cynical, I find myself increasing the distance, sticking only to those people who don't drain me physically or emotionally.[75]

She tells us about her personal relationship with her sister Kunda, "As a young girl my secrets were shared only with my sister Kunda—there was nothing I wished to hide from her."[76] And about closeness with her children she writes:

> When I had kids of my own, I vowed to be a more 'touchy-freely' parent and I'm glad I've broken tough my own inhibitions. For years I couldn't get myself to utter those three magical words ('I love You') even in romantic relationships. Today, I can say them easily to my children and mean every word. I accept their love. And I'm training myself to deal with their outburst of hostility too. I am glad they feel free enough to express their feelings—positive and negative.[77]

Even after divorce, her ex-mother-in-law respects her because she says: "You will always be their mother [for her grandchildren]. Nothing can change that. If I don't respect you, your children will never respect me."[78] While, her father still reminds her about some important things like; "Keep your nostrils clean. Pay your taxes. Love your family and country. Do morally correct thing. Choose the right path. 'A man of character always knows the difference between right and wrong'."[79] She is very cautious about children and makes others alert too when she write about them; "It's a sad reflection of the times—our children are not safe on the streets. They aren't at all that safe in the home either, without constant supervision."[80] It reflects her motherly feelings and responsibilities.

It is erroneous to believe that Shobhaa De doesn't give too much importance to marriage, as R.S. Pathak says, "Marriage is not regarded as essential in the fictional world of Shobhaa De."[81] We can easily understand how important marriage is for her in her practical life. Even though, she is the first Asian woman to win 'Reuters Fellowship Award,' one of the biggest opportunities for an Indian, she didn't leave her family to avail herself of that great offer as it amounted to "Uncertainty. Insecurity. Alienation. From family, friends and colleagues." She continues, "I'm glad I listened of my heart and stayed."[82] Secondly, just after ninety minutes of her divorce from her first husband Sudhir in July 1984, she married Dilip because she thinks, "I happen to like being married. I believe in marriage. I enjoy being a wife. I don't want to spend the rest of my life on my own,"[83] for an unmarried or a divorced woman is not respected by man. About marriage and space she feels:

> The need for 'space' makes marriage sound like a tenancy in a crowded block. Marriage means being together, even at times when the sight, smell and sound of the 'other' drives you crazy. 'Space' connotes escape, but maybe, I'm wrong. Space also obliquely refers to a strong desire for privacy, for expressing one's individuality, for putting up invisible barriers around oneself. It's a modern day invention, I don't fully appreciate or understand. Marriage to me connotes commitment and surrender—merging with, blending, overlapping, combining. It is a symbiotic relationship where one feeds on the other, depends on the other, needs the other. There is no room or requirement for 'space.' It's a misleading and mischievous concept that has let to several modern-day marriages breaking up—perhaps because the two people have misconstrued its true interpretation. Individual in search of vast and unlimited space are better off single—they can have any amount of its staying on their own.[84]

She wishes to live in the healthy harmonious and happy environment of her family, as is evident from her prayer to God:

> 'May it always be this way. May the six of them stay close and supportive of one another. May they be friends in their later years. May their children love one another. May they wish each other well always.' That's all I really want today. Peace and joy within our family.[85]

She feels safe, loved, happily in her home along with her husband and six children. She expresses her feelings:

> This and this alone was all that mattered.... Here was where my happiness was. Here was where I felt warm, loved and secure. There would be other things in life. Other triumphs. Other glories. But for me...it was perfect. Too perfect. This was heaven [for her]. It had to be.[86]

In an interview to Nandini Guha of *The Saturday Statesman*, she expresses her view about marriage as: "A bad marriage kills love, a good one can only enhance it."[87]

She is aware of the pathetic condition of women and expresses her deep concern when she says, "I fear for my generation of women—they really are like danglers, neither here nor there. They definitely don't want to be like their mothers and they desperately want to switch places with their daughters. We talk of options, opportunities and choices—sure we have them"[88] and then she concludes what modern women do with these facilities, "we earn, we travel, we splurge, and we weep."[89] In an interview, she critically comments on world and women:

> World is like that, ...nothing new. Women were never the world's priority. Why should it be any different now? We were ignored earlier. We are ignored now. And we shall continue to be ignored. It could be ten years from now or even ten centuries. We'll wait. We're patient.[90]

She considers identity crisis as the prime challenge for womankind: "Today woman faces dual challenge. Her social role has changed. She has freedom but social view has not changed, and the only solution is—economic independence."[91] For men, woman is a *Sharmeelee*[92] figure (shy figure) and if men are not able to digest her progress due to their "male mentality"[93], then women have to face the challenge ultimately.

Shobhaa De asks women to pay attention on a few but essential conditions for their freedom like honour, empowerment, betterment, health, rights (legal and political), independence (social, economical, legal, political) and security. For this she says, "I feel education and economic independence are key to woman's existence. Let her herself evaluate her freedom—self help is the greatest help. If the woman on grass root is educated, she could help herself."[94] So in all her writings, she asks woman to concentrate on: Education (for awareness, enlightenment, self-realization, self-discipline), Economics (for self-reliance, honour), Power (for prestige, decision), Experience (to enrich the life), Female integrity (for protection from abuses), Mutual Co-operation (with each other and men too), Moral and ethical values, Character, and Hopefulness-cum-courage. Here, Shobhaa De wants to convey the same thing which has been conveyed by Manu in *Manusmriti*:

> अरक्षिता गृहे रुद्धा पुरुषैराप्तकारिभिः।
>
> आत्मानमात्मना यास्तु रक्षेयुस्ताः सुरक्षिताः॥[95] (6:12)

(Even such women folk who are kept under the constant vigil by trustworthy men are not safe, only those are secure, who can defend themselves by their own virtues).

Shobhaa De's idea is similar to that of Dr. Radhakrishnan:

> Give us good women, we will have a great civilization,
> Give us good mothers, we will have a great nation.[96]

Shobhaa De believes that, only through betterment of women, a nation can progress and prosper because they will enlighten the life of all the family members. Children are the future of a nation and they (women) may be called the backbone and maker of the future of a nation, society and civilization, which would ultimately result in the betterment of entire human kind. Thus what women need today for their emancipation, empowerment and enlightenment are: "education, economics, equality, opportunities, honour," co-operation and courage.

Shobhaa De, who considers herself a "middle class"[97] and "traditional"[98] type of woman, who represents her root, culture, ideals, customs, tradition, nation, and civilization physically and mentally, is always "hungry for the experience"[99] and "learning."[100] She wishes for the liberation of women, but intellect is more important, for "Beauty is not all. So, it is secondary to intelligence"[101] and wishes for them even though it is a daydream for her. "The Indian women should be free from fetters, that too intellectually."[102]

Shobhaa De, who wants to become a grandmother, is in favour of women's emancipation and liberation, but in full co-operation with men, because without man, a woman's life is incomplete. The bra-burning phase of feminism is over which started in the 1960s in USA. So, she opts for the latest mode, which according to Nisha Millet:

> What women need today is for men to realise they have a lot of potential and are capable of reaching great heights. Despite the tremendous progress made by women in different fields, many of us are still unable to realise our full potential because of the constraints around us. Men and society need to realise that women can be independent.[103]

Today, what women need are liberated males, positive mindset, their own spine for self-respect, family support, no glass ceiling, and self-confidence. According to the novelist, a woman can get all these things through her family and society by her devotion, love, sacrifice and service plus co-operation and mutual understanding with her male partner because:

> The days of bra-burning a militant feminism of the sixties are now over. The women of the nineties are in a far more mellow mood. They have not given up their ongoing battle for equality, justice and development but there is a growing realization among the women that this journey cannot be covered on their own. That they have to work along with men, as partners and not as adversaries, if they are to achieve any of their goals [sic].[104]

This is why Angela Kind, special adviser to the UN Secretary General on gender issue and advancement of women, remarks:

> The role of men was put on the agenda at the Beijing conference on women five years ago and since then, the issue has picked up momentum. Women have realised they cannot do it alone and they don't want to do it alone. After all, what is the point of having men who are filled with resentment or with low esteem.[105]

Thus, more or less Shobhaa De wants to say nearly the same thing what has been said by Indira Gandhi in *Eternal India*:

> Women must be a bridge and a synthesizer. She shouldn't allow herself to be swept off her feet by superficial trends nor yet be chained to the familiar. She must ensure the continuity, which strengthens roots and simultaneously engineer change and growth to keep society dynamic, abreast of knowledge, sensitive to fast-moving events. The solution lies neither in fighting for equal position nor denying it, neither in retreat into the home nor escape from it.[106]

In all the novels of Shobhaa De, we find this feminist-cum-humanist feeling embedded in the thoughts and actions not only of the protagonists but also of the other characters.

Shobhaa De is harshly criticized by many critics like A.G. Khan, S.P. Swain and M.K. Naik. If Khan considers her 'Vatsyayani', then Naik is not far behind. He has written about her as:

> Most women writers seem to favour serious work, rather than entertaining popular fiction: the major exception is Shobhaa De, well known to Indian magazine readers as the queen of gossip; she was the founder-editor of *Stardust* which specialized in stories about filmstars. Her first novel, *Socialite Evenings* (1989) is a *roman a clef* about a young middle-class girl who is attracted to the world of films and modelling. It was expected to outdo Jackie Collins's *Hollywood Wives*, but the plot is thin and the narration banal. The

narrative of Shobhaa De (*Starry Nights*, 1991; *Sisters*, 1992; *Strange Obsession*, 1992; *Sultry Days*, 1994; *Snapshots*, 1995; and *Second Thoughts*, 1996) would seem to belong less to serious fiction than to pulp writing. They are "entertainments" rather than novels proper:

> Sagas of bed-hopping, chronicles of high society and low ethicality, drawing room manners and barn-door morals, "Spare-Rib-aldry" or "fuction" (to use Farrukh Dhondy's expressive term) would perhaps be an apt description of them. Empress of the Middle, De seems to tell her female readers, "women of the world, unite; you have nothing to lose except your virginity"; while her message to men appears to be: "remember your member and forget the rest; for the penis is mightier than the sword, or the head or the heart." De's works do offer glimpses of what she could have achieved, had she set herself higher literary standards; but low aim is apparently a far better fame-winner, social gainer and money-spinner, whatever the musty old proverb may say. (M.K.N.)[107]

But, in her latest interview, Shobhaa De has objected to this:

> I have a track record of credibility and openness, which I value above everything else. I talk about people who are in the public domain and whose every action is open to public scrutiny. If they cannot handle it, then it's their funeral, not mine. I am not a performing flea. It's dangerous when you become a victim of your own stereotyping. I have broken rules all my life and will never do anything predictable.[108]

Jaydipshinh Dodiya and R.K. Dhawan appreciate her and her work because they think; in her novels, all major and minor characters reflect some touching aspect of human life. They write:

> Shobhaa De as a writer is gifted with extraordinary ability to discuss very sensitive aspects of human life tactfully. The way she narrates each and every aspect of

> human relationship in general and man-woman relationship in particular, is really wonderful. The orthodox people in India criticise her for her open discussion of sexual matters. But, her fiction has got tremendous response not only from several European countries but all over the world. All classes of people read and enjoy her fiction. It is no less an achievement. In fact, as a writer she differs considerable from other Indian women novelists writing in English. She is a writer who believes in the very frank narration of the incidents and absolute open-heartedness. We don't find anything reserved in her fiction from narrative point of view. In my opinion, she is the last person to care for what orthodox readers say about the subject matter of her fiction. As a creative writer, she is becoming immensely popular day by day. Most of the readers enjoy her extraordinary narrative technique as well as her subject matter.[109]

Shobhaa De's opinion about TV serial *Sukanya*, is applicable to her novels also and their male and female characters:

> It was important to project the contemporary urban woman without making her a caricature. I placed myself in her shoes and tried to identify her problems. Today, I see a lot of young professionals with strong work ethics and ambitions who feel terrific to be doing so well. *Sukanya* was inspired by all these women I encountered in the real life [sic]. Of course, in her case, I had to dramatise the situation.[110]

Behind it, her motive is, "*Sukanya* represents the woman of today and she strongly reflects my values."[111] She goes on to say, "The character of subject has to inspire me. It's important for a TV serial to reflect what's happening around us, it has to involve your audience and engage them. I don't like talking about remote fantasy figure. I like talking about the real people."[112] More or less, her intention is the same behind writing novels including its source, matter and motto. But, in her eyes the prime goal is her home:

> I am conscious of my priorities which include looking after my home and family. Even if I give up lucrative offers and choose to spend more with my children at home, I am not on a martyrdom trip. I enjoy caring for my family.[113]

The theme of these serials revolves around the rights of women for equality and economic independence. Swetlana, the protagonist of *Swabhimaan*, is a divorcee with one legitimate son and two other children fathered by her lover Kashav Malhotra. She fights a legal battle for the rights of her two illegitimate children against a powerful family the Malhotras.

There are some critics like M.K. Nair, A.G. Khan, S.P. Swain etc., who are very harsh in their criticism of Shobhaa De and are not prepared to accept her as a serious writer. There are some like Urbashi Barat, Alexander, Monti, Nisha Trivedi, Jaydipsinh Dodiya, etc., who view her novels as genuine piece of literature having a vision. Various critics have interpreted her novels in different ways, but they seem to be either far away from the actual themes of novels except few who approach near to it and only partially correct, it is because her novels are thematically complex. Jaydipsinh Dodiya considers her a feminist writer just like Nayantara Sahgal and Shashi Deshpande, because she writes basically on women's problem and provides a new approach. Sarbani Sen views the domain of cultural politics in Shobhaa De's novels, for the vivid picture of high society and its culture painted in the works, which represent the contemporary India. According to an Italian scholar Alessandro Monti, her fiction reflects the making of modern India. Sanjay Kumar[114] sees that there are two aspects of feminism in Shobhaa De's works—an expressive and the explosive. Women in her novels face challenges and protest against patriarchy. But, for Pushp Lata[115] her novels are simply a protest against patriarchy through remarkable and superior female protagonists.

There are many other critics, like: A.G. Khan who regards Shobhaa De as Vatsyayani, because her entire acrobatics is an attempt to reduce 'fiction' to 'fuction.' According to him, her novels portray her feelings of alienation from the traditional craft to nudity and vulgarity. Ira Pande accuses Shobhaa De of vulgarising the printed word with dilettante dabbling of vapid mind. Sunil Sethi views her novels as "Boddice ripper." David Davidar lends her authenticity by regarding her attempts as discovering India through Indian eyes while Raj Reversal regards her as the high priestess of gossip and innuendo. J.M. Waghmare says, "It is true that the woman's body is much abused; Shobhaa De's writing conveys the feeling of bitter helplessness. She cannot call even her body her own's. She is an object of man's lust and sexuality. She has nowhere to go. She is confined to the four corners of the house."[116]

Writing of Shobhaa De also suffer from some of the defects and shortcomings as those of other women writers in English are susceptible to, as is evident from the remark of J.M. Waghmare:

> Most Indian women writers in English, I am afraid, rather elitist and or not very closely acquainted with Indian life and society at the grass root level. They are familiar with the upper-class urban life. The true heart of India has to be searched in the rural society. The best and truly representative Indian women's writing is found in modern Indian languages. In them, we find contemporary currents and cross currents of Indian life.[117] (Shobhaa De's works do not reflect the real India).

There are other defects such as inconsistency in the plot. It presents only one-sided view of life and society due to the use of many type of dialects, uncertainty of time, there is no co-relation between time-action-space. She has degraded her own kind by delineating poor pictures of women's life in this novel (*Starry Night*), because, beauty of art and literature lies in concealing art and symbolical representation of things for the readers and viewers.

Repudiating the above remarks of critics, Shobhaa De expresses her opinion with the help of Satyajit Ray's, *Pather Panchali*:

> I too can write if I so like on the poor like Satyajit Ray's (*Pather Panchali*). But that writing of mine will be entirely imaginary. To write about a society which is not intimately known to me and to win, some favour or sympathy would be cheating. I would call it a writer's dishonesty, because imagination in writings is more lively. The second important thing is that my writings about common people do no good for anybody. Even if it is so, there is no harm in writing such things but I would disdain taking credit for it.[118]

Thus, Shobhaa De hints at her mature thoughts and human values which are based on concrete realities of contemporary world. It seems that "Shobhaa De does not for a moment suffer from any illusions with regard to the world she inhabits. She inhabits this First World with a self-conscious assertion."[119] Her novels dissect the metropolitan Indian with such clinical success that reveals all its inner characteristics. "It is a terribly insular world, not without its titillations, but ideologically stark and barren, helplessly cocooned in the frenetic energy that wealth and social unconcern produce in the upper classes of India,"[120] therefore, we may say:

> The simple truth about Shobhaa De is that she has been successful in the very things her critics (who, incidentally, would themselves be the fish out of water outside the First World where Shobhaa De has her Empire) would like to, but have not been able to do.
>
> It is for this reason that she has always confounded her critics. For, she has understood, better than most around her, that criticism is often the other side of coin of envy, and even in the India's First World, you require hard work, ambition and talent to reach where she has.[121]

Thus, we have conflicting critical opinions about the novels of Shobhaa De and on Shobhaa De herself, who is an Indian woman, and it is the greatest tragedy in our history that the Indian woman has no ground of her own to stand on and so critics are too free to comment on her rationally or irrationally. In case of Shobhaa De, some critics have crossed the limit of civic and logic, some remain within, but few are able to read the novelist's mind and reach near the reality. By and large the critics do not rate her as a serious novelist. All her works have not received equal critical attention. Some of them have almost no criticism. Critical opinions [pros and cons] about individual novels will be mentioned in the respective chapters on them. The proposed study will attempt to show through thematic study of different novels, that most of the critics have failed to grasp the real meaning of her novels and other works. Therefore, we shall attempt to examine in the chapters that follow 'what is real Shobhaa De and what are her real concerns expressed in her novels?' Particularly in respect to Indian Ethos.

NOTES

1. Shobhaa De, *Selective Memory: Stories From My Life* (New Delhi: Penguin Books India (P) Limited, 1998), p. 13.
2. *Ibid.*, p. 33.
3. *Ibid.*, p. 84.
4. *Ibid.*, p. 89.
5. *Ibid.*, p. 95.
6. *Ibid.*, p. 76.
7. *Ibid.*, p. 126.
8. *Ibid.*, Back side of the jacket of the *Selective Memory.*
9. *Ibid.*
10. *Ibid.*
11. *Ibid.*
12. Yamuna Prasad, in *Indian Women Novelists in English* ed., by Amarnath Prasad (New Delhi: Atlantic Publishers & Distributors, 2001), p. 103.
13. Madhumalati Adhikari's, "Variations of Betrayal in Small Betrayals" in *The Fiction of Shobhaa De: Critical Studies* edited by Jaydipsinh Dodiya (New Delhi: Prestige Books, 2000), p. 284.
14. *Selective Memory*, p. 348.
15. *The Times of India*, New Delhi, Saturday October 3, 1998, p. 10.
16. Malavika Sanghvi's, "The Word Factory", *The Times of India*, New Delhi, January 28, 2001, p. 2.
17. "Days and Years of De," *The Times of India*, New Delhi, Saturday, October 3, 1998, p. 10.
18. Malavika Sanghvi's, "The Word Factory", *The Times of India*, New Delhi, January 28, 2001, p. 2.

19. *Ibid.*, p. 1.
20. Sourish Bhattacharya's, "Enter, the Supermom", *The Hindustan Times Magazine*, New Delhi, November 21, 1999, p. 1.
21. *Ibid.*, (New Delhi Edition).
22. Malavika Sanghvi's, "The Word Factory", *The Times of India*, New Delhi, January 28, 2001, p. 1.
23. *Selective Memory*, p. 386.
24. *Ibid.*, p. 402.
25. *Ibid.*, p. 302.
26. *Ibid.*, p. 295.
27. *Ibid.*
28. *Ibid.*, p. 301.
29. *Ibid.*, p. 371.
30. Urbashi Barat, "Selective Memory: Celebrity Memoirs", *The Fiction of Shobhaa De: Critical Studies*. p. 322.
31. *Ibid.*, p. 320.
32. Ravindra Nath Shukla' "Shobhaa De", (Hindi Translation) *The Dainik Jagaran*, Varanasi, U.P., May 24, 1997, p. 1.
33. *Selective Memory*, p. 229.
34. *Ibid.*, p. 230.
35. Ravindra Nath Shukla' "Shobhaa De", (Hindi Translation) *The Dainik Jagaran*, Varanasi, U.P., May 24, 1997, p. 1.
36. *Ibid.*, Rabindra Nath Shukla, p. 1.
37. Malavika Sanghvi's, "The Word Factory", *The Times of India*, New Delhi, January 28, 2001, p. 1.
38. *Selective Memory*, p. 263.
39. *Ibid.*, pp. 332-33.
40. *Ibid.*, p. 345.
41. *Ibid.*
42. Sourish Bhattacharya, "Enter, The Supermom", *The Hindustan Times*, New Delhi, November 21, 1999, p. 2.
43. Nandini Guha's, "Shobhaa De," *The Saturday Statesman*, Calcutta, August 1, 1998, p. 3.
44. Sourish Bhattacharya, "Enter, the Supermon", *The Hindustan Times*, New Delhi, November 21, 1999, p. 1.
45. *Ibid.*, p. 2.
46. Sudhir Kumar, "Artist as Vamp: A Feminist Approach to Shobhaa De' *Starry Night*" in R.K. Dhawan's *Indian Women Novelists*, set-III, Vol. I, New Delhi: Prestige Books, 1995, p. 117.

47. S.P. Swain, "Socialite Evenings: A Feminist Study" in Dodiya's *The Fiction of Shobhaa De* (New Delhi: Prestige Books, 2000), p. 140.
48. *Ibid.*
49. Sourish Bhattacharya's, "Enter the Supermom", *The Hindustan Times Magazine*, New Delhi, November 21, 1999, p. 3.
50. Sushila Singh's, "Recent Trends in Feminist Thought A Tour de Horizon" in Shushila Singh's *Recent Trends in Feminist Thought* (New Delhi: Prestige Books, 1991), p. 34.
51. *Ibid.*
52. Malavika Sanghvi's, "The Word Factory", *The Times of India*, New Delhi, January 28, 2001, p. 1.
53. Nandini Guha's, "Shobhaa De", *The Saturday Statesman*, Calcutta, August 1, 1998, p. 3.
54. *Ibid.*
55. *Ibid.*
56. *Ibid.*
57. Pushp Lata, "A Protest Against the Patriarchal in Shobhaa De's Works" in *The Fiction of Shobhaa De*, p. 67.
58. S.P. Swain, "Shobhaa De's Socialite Evenings—A Feminist Study", *Feminist English Literature*, ed. Manmohan K. Bhatnagar (New Delhi: Atlantic, 1999), p. 137.
59. Shobhaa De, *Shooting from the Hip: Selected Writings* (New Delhi: UBS Publication, 1994), pp. 111-13.
60. Urbashi Barat, "Selective Memory: Celebrity Memoirs", in *The Fiction of Shobhaa De* (New Delhi: Prestige Books, 2000), p. 320.
61. Shobhaa De, *Shooting from the Hip* (New Delhi: UBSPD, 1994), p. 110.
62. Shobhaa De, "The Sexes", *The Week*, June 30, 2002, p. 34.
63. *Ibid.*
64. *The New Encyclopaedia Britannica Micropaedia*, Vol. Six, ed. by Robet P Gwinn (Chicago U.S., 1985), p. 137.
65. *Ibid.*, p. 138.
66. Shobhaa De, *Selective Memory* (New Delhi: Penguin Books, 1998), p. 212.
67. *Ibid.*, p. 291.
68. *Ibid.*, p. 303.
69. *Ibid.*, p. 403.
70. Shobhaa De, *Selective Memory* (New Delhi: Penguin Books, 1998), p. 42.
71. *Ibid.*
72. *Ibid.*, pp. 406-07.

73. *Ibid.*, p. 408.
74. *Ibid.*, p. 409.
75. *Ibid.*, p. 415.
76. *Ibid.*
77. *Ibid.*, p. 416.
78. *Ibid.*, p. 418.
79. *Ibid.*, p. 433.
80. *Ibid.*, p. 457.
81. R.S. Pathak, "Feminist Concerns in the Shobhaa De's Work: A Study in Attitudes," in *The Fiction of Shobhaa De* ed. by Jaydipsinh Dodiya, p. 40.
82. *Selective Memory*, p. 481.
83. *Ibid.*, p. 475.
84. *Ibid.*, pp. 480-81.
85. *Ibid.*, p. 484.
86. *Ibid.*, pp. 525-26.
87. Nandini Guha's, "Shobhaa De", *The Saturday Statesman*, Calcutta, August 1, 1998, p. 3.
88. *Selective Memory*, p. 414.
89. *Ibid.*
90. *The Times of India*, New Delhi, November 25, 2001, p. 10.
91. Vimala Patil's, "Abhi door hai manjil" (The Destination is still far off), (Hindi Translation) *The Dainik Jagaran*, Varanasi, U.P., March 8, 2002, p. 1.
92. *Ibid.*
93. *Ibid.*
94. *Ibid.* "Shobhaa De's view" incorporated use.
95. *Manusmriti*, 6: 12. Quoted in *Congress Sandesh* ed., by Vasant Saathe (New Delhi: National Herald Press, 1999), p. 42.
96. *English Prose*, (Class XIIth), Madhyamik Shiksha Parishad, Uttar Pradesh, Allahabad, 2000, p. 143.
97. *Selective Memory*, p. 521.
98. *Ibid.*, p. 531.
99. *Ibid.*, p. 518.
100. *Ibid.*, p. 519.
101. Ravindra Nath Shukla' "Shobhaa De", (Hindi Translation) *The Dainik Jagaran*, Varanasi, U.P., May 24, 1997, p. 1.
102. *Ibid.*

103. "*Equality: A fair and foul deal,*" *The Times of India*, New Delhi, March 8, 2001, p. 1.
104. Anita Katyal "Days of bra-burning feminism are over", *The Times of India*, New Delhi, June 8, 2001, p. 16.
105. *Ibid.* Quoted by Anita Katyal
106. Quoted by Amar Nath Prasad, "A Brief History of Indian Women Novelists in English" in *Indian Women Novelists in English* edited by Dr. Amar Nath Prasad, (New Delhi: Atlantic Publishers and Distributors, 2001), p. 1.
107. M.K. Naik and Shyamala A. Narayan, Indian English Literature 1980-2000: A Critical Survey (Delhi: Pencraft International, 2001), pp. 114-115.
108. Farida Shaikh, "Mistress of Reinvention", *The Hindustan Times*, New Delhi, Aug. 25, 2002, p. 4.
109. R.K. Dhawan and Jaydipsinh Dodiya, in *The Fiction of Shobhaa De: Critical Studies*, edited by Jaydipsinh Dodiya (New Delhi: Prestige Books, 2000), pp. 13-14.
110. Somashukla Sinha Walunjkar's "Shobha De Storms Soap Box with *Sukanya*", *The Hindustan Times,* New Delhi, December 26, 2000, p. 4.
111. *Ibid.*
112. *Ibid.*
113. *Ibid.*
114. Dodiya's *The Fiction of Shobhaa De: Critical Study* (New Delhi: Prestige Books, 2000), p. 60.
115. *Ibid.*, p. 67.
116. A.S. Ratnam, ed., *Critical Essays on Indian Woman Writing in English* (New Delhi: Harman Publication House, 1999), p. 12.
117. J.M. Waghmare in *Critical Essays on Indian Woman Writing in English* edited by A.S. Ratnam (New Delhi: Harmann Publication House, 1999), p. 15.
118. Ravindra Nath Shukla's, (Hindi Translation), "Shobhaa De" in *The Dainik Jagaran*, Varanasi, U.P., May 24, 1997, p. 1.
119. Pavan K. Varma's, "Empress of the First World", *The Indian Express*, New Delhi, October 4, 1998, p. 4.
120. *Ibid.*
121. *Ibid.*

2

Socialite Evenings: Know Thyself

The *Socialite Evenings* (1988) is the first novel of Shobhaa De, which shot her into fame and she became a celebrity. The novel has the core message of feminist identity and independence. It tells the story of Karuna, a prominent Bombay (Mumbai) Socialite, trying to escape the nightmare of a broken marriage, failed relationships and mentally disturbed sister.

The *Socialite Evenings*, however, has not been received charitably by many a critic. They tend to criticise the novel and the novelist in a way, which is wrong and untenable. S.P. Swain, a feminist, sees the picture of marginalisation of the Indian Women in it while Subhas Chandra, considers it the portrayal of the family and marriage in the wealthy classes of urban Indian elite society which is not wide the mark as the protagonist belongs to it. Urbasi Barat has analysed it as a version of Kunstlerroman[1] 'from victim to non-victim' and feels that the most ubiquitous and enduring theme of the novel is the search for identity and self-hood. In the saga, the heroine has a quest to search about herself or her ownself, says Sheela Swarupa Rani, which emanates from her dissatisfaction with life. In the eyes of Inna Walter, it is the story of 'New Woman' who is independent in every way. It is a tale of initiation from ignorance and innocence to awareness and experience. Bhargavi Rao compares the feminine sensibility of this novel with Annes Jung's *Unveiling India*. A.G. Khan has not only negated the status and role of women in the novel but has nicknamed the novelist as the Great Vatsyayani, running and standing far away from the core issue of the novel and its essence.

About such erroneous and uncharitable remarks on *Socialite Evenings*, the novelist says that they "hurt her more than others—the sly, subversive one that tried to demolish me, my personal life and my career in the strongest possible terms".[2] She pensively illustrates that, one of the critics has suggested that "*Socialite Evenings* has been a ghost written by David himself, another that the editor had re-written so much of it, it was no longer my work."[3] But, it is not so.

Karuna, the heroine of the novel and a prominent Bombay socialite tries to escape into her past from the nightmarish present life of hers. For this, she writes a memoir of her life in a linear and flashback style. She wants to forget her bruised and battered condition due to "an unhappy divorce and succession of sordid affairs' which take place in her life and transform her character because she was not ready to accept the gauche middle-class give metamorphoses",[4] which shows her ignorance, inexperience because of her lack of guidance and ill effects of glamour on her mind. Though she deviates throughout her life, in the end she realises that "I know, I'm on to a good thing and the good thing is me,"[5] which eased her from all mortal weaknesses.

Karuna remains dissatisfied with all the three phases of her life, "before marriage, married life, life after separation from husband"[6] since her "curiosity gave way to confusion and finally to acceptance but that took an entire decades".[7] Soon after her return from USA, she felt "I need my own space. I need to find myself". (57) But the glamorous life of Mumbai has its hypnotic effects upon her and she finds herself lost once again in the morbid atmosphere.

However, she fails to get rid of a feeling of emptiness in life. During her school days, she was terribly self-conscious and resented her "middle class origins and the shabbiness of her life as the daughter of a middle-rung government official" (10) even though she got enough attention and affection from her parents and sisters. Karuna loses interest in studies and eventually not only she but also the girls of her group are given blue cards and thereafter expelled from their class for misconduct. This was a puzzling factor for her father.

Karuna's condition seems to impart veracity to Urbashi Barat's comment that the "most enduring theme in the novel is the search for identity and selfhood"[8] and it also ratifies the proposition of Rosalind Miles who says that "the novel has been and is a prime area for acts of definition and self-definition both personal and social",[9] Karuna's sense of freedom and liberty makes her rebel against her father and patriarchy and opt for the job of modelling without seeking permission from anybody. Anjali assists Karuna at every step. She becomes completely anti-puritan and anti-conservative in attitude and action due to the incommunicative attitude of her father.

Karuna becomes firmer, fiercer in her desire and determination against patriarchy, to fend females and femininity, for equality. She finds her mother's condition as very pathetic, which is always criticised and condemned by her father for nothing, which she meekly and silently bears. Virginia Woolf's comment practically suits it, that, "Imaginatively, she is of the highest importance. Practically, she (a woman) is completely insignificant".[10] The novelist here holds the opinion that man and society treat woman as a goddess or as a servile being but never as human. In general, the latter sense is preferred by men and society to subjugate entire womankind. Jane Wagner through Kate aptly expresses this feeling:

> I am sick of being the victim
> But don't even understand.[11]

Alfred Tennyson in *The Princess* expresses the same view:

> Man for the field
> And for the needle she[12].

Pushp Lata, therefore, is justified in so far as she maintains that the protagonist in the novel "raise a protest against the male dominated Indian society where women are denied the freedom to act according to their will and continue to cherish their own dreams in futility".[13] Thus, the novelist hopes that 'Men will have to come to terms with woman power'.[14]

Karuna takes an unusual and unprecedented decision of modelling without informing her father despite her mother's caution. The mother 'doesn't have courage to either protect her daughter or challenge her husband' but still she asks her, "...you tell him. Don't involve me. Later he will blame me if anything happens". (12-13) Thus, a significant fault of women has been pointed out by the novelist that woman is not courageous enough to face a man's irrational wrath.

Karuna starts looking for things outside, which she doesn't get in her home, but her hunger and quest "grew greater by the day for it was never fed" (15) perhaps due to negligence of her parents and unwariness of teachers. She becomes a problematic child at her school as well as home. Gross ignorance combined with lack of sincere love and genuine concern render her incompetent either from the point of view of taking any valid decision or facing the cunning, crafty world and still keeping her own identity. The result is that she can often be spotted wondering about in bewilderment in the modern world where tradition and modernity rub shoulders with each other. At such moments, the condition of a woman resembles more or less to a figure very aptly portrayed by Tagore:

> O woman, you are one-half woman
> And one—half dream.[15]

A vicious circle in Karuna's life is formed when Anjali enters into it with the proposal of modelling for her. With a strong impulse for the lust of life, Karuna is keen to utilise her liberty as a libertarian while at the same time envying Anjali for her lissom figure and vivacity. Anjali has a keen desire to protect Karuna from the depredations of this vulture world, but in vain.

Karuna gets an opportunity to do modelling for a Delhi based—jewellery shop. She assured her father that she would not bring any disgrace to him. Thus, here we have a glimpse of the "New Woman of Independent India",[16] who is "fearless, bright and eager to participate in work, in play".[17] This sprouts the feminist demand for liberation from the patronising castle of patriarchy which Manu, the first lawgiver of the world, advocated, "day and night women must be kept in dependence by the males of their families. The father protects her in childhood, husband protects her in youth, and her sons protect her in old age; a woman is never fit for independence".[18]

Karuna is obsessed with the word "status". So much so that she feels ashamed even of her middle class family. Karuna later realises that Anjali marries an ape-like Abe not for his money or Sweet Words, but for his generous and considerate attitude towards her. Karuna finds out that there is a striking resemblance between her status and social background and that of Anjali's as her marriage turns into a sort of compromise under the oppressive, exploitative, brutal and boorish Abe who blackmails her with "his dirty pictures". (40) So the "act of oppression not only disfigures the oppressor, it also maims the oppressed".[19]

On the basis of the foregone scrutiny of men's and women's condition in the family and society, we are forced to share Sarah Grimke's views, which certainly examines these social and sexual disparities that: "Man has subjugated woman to his will, to minister to his sensual pleasure. He has done all he could do to debase and enslave her mind".[20]

The novelist however, maintains that the proper development of a (girl) child's personality in a family needs filial love and concern of parents, in the absence of which the child is most likely to be led astray, like Karuna, Anjali and others.

The process of self-realisation takes place for the first time in Karuna's life, when she complains to Anjali about Abe's unsuccessful attempt to seduce her but she is stunned by the reply of same Anjali, who has, "lost all" her 'girlfriends to Abe' but doesn't 'Want to lose' (43) Karuna, this sudden and sharp slap in Karuna's face snaps her conscience, to search her own heart and within no time she "realised, the ridiculousness of" her 'position in their lives,' which is nothing more than a 'toy,' a thing for their amusement. She instantly "reasoned and decided to get out" (50) of their life.

After this incident, Karuna feels impelled to establish her as an independent model. She also collected enough money for her virgin trip to foreign lands, free from all strings and influences either from family, father or Anjali. Karuna, for the first time, in her life feels 'adventurous and liberated'. (50) Karuna dominates the patriarchy as well as tries to 'search' her 'identity,' which has been a theme in the fiction.[21] But she does so on the principle of *Ekam Gyaten Sarvam Gyatam Bhavati*, as enshrined in the "Chhandyogyopnishada", which is nearly parallel to the Chinese proverb, "who knows himself knows others".[22] Karuna herself emphasises this when she says about her brave new world trip that through it "I was going to find out about myself."

Karuna loses her virginity in her virgin trip. The same Sindhi stranger assists her to cancel her decision of unofficial engagement and marriage plan with Bunty, her "loving, affectionate, accommodating" (51) boyfriend. On her return to home from U.S.A., she firmly, convincingly and in an unrecognised voice commands him not to disturb her privacy. "You know—SPACE—I need my own space. I feel claustrophobic. I need to find myself". (55)

The above condition of Karuna is quite identical to what Charles Lamb points to Thomas Maining, "Nothing puzzles me more than time and space, and yet nothing troubles me less as I never think about them".[23] Thus, to kill her boredom, she decides to get married to a suitor, who proposes to her in a restaurant, not well acquainted with her. Karuna with her fanciless and fancy-free marriage "pushed herself by an acceptable male who wouldn't take no for an answer", (58) which makes her life even emptier, meaningless and boring, due to lack of communication. The novelist here offers a fitting comment about her marriage:

> A woman could walk out of a perfectly secure marriage out of boredom? Karuna the main protagonist, is not a bitch, if anything she is far too sensible and controlled.

> But she's one who recognises her marriage for what it is—empty. Her husband isn't a wife-beater, a drunkard or a gambler. There isn't any reason to leave him, yet that is what she does. Lack of communication is a valid enough explanation for her. She doesn't justify her decision, point fingers or attribute blame.[24]

The protagonist, however, remains dissatisfied with her married life due to its emptiness, lack of communication especially with her husband. To overcome her problems, she deviates in search of identity, enjoyment, communication and belongingness. Her ignorance and inexperience ultimately bring her divorce, when her husband catches her red handed.

After a year or so, the status of Karuna in her husband's house and family becomes insignificant. This affects her moral and womanly pride. Her frequent chats with her husband about his plans for the firm fade out "to nothing by the end of the first year of our marriage." (62) She is further "studiously excluded from the cosy mother-and-son dinner business chats." (63) Though her marriage pleases her parents, but for Karuna, it proved to "be a pretty terrific marriage." (63)

The novelist's views about the social inequality rampant in society can easily be gleaned here. The pertinent point, however, is as to how can this social inequality be remedied? If the adage 'money makes the mare go' has any social relevance, it is applicable here as nowhere else. Unless a woman is economically self-dependent and unless she contributes economically to the family budget, no improvement can be suggested to her social status and she will remain subservient to man's ego and superiority complex. Empowerment of women in different walks of life is another deterrent to woman's slavery and degradation. Both combined together will go a long way to make her socially more acceptable.

Karuna finds herself trapped into a "meaningless marriage" (64) like Anjali's divorce, because both are "loveless, joyless and bridgeless",[25] due to lack of understanding and trust among the spouses. Karuna and women of her group are "reduced to being marginal people"; (69) they are considered "dependent dolls" (69) to show "the status quo" (66) of their respective husbands. Through Karuna's dissatisfaction with her empty married life what the novelist wants to convey, here is akin to P.N. Tickoo's conviction that, "Marriage is not all love. The grand edifice of happy married life is based upon genuine love, deep respect, gratitude and sense of duty towards others".[26] The novelist decodes and declares the meaning of 'love' in a decisive epithet, through a French male character of the novel Perre, "Love is music and food and wine and touch." (81) The novelist here peripherally expresses her concern about, "the place of women's...in the existing system of values, just as the feminist questions the situation of women in society".[27]

Here the novelist tends to raise questions to demand equality for womankind as she has once, "When will our women be in a position to regulate and negotiate sexual intercourse in marriage on their terms? Or at any rate on more equal terms"?[28] In the present day, a woman who favours her husband in each and every aspect of his life is basically insecure, inferior to man. She not only faces sexual discrimination but also becomes a sex bait of the male and male dominated society. The only way to its solution, therefore, is the unforgettable lesson given to Karuna by Ritu. Karuna recalls it, "Men like dogs, could be conditioned through reward and punishment. It was a lesson I'd never forget." (87)

Karuna is not sure about the longevity of her marriage and, therefore, she doesn't want any child in her life, for "the children always come off the worse in a divorce". (106) Being a dependant doll, Karuna is mercilessly humiliated by her husband as "unfaithful, selfish, treacherous". (150) While her mother-in-law directs her through her husband to "do something", (151) this stresses the point that "a woman has to be self-sufficient these days". (143)

During her religious devotion, Anjali organizes a *janmashtami* (149) celebration at her home. In it she invites Karuna along with her husband to attend the party; but Karuna goes there with Ritu, because her husband spurns Karuna's request and denigrates Anjali as "a real bitch". (151)

Here through this "*Janmashtami* party" (153), the novelist conveys the very idea and ideal of patriarchy which Sudhir Kakkar, the psychologist, has also conveyed that in Indian tradition, "a woman knows that motherhood confers upon her a purpose of identity that nothing else in her culture can. Each infant born and nurtured by her safely into childhood, especially if the child is a son, is both a certification and redemption".[29]

In this party, Karuna feels a kind of attraction for Krish Mukherji, "a hot-blooded Bengali rebel from the late 60s, who had flirted with all the right things—poetry, theatre and politics"; (164) he is also a "pretentious adman, whose wife actively helps him in his extra-marital affairs".[30] Her husband introduces Krish to Karuna as "a great guy" (167) at her house. She finds him "a shy, sensitive, mixed up man whom she 'instantly' fell in love with". (168) Krish Mukherji starts seducing Karuna from his very first meeting by offering her a "chameli gajra", (168) appreciating her feet that "they have a lot of character in them" (169) and by inviting her to attend "a little workshop" (169) at his theatre. Karuna's husband, however, remains too simple to suspect his wife's three years long "torrid affair" (170) with Krish, which they conduct through letters.

The novelist through Karuna's case wants to draw the attention of her readers to the all-pervading malady known as 'lack of communication' between husband and wife or between two near and dear ones. This malady is more prevalent in our cosmopolitan towns and cities. Psychologists like Eric Fromm hold this state of affairs directly responsible for many of the mental illnesses of the modern man. Man being gregarious by nature, mechanical living and style of life is repugnant to his nature and psyche and sooner this anomaly is removed, the better for the future generations yet to come.

Absence of progeny between the spouses is also one major cause for discordant notes between the couple and is one potent reason, which eventually breeds permissiveness. What then is the remedy for such deviation and extra-marital misadventure? In a country like India, which is bursting at the seams due to its teeming millions, there is hardly any need for extra mouths to be born but this fact of life is not comprehensible to the unwary and ill educated. Conscientisation, therefore, is the only way open to India's milling crowds. But before any scheme for conscientisation is embarked upon, food, clothing and shelter is a must and only then can any plan for higher living can have any chance of success. The novelist gives an identical message through the protagonist who feels awful that she has joined the rank of "an adulteress", (175) the very thing she used to condemn in her recent past.

Karuna doesn't opt for the policy of "silence is the best defence", (180) when her husband scold her for her present adulterous affair with Krish, "If you hadn't forced him on me, this would never have happened". (184) Further, she announces about emptiness and end of her marriage. "I think our marriage was over the day our honeymoon started. We have got nothing going. I don't love you—never have", (184) because of his "smugness and irritating mannerism" (185) and the way he takes her for granted.

Here, the novelist suggests woman to be practical in life. For this, she has to know and decide 'her main priority desire, destination, keeping things round about her daily life in her mind.' She must have control over her passions and desires and must have the civil behaviour, that is, respecting the personality of others just as we have respect for our own. This is quite necessary so that she is neither deviated nor humiliated by any being just like Karuna, who realises soon after her husband's departure that Krish really, is "a shallow, exploitative, utterly ordinary, no he is even less than that, human being." (191)

Karuna's "grand passion—stupidity" (191) comes to an end, when Krish regrets to challenge her husband to "a duel" (191) to express his love for her. For this reason, she does not accept his love symbol 'chameli gajra' or "chamelis." (191) Krish rejects her plan to stay any more in Venice, when he comes to know about the presence of her husband. A person like Krish is an example of 'green-world lover, who "is certainly no ideal non-patriarchal man—no man in De's fictional world ever is—unconsciously and unintentionally he is the precipitating factor behind her realization that the woman has no-one to turn to but herself".[31] So, through Krish, the novelist vehemently criticizes opportunists present in the society. Here, Krish's nature serves as a source of self-realization and scrutiny. This is the second opportunity for Karuna to know about herself, her mind, her motto and the way of the world, after her school and college life.

The worst part of Karuna's life starts with the sudden problem of pregnancy, which surprises even her when she says, "How could I be pregnant"? (212) She is afraid of her non-aesthetic figure "with a gross, disfigured body? And, the pain, blood and slime, 'a very distasteful process' with life-long responsibility attached to it"; (214) which she does not like. The child issue or pregnancy becomes an apple of discord between the protagonist and her husband. He not only disowns the unborn child, as he blusters his way out of this difficult situation by saying, "It cannot be mine anyway"! (215) Because he has no more 'trust' in her any longer" (215) due to her affair with Krish "right under his nose", (215) he accuses her of adultery which according to him "is an addiction—it's only the first time that is difficult". (215)

Karuna's father who was previously all praise for her has turned quite antagonistic and all of a sudden becomes totally indifferent to her pains and pangs by making an excuse and accuses her of betrayal and or serious offence: "What you have done is totally unacceptable, nobody in our family has done it before, nobody will do it in the future. You've made the mistake, now you pay the price". (219) So, even her parents want to absolve themselves of any responsibility by leaving their own daughter in the lurch and thrust her to face the atrocities of the male world. They are not courageous enough to accept adultery as it is against all types of civilised norms. Here the novelist not only portrays the pathetic and abject condition of womankind in the Indian social set up but also exhorts women to help one another in their "poor battle of survival",[32] for their identity, existence as human beings and equality with men.

Karuna's second phase of self-realization begins when her husband advises her, "it is better to be independent". (222) Later, for the sake of identity and belongingness she toys "with the idea of keeping the baby" (222) which is outright disapproved and cancelled by Anjali, who put her daughter Mimi's case as an instance before her, and cautions her against motherhood because "a baby is a life-long responsibility" (222) and will be responsible for her permanent deterioration.

Karuna feels most "lonelier" when 'fibroid' (223) is discovered in her womb which meant that she has became barren and can "never have children" (223). Karuna now realises that, "there is something like divine justice. I've never been a believer—but now I'm beginning to wonder. I'm being made to pay for my sins. This wouldn't have happened if I hadn't got involved with Krish". (224) She atones for her guilt and decides to live a simple, lonely but thoroughly independent life. Her childhood innocence and rest for life revive her from her physical and mental illness in the caring company of her mother who was earlier disowned by her. Karuna undergoes transformation in her character and nature, which is the direct outcome of self-realisation; resurrection of identity, hope, belongingness and her life journey from innocence to experience.

Karuna is in the grip of poverty, "no money, no job, no nothing. Not even a cupboard to call her own". (234) Krish tries to entrap her once again through a new offer, but Karuna who has learnt a lot through her life and experience rejects the offer "why don't you be the creep that you are and creep the hell out of my life". (237) Karuna is able to resurrect herself by her hard labour and the emotional support provided by her father, "our doors are always open to our children" (254) and she realised to experience "cultural affinities" (254) which she had missed all these years by disregarding her parents. She rejects a prestigious offer to act in the film titled *Shakuntala* (modern version), which was being directed by a noted film director Mr. Girish Shridhar to enjoy her "little patch of independence" (255) in the presence of her "parents". (256)

The novelist has portrayed the pathetic condition of Karuna's husband, who has now kept Winnie as his woman, and plans to marry her after sometime. Winnie's "assertive, bossy and flagrantly sexual" (238) nature once again brings him at the door of Karuna with the request to rescue him from the grip of Winnie by announcing that she wants to "come back". (264) Karuna remains indifferent and tells him, "Just get the hell out of my house and life. I don't ever want to see you again. I let you in this time—but never again. I'll call the cops if you try and invade my home in future. You are a worm. You deserve Winnie". (264) Thus novelist has emphasised the need of loyalty amongst spouses, so that they may lead a happy and harmonious life as usually second marriages may not bring in the desired happiness in their lives.

The gossip news published in the newspaper that Karuna is having "an affair with both, father [Girish Sridhar] and son [Kunal Sridhar]" (267) upsets her. She is further "confused and happy at the same time", (270) when Kunal comes to her and conveys his father's desire to marry her. However, she is emotionally moved by the pathetic condition of her parents and declines the offer of the marriage for the time being, because "gossip" (270) cannot be

> a reason enough to get married. Not now, at any rate. Living with my parents had opened up a new dimension for me. I felt like a responsible, caring daughter for the first time in my life. They need me. And I needed them. We had arrived at a happy situation. They didn't have a son to look after them in their old age. They had the enormous burden of an invalid daughter to cope up. Each day in their life was a major struggle to just get on with the living that remained. How could I abandon them at this point? It would have been a callous, cruel thing to do. Walk in. Walk out. No. There was just no way I was going to stride into my room, fling my few belongings into a suitcase and take off. (271)

Karuna now does some introspection, which is a great help in unravelling her own personality and thus fix her priorities for life. Karuna decides to serve her parents as a son, as service to man is service to the creator Himself and since benevolence must begin at home, parents are the first beings who deserve the service of their progeny.

Karuna has been working for a firm, which "bagged the Ad Club award for the Best Ad of the Year." (273) She also gets the award individually, "an individual citation as copywriter of the year". (273) She is suggested to go full time and professionalize in advertising business, as her market is up, "Capitalize on your award—now is the time". (273) But she resists the temptation as her priorities have changed, "It wasn't money or success I was looking forward to in my life" but "it is the freedom to do what I wanted", (273-274) which she very easily gets through her part time job. This shows that at long lost she has come to have some serious purpose in life and that is, herself.

She is sincerely advised by her mother to marry, "Take your time, but marry. And marry the right one—that is important". (275) The mother's notion about marriage is the traditional one. She believes that a woman cannot live alone as society is very cruel and therefore "a woman needs a man's protection, a woman's real place is in her husband's home—not in her parents". (275) Karuna, however, finds herself far more "secure and at peace" (276) in her present condition. She question her mother "Why does [a woman's] security rest with a man"? (276) She tells her mother very plainly that she can look after herself, as she has a roof over her head and she was earning equal to a man, "I'm at peace with myself. I don't feel like complicating my life by getting into a second marriage. I can't make any 'sacrifices'—not now". (276)

Karuna, with the passage of time, has developed self-confidence, which is evident from her snubbing Varun, a very powerful editor of the *Outlook* who had been slinging mud on her character to defame her, "How dare you. I'm not afraid of your threats. You can bloody well go ahead and print what you wish". (279) The same self-confidence is noticeable in her dealings with an America based NRI Randhir Roy "a roving correspondent" (281) of *The Washington Times*. She rejects a lucrative offer from Randhir Roy to figure in a documentary on the theme of "the *desi* lib movement" (305) on dowry death with Indira Gandhi angle for American viewers. Through Karuna, the novelist has tried to present a picture of modern liberated woman, who is upright, active, smart and scrupulously avoids two pests—sloth and indecision—such a woman who is economically independent "I had no one to rely on but me". (240)

Anjali, who remains an ideal and idol for Karuna from her teens to her present state of maturity and brimming self-confidence, is always in a mess due to ignorance and her love for the life of senses. After her divorce from her husband Abe with whom she has been leading a loveless unhappy marital life, she feels that she cannot "face the world alone without a man by [her] side". (57)

Anjali commits her second mistake in marrying Mr. Kumar, a 'homo' who needs her as "a front" (125) in the society. This frustrates Anjali's desire to lead "a proper married life with a proper husband and a home". (126) She turns to spiritualism and religion to seek relief from her mundane existence. She shares her feelings with Karuna:

> What is sex compared to religion? Nothing! The ecstacy I experience when I'm praying or listening to my *bhajans* is far better than an orgasm. I'm into this totally, and sex has become irrelevant. In fact, I hate to use the sort of language we used to—you know—fuck-shuck and all that. I feel impure. (140)

Anjali recovers through her faith in religion and self-realisation and finds that "Peace and love" (140) are essential for harmonious development of entire humanity. Anjali who is now overflowing with love for all, forgives every body, even Si, who always criticised her—vehemently. However, she has not been able to rise above her desires as she admits, "I made a complete fool of myself", (295) in the anniversary celebration party of *Outlook*. Though "Anjali did become a star of the party and it took Anjali years to recover from the aftermath",

(288) Karuna at once realises that she is "not Anjali" (304) who was once her ideal and who represented the "height of good living." (27) Anjali is one character in the novel, running from pillar to post—in search of peace and happiness, but they elude her grasp. Her life is a reminder to the readers that they should opt for a life of simplicity and self-introspection if they are in the search of real happiness.

Another character of some importance is gorgeous, vivacious Ritu who leaves her second husband for a smuggler Gul and becomes his pimp, procuring "virgins for his and his friends". (220) She lives a sick and servile life and to get deliverance from it, she makes a "half-hearted suicide attempt" (221) by taking a handful of pills along with whisky. She is timely saved by Gul and his henchmen. Ritu is a sadomasochist and has a quality to entice men of all ages. She has firm faith in manipulating 'sex' and advises Karuna to enjoy "a boring husband in the home and an exciting lover on the side lines—perfect...can have both" (173) and inspires her to take "a couple of hard decisions." (173) She does not understand the difference between "a wife and a mole" (131) like Anjali which ultimately turned her life nightmarish.

Ritu returns to her husband after her suicide attempt who "accepted her without any questions asked and they'd gone off to the hills for two months to get away from everything." (228) Though her husband is boring as ever, but she now realises that he is very "sweet about everything". (229) In the lap of nature, her process of self-realization starts and she worships the "Original Earth Mother" who mends her. Thus the novelist has repeatedly emphasised the importance of self-introspection (To know thyself) as it has the unlimited capacity to transform oneself. The novelist is also in favour of marriage, which is based on mutual understanding, respect and sense of sacrifice between spouses. The novelist does not approve divorce as "The children always come off the worse in a divorce". (106) Finally, the novelist suggests the readers that self-introspection, meditation, rumination over nature of things and a ceaseless effort to find light are the keys to a peaceful and harmonious social life.

NOTES

1. "From Victim to Non-Victim *Socialite Evenings* as a version of Kunstlerroman," in Jaydeepsinh Dodia, ed., *The Fiction of Shobhaa De: A Critical Study* (New Delhi: Prestige Books, 2000), p. 119.
2. Shobhaa De, *Selected Memory: Stories from My Life* (New Delhi: Penguin Books India (P) Ltd., 1998), p. 398.
3. *Ibid.*, p. 328.
4. Shobhaa De, *Socialite Evenings* (New Delhi: Penguin Books India (P) Ltd., 1969). Back side of the jacket of the novel.
5. Shobhaa De, *Socialite Evenings* (New Delhi: Penguin Books India (P) Ltd., 1969), p. 306. All further references to the novel will be incorporated in the text.
6. Jaydipsinh Dodiya, ed., *The Fiction of Shobhaa De: Critical Studies* (New Delhi: Prestige Books India (P) Ltd., 2000), p. 161.
7. Shobhaa De, *Selected Memory* (New Delhi: Penguin Books India (P) Ltd., 1998), p. 331.
8. Urbashi Barat, "From Victim to Non-victim: *Socialite Evenings* as a version of Kunstlerroman," *The Fiction of Shobhaa De*. p. 119.
9. *The Female Form: Women Writers and the Conquest of the Novel* (London: Routledge and Kegan Paul, 1990), p. 61.
10. Virginia Woolf, *A Room of One's Own* (New York: Harcourt, Brace and Word, 1992), p. 45.
11. Jane Wagner, *The Search for Signs of Intelligent Life in the Universe* (New York: Harper and Row, 1978), p. 53.
12. Alfred Tennyson, *The Princess*, V.L., pp. 426-27.
13. Pushp Lata, "A Protest against the Patriarchal in Shobhaa De's Works," *The Fiction of Shobhaa De: Critical Study* (New Delhi, Prestige Books, 2000), p. 62.
14. Shobhaa De, *Shooting from the Hip: Selected Writings* (New Delhi, UBS Publication, 1994), pp. 111-13.
15. Quoted by S.P. Swain in his article "Socialite Evenings: A Feminist Study," Dodiya's, *The Fiction of Shobhaa De: Critical Study* (New Delhi, Prestige Books, 2000), p. 132.
16. Chittaranjan Mishra, "Shobhaa De: Autobiographic Strategies in Selective Memory," in *The Fiction of Shobhaa De*. p. 330.
17. Dorothy Schneider and Carl J. Scheneider, *American Women in the Progressive Era, 1900-1920* (New York: Facts on File, 1923), p. 148.
18. *Manu Smriti*, Vol. IX, pp. 2-3. Quoted in the *Encyclopaedia of Women in India* edited by B.K. Vashista (New Delhi: Praveen Encyclopaedia Publications, 1976).
19. Sheila Rowbotham, *Women's Consciousness, Man's World* (England: Penguin Books, 1988), p. xvi.

20. Sarah Grimke, *Letters on the Equity of the Sexes and the Conditions of Women* (New York: Burt Franklin, 1970), p. 10.
21. Nisha Trivedi, "Search for Identity in Shobhaa De's *Starry Nights*" In Veena Noble Das and R.K. Das and R.K. Dhawan, *Fiction of Nineties* (New Delhi: Prestige Books, 1994), p. 62.
22. Rosalind Fergussion, *The Penguin Dictionary of Proverbs* (London: Penguin Books Ltd., 1983), p. 214.
23. Charles Lamb, "A Letter to Thomas Maining," January 2, 1810. (*Brihat Vishwasukti Kosha* [International Thesaurus of Quotations], Vol. II, New Delhi, 1996. ed. by Dr. Shyam Bhadur Verma, Prabhat Prakashan, 4/19, Asaf Ali Road, New Delhi, p. 462.
24. Shobhaa De, *Selective Memory: Stories of My Life* (New Delhi, Penguin Books India (P) Ltd., 1998), p. 330.
25. S.P. Swain, "Socialite Evenings: A Feminist Study," in Jayadipsinh Dodiya's *The Fiction of Shobhaa De: Critical Study* (New Delhi: Prestige Books, 2000), p. 130.
26. P.N. Tickoo, *Indian Woman* (New Delhi: B.R. Publishing Corporation, 1985), p. 72.
27. Olga Kenyon, *Women Novelists Today: A Survey of the English Writers in the Seventies and Eighties* (Brithon Susex: The Harvested Press, 1990), p. 7.
28. Shobhaa De, "Powerless in a Last World" Published in *The Week* January 23, 2000, p. 10.
29. Sudhir Kakkar, *The Indian Psyche* (New Delhi: Oxford University Press, 1998), p. 56.
30. Shobhaa De, *Socialite Evenings* (New Delhi: Penguin Books India (P) Ltd., 1989). Back side of the jacket of the novel.
31. Urbashi Barat, "From Victim to Non-Victim *Socialite Evenings* as a version of Kunstlerroman," in Jaydipsinh Dodiya's *The Fiction of Shobhaa De: Critical Studies* (New Delhi: Prestige Books, 2000), p. 126.
32. Shantha Krishnaswamy, *The Woman in Indian Fiction in English (1950-80)* (New Delhi: Ashish Publishing House, 1984), p. VIII. (Abstract)

3

Starry Nights: Hope and Struggle as Essence of Life

Starry Nights (1991) is the second novel of Shobhaa De, which has been viewed by critics variously. The novel basically deals with the Bollywood life, which has been portrayed through the protagonist Viji or Aasha Rani. She acquires success and status in her life through hard labour, sacrifice, slavery and sexual exploitation, for which men have been held responsible by the novelist. But, Jayadipsinh Dodiya and R.K. Dhawan are of the opinion that this novel is a "frank and candid expression of love and lust". Sandhyarani Dash pays attention to the protagonist; she takes into account many factors about Aasha Rani, such as, "her exploration vis-à-vis her sexual exploitations in a male-dominated society". Geeta Barua is of the opinion that the novel is about the rise and fall of the protagonist Aasha Rani. Nisha Trivedi feels that, the novelist has presented different models of women characters in this novel, and, each and every character like Aasha Rani is strong enough to take decision boldly to survive in the society. Sudhir Kumar interprets this novel on the basis of feminist theories propounded by M. Gilbert and Susan Gubar. Lastly, Prabhat Kumar Pandeya sees in it the theme of lesbianism, and tries to exemplify it through the character of the protagonist.

About this novel, the novelist is of the opinion that, it is "a ringside view"[1] and "a fictitious account of Bollywood".[2] She admits that it is slightly based on the romance of Rekha-Amitabh. She writes: "their relationship did provide a take-off point for the novel but was by no means a faithful retelling of their off-screen lives. There are undoubtedly a few shades of Rekha in Aasha Rani, while Akshay is a pale reflection of Amitabh Bachchan".[3] Further, she writes that, "The events in the book are not real but are based on reality. Most of the characters in the book are based on actual individuals I've encountered or whose existence I was aware of, but the key word is 'based'".[4] As in the novel, she illustrates the underworld 'dons' with *seths* and Divya Bharti with Sudha Rani. She has delineated women's degradation and exploitation in the novel, "The language employed was harsh, crude and explicit. It was the only way I knew to capture the underlying tragedy of Aasha Rani, to underline the depth of degradation she is subjected to, to better define the extent of exploitation that dominates this world of sham and make-believe".[5] In a nutshell, she is against all sorts of discriminations against women.

According to an Italian scholar Alessandro Monti, *Starry Nights* is a novel about Bollywood's hellish life as he writes:

> The safe measure is heavily discounted in the novel *Starry Night* (1991), with its derogatory sequences of *sthalas* (places) devoted either to wholesale corruption or to temporary escapes from the Bollywood hell. *Starry Nights* makes a valuable test-case, spotlighting as it does the career of the film star Aasha Rani, who whore her way to ephemeral stardom. The pressures the filmi milieu exacts on the heroine of *Starry Nights* are toned down to a more intimate quest for self-expression and identity.[6]

"The Pasha of the pulp",[7] who claims herself to be "among the first to explore the world of the urban woman in India",[8] in a way justifies the comment of Anita Desai about the art of writing, which "is an effort to discover, and then to underline, and finally to convey the true significance of things",[9] through her second novel, *Starry Nights*. Although the novel seems to be full of "female homosexuality, lesbianism, sapphism, tribalism",[10] with pornographic details, yet it "has all the ingredients of a *masala* production, sex, violence (that is, in both the categories—sexual violence and violent sex) in it".[11] But, the feminist charge against men is, "whichever way one looked at it, there was always a man in the picture. A man using, abusing and finally discarding a woman";[12] and the message of hope regarding the betterment of the womankind is given by the novelist through it, when she writes, "It was Diwali tomorrow. The festival of lights". (234)

Though Geetha Devi wants to protect her daughter Viji or Aasha Rani from "Men", (4) but she fails to do so. This happens because the father of the protagonist has "deserted them. The mother had been left with three girls to raise—the poverty, the deprivation, the struggle". (4) This compels Amma to opt for the profession of prostitution. It eludes comprehension why only this much poverty forces a mother to compel her daughters to adopt prostitution. The mother along with daughters could take up menial jobs: cleaning utensils, sweeping, washing clothes even spinning and weaving or selling fruits and vegetables, ground nuts, parched rice, gram and other eatables. Selling away body for favours of pecuniary gains is world's oldest profession. It is a matter of regret and surprise too why a seasoned writer like Shobhaa De has directed her female characters to take up prostitution instead of asking them to opt for menial jobs and earn their daily bread by the sweat of their braw. Aasha Rani recalls it, "She'd come back late in the night, smelling strange and looking sleepy". (69) She forces Viji, "to 'perform' in blue film when she was not quite twelve" (19) just to "make her a star". (19)

In Mumbai, Viji becomes the first prey of Kishenbhai, who considers her his personal property when he says, "you are mine. Only mine, all mine". (6) Such difficulties in life by men arouse a voice and feeling of protest even rebellion against men. The protagonist openly challenges men and their social system through Kishenbhai, when she diffidently warms him, "I will do to men what they try to do to me. I will screw you all—beat you at your own game".(8) She says so because she has full faith and hope that her future will be certainly bright. The novelist expresses this anticipation as "The extra 'a' made all the difference between success and failure". (14) This hope sustains her and keeps her spirits high to emerge victorious from the pains, problems and challenges to her.

In this novel, the novelist seems to be of the opinion that, "feminism continues to challenge itself as well as its 'enemies'".[13] It can be verified from the novel through conflicts between different women characters, though the prime source of the problem behind them is a man who drives a wedge and creates differences among them. She starts her aggression, therefore, against patriarchy. Kishenbhai becomes its first victim, when he objects and abuses Aasha Rani for her affair with Seth Amirchand. This provokes her into giving a trenchant and fitting reply to him, instead of being apologetic for it. She counters him, "You financed and produced my first film, Kishenbhai, but you extracted payment from my body. You call me a prostitute, but you forget that you were my first pimp. So don't throw *ahsan* on me. I owe you nothing". (13) At this juncture, Amma supports her daughter's view and her liberty, "She is free to go with whoever she wants". (13)

So it is clear that, Aasha Rani's mental agony has a regressive link with past—innocent days of her childhood, when she faces the agony of child abuse by her Appa's assistant producer Gopalakrishnan. She remembers, "Soon her hand had been slyly slipped into his *mundu*, his hand had been replaced by what felt like a firm, hard stick. Aasha Rani had wanted to scream. But, she was terrified. Finally, he had turned limp, she had felt her small hand go damp with something sticky and smelly". (196) Owing to this, Sandhyarani Dash correctly comments that, "Aasha Rani's irresistible sexual desire is not inherent, but, the manifestation of a suppressed sense of vengeance of the male world which has its roots in the ill-treatment of her Amma by her Appa, or it is because of her own exploitation by the male world since her childhood".[14]

Aasha Rani is so dependent on her mother that her each and every sentence begins and ends with "Mummy says". (3) Owing to this dependence, "Aasha Rani's first lesson in exploitation begins with her scheming mother who, for the sake of money, uses her fifteen-year-old daughter, forcing her to be the bed-mate of producers and distributors. She also thrusts Aasha Rani into the orgy of blue films".[15] And, "for the hungry people of the film world, it is the forty inch bust of this fifteen-year-old girl, which becomes the centre of attraction".[16]

In the novel, Aasha Rani remains a passive character who is always acted upon, even by Akshay, "Who has no courage to take a bold step".[17] He has started his "Screw Aasha Rani campaign with a vengeance". (52) He exploited her physically, emotionally and sexually, and even then he remains dissatisfied with her. He, therefore, opts for two ways to harm her. First, by demanding and threatening Nitesh that, "Aasha Rani be dropped from his forthcoming film, or else! *Industrywallahs* know all about the Nitesh-Aasha Rani *lafda*". (52) Second, by propagating a scandal against Aasha Rani that she "in her *Kadka*, hard-up days, ...was forced to act *nanga-panga* in those sexy *sambar* films shot in sleazy Madras hotels". (52) Owing to this, she finds herself in "desperately alone, and sick" (52) condition and finally, her romance with Akshay was off "as suddenly as it was on". (52)

Money plays an important role in the life of the protagonist and her lover, "All these relatives were just the same. Like *amma*. What do they care about the people who slave in the studio to make money for them? Nothing. But they want to control their lives all right". (16) But, money is not everything as with all the opulence, fame and luxury, Aasha Rani misses one thing one vitally important thing, "genuine love".[18] "Deprived of true love and sympathy, she seeks shelter in Akshay's bosom".[19] Her yearning for freedom from the world of bondage seems obvious when she says with irritation to her mother "Money, money, money. That's all you think of. *I'm fed up of being your money machine. I've done enough for everybody now, I want to live for myself*". (106-07) Thus, the protagonist here longs for two things 'true love and liberty' for the sake of equality with men.

After being beaten and kicked out by Akshay, Sheth Amirchand goes to see Aasha Rani at her residence. He assures her "Now your career has taken off; it's stupid to throw it away". (56) Aasha Rani feels happy because "she needs a backer, some one with muscle. And money". (58) And her Amma is "interested in what is best for my daughter for her career, her future. I want to see that she has enough money. That she settles down properly. Let her go to Shethji". (58) But, Shethji is interested in her because she is "different. Intelligent and *bindaas* [and hopes that], this *chidiya* will go far". (56) More than this, Aasha Rani's "sex-appeal" (145) touches him, which according to him, "A man had only to take one look at her and he'd feel aroused—like an animal". (146) So, Amirchand poaches on the keep of Kishenbhai and becomes her new pimp. Aasha Rani prospers financially, which "she badly needed". (61) She also gets an offer on behalf of Sheth Amirchand for shopping in Dubai to "forget Akshay". (65) But, "Dubai had still not prepared her for life without Akshay". (67) While her worldly status remains the same as before, even the eunuch Mastaan comments on her, "All you women are the same—screw a thousand men get your womb filled by one of them and then come and *phasao* the rich one". (59-60) It is later confirmed by Shethji, who openly says that, "I have not decided yet whether to make you my permanent keep. Women create too many complications. It is easier to use them and discard them. Replacement is always more stimulating for a woman to hold a man's interest, she has to offer more than just her body". (62) So, here the novelist presents woman as commodity. It is another thing that *shethji* himself like others is not so possessive in nature as Kishenbhai, because he grants her liberty, "You are free to sleep with anybody you choose". (62)

Akashay and Asha Rani feel attracted towards each other, for "sexual gratification"[20] and Aasha Rani for love and company. But Akshay is a sadist by nature, which is evident from his striking on the "naked" (70) body of Asha Rani "with his belt" (70) in the studio's make up room. She is rescued by Geetha Devi [Amma] her mother. At this moment, the utterance of Gita Devi is very significant: "You—shameless fellow—running after women when you have a wife at home! My daughter is free to see any one, any time! She is not your property, understand?" (70-1) Here, two things are noticeable:

liberty and freedom are as much the prerogative of women as of men and a woman has an identity of her own, which by no means can be subjugated by man.

Owing to her "lonely and bored" (75) life and impelled by the womanly instinct to conceive, Aasha Rani proposes Akshay to marry her even by proselytising, but the latter rejects it as he lacks courage and is mortally afraid of his brother, "Ajay will kill me". (108) He slyly puts the excuse that, "*I don't want to become a Muslim.* I believe in my religion. I don't want to give up my faith. *I was born a Hindu. I want to die a Hindu.* I want to be cremated; not buried". (108) Here, Akshay makes religion a scapegoat for duping and betraying Aasha Rani. Upon this, she infuriatingly replies him, "You've just taken me up again because your career is in the doldrums, and you're scared shitless of your wife". (108) After this in a fit of rage she tries to commit "suicide", (109) by taking an overdose of sleeping pills but thanks to timely help by Kishenbhai and Geetha Devi (*amma*) that she is saved. It "gave a little boost to Akshay's career", (114) but not to her.

The next man in Aasha Rani's life is Suhas, who has a "civilized divorce" (83) with his ex-wife Suhaila. "Which meant that they still sleep together when the night got lonesome". (83) He assigns her to an art film "*Bechari Begam*", (81) to be shot at Jaipur. Suhas is an impotent. "Suhas's inability to perform made him crabby [and therefore, he decries Aasha Rani and her effort by saying] Bloody bitch!" (86) He snarls at her, "Take your filthy fingers off me". (86) Suhas is followed and superseded by Abhijit Mehra, son of Amrish Mehra, a man "as powerful as the Prime Minister, as ruthless as hangman and as wealthy as the dictator of banana republic". (89)

Abhijit loves Aasha Rani passionately. But Aasha Rani doesn't give him much importance because he is "a married man with a lovely young wife". (97) He comes to her "For sex. Nothing else! I'm just your celebrity—just a sexy *Madraasi* girl with big tits. You are not making love to me! You are screwing my image—my screen image". (97) She commands him therefore, to "Get out of her life here, Abhijit. Go back to your wife and make a man of yourself! It's all over between us. I never want to see you again". (97) Behind this, there is one more reason also and that is that Aasha Rani wants her "own life to lead". (97)

"It was Akshay she wanted.... All the time". (103) It makes her a reluctant actress. Just on time her Amma comes back to her from Madras, whom she needs "to organize her future". (104) Amma asks her to keep herself always engaged in some work because "**work is the best cure for everything**". (118) Though she is engaged in the role of "Sita—A real goddess!" (119) Which symbolises sacrifice, but this time this role is quite different as it has been changed "into a modern woman with lib Ideas", (119) which means no more sacrifice for any man. Aasha Rani is fascinated by the carefree life of the fisher folk. She wonders about them, "Did these women ever worry about their future?" (118) She also recalls her romance with Ramesh a "gallant sportsman" (121) who chanced to meet her in Dubai.

At this time of her life, Abhijit meets Aasha Rani once again and proposes to her a plan for elopement with him. "Come away with me. Some place where nobody knows us. In fact, even the old man won't suspect a thing—New Zealand—that's where! Let us go to Auckland". (121) They are "safely airborn", (123) this news has been conveyed by Malini to Amrishbhai "through a common source". (123) At Auckland Airport, Amrishbhai located his son and comes back to India along with him. He is munificent enough to leave for Aasha Rani a sizable amount to pay for her hotel bills and her sojourn. He also promised Aasha Rani to give her more if she required on her arrival back.

Aasha Rani spends ten days in Wellington. "She hadn't ever been alone before. Entirely alone—like she now found herself". (125) There by a quirk of chance, she meets Jamie Phillips (Jay) on her sixth day in Wellington in a disco. He astonishes her through his knowledge of Hindi films and film stars, dialogues and lyrics. He mimicked her also and acted in Akshay's style. At this point, he asked whether she has married Akshay. After learning from her that Akshay has disappointed her, he came out with a flourish. "Would you do me the honour of marrying me? I am yours, single, AIDS-free and considerably well off. I've been a little in love with you for years, and this seems like a dream come true. Would you make me happy and be my wife?" (127) Jay tells Aasha Rani to think over his proposal and requests her to convey her decision by Thursday. Duped and desolate, forsaken and forlorn, Aasha Rani accedes to his impassioned pleading and consents for marriage. It may be pertinent here to remark that the novelist is a consummate psychologist. It is commonly felt that there comes a period in every woman's life, and in a man's as well, when she yearns and craves for marriage and progeny; she instinctively desires an offspring and opts for wedlock. Aasha Rani was desperate for such an offer and she grabs the very first opportunity to become a spouse. But it was not to 'save' Aasha Rani as she tended to think later that Jay opted to marry her. He himself made it amply clear at a later stage when he said, "I did it for myself. I find you impossibly sexy and...exotic. I was sick of bland with girls from proper English school. I liked you the way you were with your funny Indian accents. I miss that old you". (170) He says further, "I miss your saris and all those fussy clothes, all the little rituals and *pujas* you used to perform in the beginning. I still find you indecently sexy". (170) Though once Jay tries to convince her of that, "we white men are not exactly sex maniacs. And all the white girls aren't nymphos". (131) But his statement is contradicted when he acknowledges his affair with Nanny by betraying Aasha Rani. "I won't deny that she and I were having an affair. I love the girl. She loves me. I guess it was Sasha who was the common factor". (209)

After a gap of five years when Aasha Rani returns to India along with her husband and daughter, her hatred for her Appa, which had reached its high water mark, expressed through sentences like, "let him die like a dog". (72) "A real bastard who abandoned all of us and never showed his face again, wasn't it enough that he ruined *amma's* life and ours?" (72) Now changes into love, empathy and sympathy for him. "Aasha Rani was shocked to see *appa*". (160) "I will not allow you to stay here for one more minute. Who put you in this hell? Why is not anyone looking after you?" (162) After this sea change in Aasha Rani and also because of the need of the time Jay advises her to stay in India. "This is where you belong. Your father needs you desperately. It would kill you if I force you back. It would also finish off our marriage". (170) Here we find that Indian "feminism is based on the concept of humanism".[21] This apart, care and concern for members of the family has been a major aspect of Indian culture. Although under the impact of Westernization, Indian traditions are fastly crumbling, yet some remnants of the past still constitute the dominant trends.

Owing to her stay in Bombay, Aasha Rani signs to play the role of "Mother-in-law" (175) in Jitendra (Jojo) Mehta's film. She signs it because the monotony and tedium bred by absence of some serious engagement make her ill at ease. "I'm bored. Film are all I know. I'm not educated. I'm not a clever business woman". (176) For which indirectly her family atmosphere and more especially her parents are responsible here as they failed to provide her any formal education worth the name, even though Appa with his uncanny sense suggests her not to do that role. This contract results in an illicit sexual relationship between Aasha Rani and Jojo. "He did nothing for her ego as a woman" (185) and everything is on his "terms making her feel like a hard up, frustrated, discard". (185) Jojo's wife Neelum sends *goondas* to teach lessons to Aasha Rani. She is advised by them very sternly to keep away from Jojo. One of the goons sprains her wrist and warns, "Stay miles away from Jojo—or the next time I'll spread open your legs and slash your Vagina". (188) This is why it is said "if character is lost, everything is lost". A person is easily and frankly criticized with degraded remarks, like Aasha Rani.

This is an important happening and it is through this incident that the novelist has highlighted the highly adverse and deleterious effects of illicit and extra-marital sex. Extra-marital sex is very definitely one of the post effects of Westernization although even in the West, sober opinion has always condemned extra-marital sex as lecherous and pernicious. Indian culture has always emphasised purity in sex. As a matter of fact, Indian scriptures hold 'lust, greed and anger' as the gateway to hell. And rightly so, any untoward situation in this novel is a direct outcome of any of these three.

The last man in her life is Gopalakrishnan, the same man who had abused her when she was an innocent child. He meets her again in the aeroplane and abuses her sexually once again in the "loo" (198) of the aeroplane. So, Geeta Barua's opinion must be critically examined, here. 'Where is the question of frustration in love when she has already married Jay? The marriage has not yet ended. The question of loneliness is also not relevant. Can't married woman spend at least some days without her husband? Besides, should sex be always treated as such a violent factor as needs be satiated with means, fair or foul? What is the role of a cultured mind then?' Therefore, Geeta Barua is unjustified when she writes that Aasha Rani is "frustrated in love, dejected because of loneliness, she goes on sleeping with various men".[22] Sudhir Kumar is of the opinion that the protagonist is a vamp and the novelist belongs to the category of "the vamp school of feminism",[23] by quoting in his support Gilbert and Gubar:

> Delectably sensual and transgressive as some of the writings of the vamp critics have been, it, too, has the faults of its virtues. The vamp is glamorous, an actress in a kind of guerrilla theatre, but the drama of seduction and betrayal that she enacts in her foray against patriarchal structures may end up being as seductively treacherous to women as to men.[24]

It is because, the protagonist is neither prepared to live "as Sita did [nor] as Draupadi did".[25] She is also not prepared to accept the status of "*Durga* incarnate [for] myth keeps her bemused, bound hand and foot".[26] She "rebels, [therefore], against it—either in speech or action [which] would mean that she is questioning the myth, attacking the legend, and that can't be permitted: it is the cornerstone on which the Indian family and therefore Indian society are built".[27] The novelist, who claims to write on the basis of "reality"[28] has been assigned to the category of the Vamp School of feminism by Sudhir Kumar. We feel that Sudhir Kumar has a biased attitude towards the novel, because the protagonist in the novel is not a vamp. His comments are uncalled for in the context of a suffering woman, by ignoring the role of men and society. More than this, the protagonist is "sick of living, sick of deception [sic]. So many people had betrayed me so many times. I too had lost my head and became a loose woman. In India, no decent man, would have married me, given me his name, looked after me. Most probably, I would have ended up like *amma*". (169) This comment of the protagonist is a castigation of the male dominated chauvinistic society, which hurls a woman into a deprived, devastated and pitiable condition.

Now, we will see another side of women's exploitation by men, the indirect one, because behind the conflict between women or exploitation of a woman by another woman, there is always a man, according to the novelist's view. Galores of examples are there to testify to this view.

The first woman character in the novel is Geetha Devi or Amma, a mistress of a big film producer of south. She is slandered and humiliated by Girija, the wife of the producer. She reviles her as "a common prostitute". (68) Owing to the conflict, the producer has "abruptly cut off all money" (69) and "that was when the nightmare had begun". (69) This has driven her to opt for prostitution, "She'd come back late in the night, smelling strange and looking sleepy". (69) She embraces this degradation to raise her three girls amidst "poverty, deprivation [and] struggle", (4) which become her lot after being 'deserted' by the producer. She survives the penury and the struggle and fights against every quirk of fate with her only longing and hope that she has to see her daughter "a big film star" (19) of Bombay. Other two things that attract her attention and capabilities are the "future" (104) for her daughters and "money". (106) Since she has already tasted life with its bitter dregs, Viji Aasha Rani noted painfully that, "when *appa* had left, *amma* had aged overnight". (69)

Although, Amma is well aware of the dirty film line, yet she prevails upon Aasha Rani to join it. She looks "the other way" (32) when she sends her to some "client". (32) She does this just to protect her younger daughters who are "pure" (104) and she anticipates that "any good Iyengar boy will be proud to marry" (104) them some day. She desires to protect her other two daughters and concludes that, "one child was enough" (104) to enter this dirty profession. That is why when Aasha Rani elopes with Abhijit and eventually gets married to Jamie Phillips she repudiates her, " 'My daughter is a whore' 'Aasha Rani betrayed me.' 'Mother Disowns Aasha Rani,' 'Sweetheart of Millions turns Vamp'. 'Aasha Rani in any case, is dead to us". (145) She curses her that she "will never be happy". (144) But behind all these trials and travails in life, those who were instrumental in shaping the course of life for Asha Rani included are *appa*, Akshay, Abhijit, Kishenbhai and to some extent, Sheth Amirchand and Amrishbhai too. It is obvious by the bitter remark of Aasha Rani, which she makes about Kishenbhai after her unsuccessful suicide attempt, "I hate him for getting me into the industry; for ruining my life. I will never forgive him, never". (113)

Akshay's harsh comments on Amma, "you can't call yourself a mother—you are scum. A wretched exploiter of your own child. You think you have made your daughter a big star—but it is her life you have ruined! How do you sleep at night? Doesn't your conscience kill you?" (70) And castigation by Sheth Amirchand that, "Their mother is a shameless bitch. She has ruined her innocent children" (146) and perturbed her to an extent that Amma "The feisty old battle—axe was reduced to a bag of bones. A depression with fading memory and humiliating incontinence". (228)

Malini is extremely possessive of her husband Akshay and therefore, she accuses and abuses Aasha Rani for entrapping her husband. She is extremely indignant. She screams "Sex! That is all you have—Sex! That is what women like you use. Cheap Bitches—part your legs and let any man in. Sex, Sex, Sex, dirty filthy sex! Perverts! You must be a pervert. What do you do to him? Suck his cock or suffocate him with your breast?" (49) Thus Akshay, the sex pervert, is the man behind the conflict between two women Malini and Aasha Rani. Malini realises the grimness of the situation and concludes that, "Men are all the same—animals, and we women, such fools". (50)

Another instance of sexual perversion is Gopalakrishnan, who "track [s] down". (215) Aasha Rani is in London with the help of Sonali, an extremely attractive Indian woman. He tells Aasha Rani, "I was the one who alerted her [Sonali]. I made discreet enquiries through my associates in Wellington. I was told you were headed for London. The rest was easy. Sonali is an old friend". (215) So a man tracks down a woman with the help of another woman for a work nothing better than a decent prostitution or sexual slavery of the socialites. Sonali lays the truth with her exhortative speech as about bureaucrats and diplomates:

> These men who seek out company are powerful, rich and influential. They control the world. They find us relaxing, charming and desirable. We are doing them a favour—they spend their days under stress and tension. Their lives are complicated, their wives are bitches, their children hate them and their English girlfriends use them. We are safe. We give them what they want. That's why we are successful. (213)

So, the protagonist is here "nothing better than a high-priced whore", (214) and it is man who makes her so, with the tacit approval of the woman who falls an easy prey to the lure of lucre and sexual gratification. But then it is 'Sonali' who saves Aasha Rani's life from Bhaskaran "a trained guerrilla fighter", (218) deployed by Gopalakrishnan. Sonali assists the protagonist to get out of the wicked-web of Gopalakrishnan, "a wanted man, a killer". (220) She informs Aasha Rani that, "Bhaskaran is dead and you had better get out of here fast. Here's your plane ticket—the flight leaves in two hours. You know darling, you're lucky to be alive. I'm doing this as much for myself as for you". (220) Through this, the novelist seems to hint that the betterment and emancipation of womankind is possible through their own efforts. Another thing the novelist holds is that it is mostly man, who hurls women into prostitution and sometimes, vicious men directly throw them into harlotship.

Neelam and Aasha Rani's conflict takes place due to Jitendra Mehta (Jojo). Neelam sends three ruffians to Aasha Rani's house who threaten Aasha Rani of dire consequences if she does not withdraw from the life of Jojo. Their leader in a dramatic way pulls out some papers from inside his jacket and shows them to Aasha Rani and says, "'Your contract *Khatam*'; after it he flicked a lighter and lighting it, tossed it at her. Aasha Rani jumped back and the flaming papers fell on her synthetic carpet which burst into flames" (188-89) and Aasha Rani's house was put to flame.

Jay is the cause of another conflict in Aasha Rani's life, and it is between Nanny and Aasha Rani. Aasha Rani asks her, "You were sleeping with my husband, weren't you? I want you out of this house and out of our lives this minute. I'll mail you your wages. But get out now!" (201) Jay concedes to his infatuation and tries to rationalise it in this way. "I won't bother to deny that she and I were having an affair—well, it's a little more than that. I love the girl. She loves me. And she loves Sasha. I love you too, but differently. We've grown part.... I guess it was Sasha who was the common factor". (202)

Lastly, it is Amar, the cine actor, who becomes the bone of contention between Aasha Rani and Shudha Rani. It is reflected in the statement of Sudha Rani, who blurts out to Aasha Rani, "Take everything I have. It is rightfully yours, I grabbed it from you. There is nothing I want. Take the bungalow, take Amar, my jewellery, whatever there is". (232)

Thus, on the basis of instances cited above and the novelist's minute observation of society, it is apparent that the male dominated society creates snares and conditions for women which hold them in perpetual bondage and relegate them to a position subservient to men. Kishenbhai reminiscences about it: "Most men are haramis". (8) *Appa's* remark to Aasha Rani, which emanates from his disillusionment and study of human psyche, is that, "Men are very cruel. There is no justice in this world. And no equality between men and women". (193) Aasha Rani's own image and recognition in society after so many years of trials and travails, agony and suffering: "She is a *chudail*, a *bhootni*, after other people's husbands! Already killed one man [Akshay Arora] and widowed our *bhabhiji*! Now she wants to murder another victim", (188) these and similar other instances will suffice to support the novelist's views against male chauvinism which is highly detrimental to woman's natural growth and efflorescence. It gives credence to the view of the protagonist and justifies her words: "Whichever way one looked at it, there was always a man in the picture. A man using, abusing and finally discarding a woman". (157) Justifying that, 'Indians are high in hightech, but low in liberty.'

Thus, the novel portrays certain serious issues and is contrary to what A.G. Khan thinks about this novel:

> In fact I would regard her entire acrobatics as an attempt to reduce 'fiction' to 'fucktion.' She has no literary pretensions. She sells the *Chaat masala* with abundance of violence, stunt film action and her plots are mere excuses to depict the different techniques which Vatsyayana could not imaging. She has improvised *kamasutra* by inventing orgies in airplanes. The *asaba* she describes would make whores blush and males shout in ecstacy. There is little of lesbianism in Vatsyayana but Shobhaa De's portrayal brings us an inch-to-inch account of 'lesbo' game.[29]

In the same way it is also incorrect to say that the novelist has vulgarised "the printed word with dilettante dabblings of vapid mind";[30] or to consider her work as "Boddice ripper".[31] It is also not what Sunanda Swarup feels to be "equivalent of Hindi films with their peephole voyeurism".[32] And to some extent V.M. Madge is only partly correct, when he writes:

> Like any run-of the-mill Hindi film, the novel has all the ingredients of a *masala* production: sex, violence (that is in both the categories sexual violence and violent sex) and imperfectly rendered supposedly exotic locales and

> like New Zealand and, in the end, in spite of all brutality of ethos painted, the indulgent fine sentimentalism.[33]

The aforesaid opinions have some points of validity no doubt, but they cannot be held as conclusive. There are other critics too who have the same opinion about the novel, the novelist and the feminist writings and writers. J.M. Waghmare writes about the works of Shobhaa De:

> "It is true that the woman's body is much abused. Shobhaa De's writing conveys the feeling of bitter helplessness. She cannot call even her body her own. She is an object of man's lust and sexuality. She has nowhere to go. She is confined to the four corners of the house".[34]

He further writes that, "Shobhaa De's *Starry Nights* sprinkles rose-coloured light on the darkness which has enveloped a film actress, Aasha Rani. Her odyssey to stardom is most painful. She experiences emptiness at every step in her life. She swims across pent-up emotions".[35] About the protagonists he writes:

> The protagonists of the fictional works of Shobhaa De have some sort of schism in their souls. They do not have a cohesive and positive identity of their own. Their voices vibrate with profound grief and anguish. They suffer from a deep sense of betrayal and alienation. Their identities have cracks in them. This is the burden of the song of their life.[36]

But as the critic maintains, eliterature is supposed to be the mirror of life where everything concerning life whether good or bad, cultured or uncultured, pernicious or delectable is portrayed in an objective and detached manner. India's new woman today is in search of her identity. Customs and traditions, norms and principles, etiquette and behaviour, all are undergoing subtle changes today. No longer one norm of behaviour can be given for men and quite another one for women. "The prevailing norms of purity and chastity for the woman and promiscuity for the man [says the critic,] are giving way to more considerate points of views".[37] No doubt demands of the soul are to be accorded better attention and, consideration, but the raw call of the body too cannot be overlooked or looked down upon. Extra-marital sex, which has been tabooed and considered abominable so far has come to be treated 'with greater understanding or flexibility' depending upon the circumstances in which it is committed. Men and women are treated at par today and if men can justify a particular action of theirs, women too can claim to same justification and immunity.

R.K. Dhawan further maintains that Shobhaa De has now come to occupy a significant place in the realm of Indo-Anglian fiction, "The De phenomenon has come to stay".[38] The woman in De is the representative of the "confident, enterprising, ambitious, and individualistic new women who demands attention, equality and peace"[39] not as a matter of concession, consideration or kindness but as a matter of right, at par with men. She can be equally assertive as well, as and when the situation so warrants. *Man is no more superior to woman, in any respect physically, mentally and morally.* He is no longer wolf to the woman lamb, and both in their respective places are deemed to belong to the same species and social order.

Jeremy Hawthorn gives his opinion on the feminist approach. He says that, "Feminist critics have argued that not only have women had to overcome sever difficulties to become writers, but that once they have produced novels these have consistently been read in negative ways by male readers".[40] And, according to Rosalind Miles, "The sex of a novelist is always in question somewhere, sometime, in the course of the critical response—the sex of a woman novelist, that is, whatever a woman produces as a writer, she is still judged as a woman".[41] So, in a nutshell, it can be said that comments and views of some critics like, A.G. Khan, Ira Pande, Sunil Sethi and V.M. Madge may have some cogency but they are by no means final and conclusive.

The misjudgement about the protagonist has occurred due to two reasons. First, the patriarchal system and the male dominated norms of society; second, which is made abundantly clear by what *appa* of Aasha Rani says:

> Men are very cruel. There is no justice in this world. And no equality between men and women. Don't believe that a marriage alters that balance. Sometimes it only makes it worse. Power lies with purse and whoever controls that, controls the relationship. Some men can control their true feelings of superiority. These are called "cultured". Other men display them openly. They make their wives feel under constant obligation. That is the best way to keep them suppressed. (193)

While, witnessing Akshay's funeral proceedings on the T.V. set, Aasha Rani feels bitter because, "Nobody ever thinks of condoling the other woman. Nobody sympathizes with her, not even in death, for in the eyes of the world, if he wasn't husband, he was nothing. Their closeness, their sense of belonging to each other, their unique chemistry, was of no interest to anybody". (187)

The novel has been vehemently criticized for its pornographic and lesbian subjects portrayals. It is specially criticized for a "Sandwich massage" (66) and lesbian relationship between the journalist Linda and Aasha Rani. (79-80) Aasha Rani demands half-jokingly from her husband, "I prefer girls. They are so sensitive and soft. This, only another woman can know—how to turn a woman on, can't you find me a sexy girl friend here?" (128) It may be cited as an example of her preference for lesbian relationship. Scholars hold different opinions about lesbianism.

Alfred C. Kinsey believes that lesbianism is a natural phenomenon because the perversion of natural desire has no scientific validity. He elaborates his viewpoint:

> The impression that infra-human mammals more or less confine themselves to heterosexual activities is distortion of the fact which appears to have originated in a man-made philosophy, rather than in specific observations of mammalian behaviour.

> In actuality, sexual contact between the individuals of the same sex are known to occur in practically every species of mammals which has been extensively studied. Homosexual contacts in infra-human species of mammals occur among both females and males. Homosexual contact between the males have been observed in such widely separated species as rats, mice, hamsters, guinea pigs, rabbits, porcupines, martens, cattle, antilope, goats, horses, pigs, lions, sheep, monkey and chimpanzees.[42]

Man is macho in nature and therefore he is harsh and rough in approach and his body can never be soft like that of a woman's. About it Pierre Louys, the late nineteenth century French novelist wrote in his novel *Aphrodite*:

> A woman is a perfect instrument. From head to toe is made solely and wonderfully for love. Only a woman knows how to be loved. Therefore, if a couple is composed of two women, it's perfect; if it has only one woman it's only half as good; if it has no woman at all, it's completely idiotic.[43]

An Arabian poet Sheikh Nafzavi, has also written in the same vein:

> My source of happiness is a soft skinned girl. Praise be to Him who has moulded such beauty. My night was one of sucking at her mouth and throat, and if to love a girl in such a way is sinful, to love a man's unlawful.[44]

Simone de Beauvoir observes a sort of mutuality in this relationship, she writes:

> Between women love is contemplative, caresses are intended less to gain possession of the other than gradually to recreate the self through her; separateness is abolished, there is no struggle, no victory, no defeat; in exact reciprocity each is at once subject and object, sovereign and slave; duality becomes mutuality. Says Colette in *Ces plaisirs*: 'The lover takes delight in being sure of caressing the secrets of which she knows, and shoes preferences her own body indicates to her.' And

> Renee Vivien's poem (*From Sortileges*) expresses the same idea: 'Our bodies are made alike, our destiny the same. In you I love my child, my darling and my sister.'[45]

Lesbianism is not the central theme of the novel. It finds place in the novel as an expression of *Women's lib* and *true equality with men* as Prabhat Kumar Pandey maintains with the emphasis that a woman is sexually aroused better by a woman in comparison to a man. In a sexual union between a woman and man, it is the man who is the more active partner and when the orgasm is achieved and ejaculation takes place, the man feels satisfied; he cools down and does not then bother for his partner, the woman, whether or not she also feels sexually equally satisfied. Pandeya refers to a recent survey where a woman, when interviewed gives her reasons for her lesbian preference. The first reason she gives is that "it is much easier to give emotionally to a woman, to surrender ego".[46] Secondly, the woman finds that the skin of the woman partner is soft and smooth, which is much more sexually gratifying as compared to the coarse and rough skin of the male partner. This apart, in lesbian relationship, no partner has to worry whether or not her body is adequate for sexual gratification which is an important factor in, man-woman relationship. Thirdly and quite importantly, the woman feels free from any social or moral stigma usually attached to man-woman sexual relationship. Lesbian relationship saves women from any Value-judgement, 'Where I was going to be placed on spectrum of female frailties (angel or whore).'

Pandey maintains that, 'here surrendering of ego is important' which implies that a woman always finds it easier to surrender to a woman, than to a man who is always domineering, exploitative and chauvinistic to a woman. Pandeya hereafter mentions 'another facet of lesbian behaviour' and this is independence from the male. This is an important principle of *feminism* or *Women's Lib movement.* The liberated woman today does not want to be subservient to man in any walk of life; she wants to get rid of the indispensability of man. Man, she thinks has exploited, dominated and discarded her identity for much too long and the sooner she gets rid of him the better for her species.

Pandey here refers to political implications of lesbianism. He cites the *Hits Report*, which says that 'lesbianism can be political.' Sex with another woman could be better because it assures equal relationship and there is absolutely no question of superiority or inferiority. Sex with woman can also be 'reaction against man and our second class status with them in society.' This makes it implicitly clear that woman is sick of man's domination and she wants to be free of the hegemony of man, come what may.

The Hits Report has one subject saying 'Sex with a man is often the beginning of a political education. Sex with a woman means independence from man.' This is an important factor. This means that independence from man is in the uppermost of woman's mind, as she wants to be free of man at any cost. Another noteworthy aspect of lesbianism, is that 'there is a kind of reciprocity and similarity between two women'.

Here the Professor has given the opinion of a psychologist who says that 'only another woman knows' meaning thereby that the erotic pleasure felt by a woman through another is a matter beyond the comprehension of any man, because man himself is not the partner: he can at best only guess and surmise. The subject in the *Hits Report* further throws light on the lesbian sex and says that sexual pleasure apart, the woman's body provides a sort of security as well which can be had nowhere else. A woman's body is superior to man's in one more respect, and that is its capacity of providing satisfaction uniquely its own which cannot be provided by a male body. The male body undoubtedly may be highly sexually exciting and elegant but 'it lacks the obvious physical attributes of our first source of love, mother'.

The question here involved is not about the mother's breasts only. It is something about her total personality: the texture of the skin, the smell emanating from the body, 'the whole mysterious aura of that first body' which fed, warmed and over to helmed us in our infancy. The veracity of this observation is upheld by what Linda says to Aasha Rani. "Let me make you come like you've never come before. This is love making not what those bastards do to our bodies". (79-80) Thus, it is brought to our notice that Linda provides Aasha Rani a sort of pleasure, which so far was beyond her imagination. The initiative was also Linda's, and not her. Aasha Rani becomes convinced and she admits that 'lesbian pleasure is definitely superior to that of man-woman union.' She admits it explicitly and says, "yes, this is what it should be, tender, beautiful and erotic". (80)

Aasha Rani's lesbian relation only denotes her escape from lesbianism. Not finding any fulfilment at the hand of any man whatsoever, she is irresistibly drawn to this technique of self-gratification and one single union with Linda leaves such a powerful impact on her mind that she blurts out "it could never be with a man". (80) On a deeper level of her consciousness, this experience also symbolises her disdain and escape from man.

While concluding his remarks and opinion about Aasha Rani's lesbian experience in *Starry Nights*, P.K. Pandey says that it is 'not just a variant sexual behaviour', but it is related with the heroine's character. As has been pointed out before, Aasha Rani is deceived and duped by men every time she comes in contact with them and, therefore, yearning for genuine love and concern grows stronger and stronger in her. At this time, the 'short-lived abandon in the arms of another woman,' Linda, provides her fleshy warmth, security, love and of course sexual pleasure which she had failed throughout to get from any of her contacts with man. Aasha Rani had received sexual pleasure with complete abandon in Dubai also with the Thai girls when she had experienced some of the greatest orgasm of her life. This experience was for her the fulfilment of a long felt need, as P.K. Pandeya writes, "In the turbulent life of the heroine, it was something fulfilling, an emotional oasis".[47]

The foregoing discussion makes it amply clear that lesbianism in the novel is only an expression of women's desire for equality, liberty and security. It has become a synonym for "Feminism" or "Women's Lib". The novelist suggests that one of the best ways to achieve equality is through acquiring money. Appa guides Viji (Aasha Rani), "Take my advice and come back to Madras. Revive the studio. You'll make a success of it. I'm sure". (193) The sane advice of Appa impresses Aasha Rani. It makes her think, "Of course money solves problems that much faster". (170) Aptly so, the novelist has taken up the pragmatic position in life and given some importance to money in the social life of human beings.

Another important thing, which we find in the novel, is the novelist's views about the institution of marriage. She expresses it through different characters in different ways. She makes the protagonist say, "the husband-wife relationship...of the perfect understanding that two people shared within this sacred relationship". (230) This feminist view is sufficient for cancelling all the patriarchal and dominant views. Akshyas' fervent plea, "I want a home-maker, a good mother to my children". (40) Malini's candid confession "My husband means more to me than a career, a wife's place is in the home". (40) Aasha Rani's pragmatic views, "being a wife and being a whore were not all that different". (43) Rita's realistic statement, "All wives have to pretend. A wife is acting all the time—this is the world's best-kept secret" (50) and, "Everything is decided by the bed". (50) According to Kishenbhai, men marry "For status, prestige and acceptability. A successful man in any field, needs a grand home. A wife to look after it. Two good-looking children—a boy and a girl—and all the other domestic trappings". (192) While, Jay is of the opinion that, "You just relax, enjoy yourself, make me a good wife, be a good mother. That is what a woman is all about". (194)

The novelist's view that a woman is incomplete without having a child, finds expression at different places. It can be well evaluated in two comments, one by the protagonist and the other about her. The first comment she makes is by way of an introspection, when army men's women taunt her, "What about a family? What about a husband? Children? You may not miss these things now but later, when your looks and popularity fade, then you'll think, 'My life is so empty and these women are so lucky'". (97) Aasha Rani realizes this, "they were right". (97) But, she spares herself at least with the feeling that, "She had married. Her womb had been filled. She had a daughter. She had escaped". (231)

The protagonist gets her feminist victory due to her hope amidst all sorts of sufferings, which were inflicted upon her directly or indirectly by men and their society. First, it is Akshay who apologizes, "All these years, I've been living for this moment. All through my bad days, one thought kept me going...I couldn't leave this world without saying goodbye". (137) Here, he wishes to "apologize Akshay wanted to say he was sorry. It had taken him five years to realize". (138) Its climax is seen when some unidentified voice asks her, "Akshay is critical. He needs your prayers. He has been asking for you. Pray for him". (185)

Appa of Aasha Rani is the second person who, apologized to her in writing for his past errors. "It was a letter—a farewell letter. In it, *Appa* had begged her forgiveness and tried to explain some of the circumstances in his life that had led to ugly decisions. Decisions that had hurt her and her mother and the other". (228) He accepts it verbally too when he talks with Aasha Rani. He wants to tell her "how sorry I was for whatever had happened. I had done all of you great harm. Behaved unforgivably. Cruelly, your *Amma*'s life—I destroyed it". (172)

Even Amma also realizes her errors. She thereafter changes her behaviour towards Aasha Rani. "Your *amma* has changed", she says in a penitent mood. "I have realized my mistakes. Now I'm no longer thinking of your career, I'm only thinking of you and your happiness. You know what this industry is like. It is vulgar, cheap, cruel—not meant for decent people, certainly not meant for married women!" (152) Then with the appraisal of Aasha Rani, she surrenders herself. "You have a soft heart. You are kind and good to people who have done so much for you. I know you will not throw out your *amma*. You will look after her in her old age. Where can I go now? How will I live?" (153) And finally she utters, "I'm tried. My joints pain. The doctor says I'm suffering from hypertension. I've got diabetes. God knows how many more days I have on this earth. But I'm not complaining. I want to live in peace". (153)

The last person who asks Aasha Rani for her pardon is her own sister Sudha Rani. She is the last person to apologize to her. "God has punished me, I deserve it. I have been evil. I have sinned, I have done you so much harm. You don't have to forgive me. Take everything I have. It is rightfully yours, I grabbed it from you". (232)

The keynote of the novel is "Hope", which always keeps the protagonist's spirits high, despite many bad situations she faces in her life. Geetha Devi Amma struggles hard for her girls. She brings Aasha Rani to Bombay to help her become a big film star. Sudha becomes her only hope, when Aasha Rani elopes with Abhijit Mehra and finally in Wellington gets married to Jay. But, when she returns to India, her hopes once again centre round Aasha Rani. Aasha Rani thinks tiredly, "We all have to look out for ourselves in the end. Each person finds his or her own way to survive. Poor *Amma*—her only hope is me. And as for me, I'll find out soon enough". (153)

Appa of Aasha Rani has lost all his hopes and dreams after the tragic incident in the past at his own theatre. But, after seeing his daughter, his hopes "have been reborn. I can tell myself, all is not lost yet. You have a daughter. A clever daughter. She will revive your banner. She will reopen the studio. She will once again restore that lost glory of your name". (173) He implores her to "Do it for a father who is dying. Who is broken. Who is a very unhappy man. I had lost the will to live or even to speak. But now, with you by my side, I feel strong. I feel young again—in my mind, at least". (173) His only hope from his daughter is, "I want to see the studio prosper once again. Become the pride of the industry". (173) So the atmosphere charged with emotion, of hope struggling against a sense of doom, is discernible here in the novel.

After coming back from her second foreign tour, Aasha Rani finds the situation very grim. "Sudha had sustained severe burns all over, including her face", (226) by the handiwork of underworld miscreants while the "two wounded veterans waiting to die". (228) At that critical moment, she decides, "Nothing could get worse than this. And all this while a single thought kept surfacing: it was up to her to resurrect the family. She didn't have the strength, the resources, the courage". (226) And, in the late afternoon, she makes her decision, "She wouldn't run again". (227)

She gathers her lost strength by recalling Akshay's comment, "India is also beautiful. We can make it beautiful, you and I". (227) Jay's comment, "I believe a person should not live with regrets. A frustrated person is an unhappy person", (170) also reiterates the significance of hope. Even the farewell letter of Appa boosts her a lot. It is the last paragraph of the letter, which stuns her and also outlines his master plan. "The studio was hers all along. Only the solicitors knew it the name and the premises—they were both Aasha Rani's—the name that had given so many super hits—the name that now belonged to Aasha Rani". (228-229) The only condition is that she will not "sell the property". (229)

Aasha Rani promises her Appa that, "she would resurrect the family banner and re-open the studio". (229) While her Appa has full confidence in her, "She could do it. She would immortalize their family and make a permanent contribution to cinema. That was his legacy to her. The only legacy he had left to give". (229) This makes the old man shut his eyes in peace and contentment. "And, for the first time in the last couple of days, she could see a glimpse of how the future might work". (232)

The protagonist's consolation to her sister is full of hope, sure success and demands for mutual co-operation and understanding among them. The protagonist's exhortations to her sister rebounds with hope:

> First you have to promise me one thing—that you will stay with me. I will look after you and you're going to help me. The two of us together will reopen *appa*'s studio—our studio. We will make films, good films, and we will survive. Not just survive, but prosper. Ours will be the most up-to-date, high-tech studio in India. You have excellent business sense. I will need that. I will

> concentrate on the technical side, handle production details. Appa will be proud of his daughters. Amma too. Look at me, Sudha. This is our chance, your and mine, to start new lives, begin again. Sudha are you with me? You're going to make it. Make it just fine. There is nothing good plastic surgeons can't do today. And I'll be with you, for however long it takes and wherever in the world it is that we have to go. Show your face to me Sudha, my dear, little Sudha. Let me look at you. (233)

Here, through the term plastic surgery, the novelist suggests to women to overcome their inferiority complex and other weaknesses of the mind and heart. Only then they can get the best results out of it, like that of a farmer who skilfully uses rainwater for nurturing his crops. It is owing to his sacrifices that even destructive things change into creative and constructive materials. This is why in the novel the protagonist keeps on repeating and reassuring before her Appa that, "Everything is going to be perfect, *appa*. It rained last night. Good omen". (233)

Just as a seed sacrifices itself for its offshoot (future), so is the protagonist who hopes and sacrifices for her offspring Sasha. Though Sasha at the moment is in New York, but she cherishes her in her mind with plans of freedom and futurity. She tells herself:

> It was Sasha who needed her the most. Her beautiful daughter with her tawny skin and those special eyes that had the sun and the sea dissolved in them...Sasha with her innocence and guilelessness. Sasha would come and live with her. Together they would conquer the world. Together, her little daughter and she would carve themselves a niche. With no one telling them how to live life. No heart-breaks, no disappointments, no compromises. Sasha would live life on her own terms. And she would bring her up as *amma* never had. Sasha had the makings of a star. An unforgettable star. The Golden Girl of the silver screen! Sasha would be tomorrow's Lover Girl! (234)

And the protagonist expresses it through the light of hope, prosperity and knowledge of futurity. The novelist also utilises the age long symbol of the Dipawali's *Diyas*. Here, *Diyas* also sybolise the son of a house or family. But the novelist through the protagonist wishes to equalise the status of a girl and a boy from the very primary levels, from where this difference originates in the society. The protagonist never loses her heart or hope. She becomes the light of hope for her parents, while, Sasha becomes for her. So the girls serve her as *Kuldeepika* or light of the family as *Kuldeepa*, or lamps of the family. The remarks of Sandhyarani Dash command cogency:

> In a twilight between dream and waking, Aasha Rani has a vision of her daughter's future. She dreams to fulfil her dreams through her daughter by making her a superstar. Sasha will live her own life on her own terms. Aasha Rani thinks of bringing up her daughter in a different way than her *Amma*. With her daughter she would conquer the world without any heartbreak, any disappointment and compromise. A series of misfortunes, circumstantial compulsions and the failure of her marriage do not let her down. She emerges as a phoenix from the debris of the past with a beautiful dream for the future which she wants to share with her daughter. Thus, the novel ends on an optimistic note.[48]

And the most symbolic-cum-optimistic lines of the novel are, "It was [is] Diwali tomorrow. The festival of lights; she would need to tell Laxmi to prepare the *Diyas*". [sic] (234) Here, the novelist fervently hopes that with the advancement of time and the spread of education in coming future, women will certainly achieve the concept of true equality with men. With passage of time, there will be no sort of difference between them, just like: "*Waqt ne Kiya kay haseen situm:/ tum rahe na tum, hum rahe na hum*", meaning there by that, the impact of time obliterates all differences and drives away all antagonisms.

Thus, this novel is not only anti-patriarchal in nature but is also just opposite to what Manu has said in the *Manusmriti's* ninth chapter:

Pita Rakshati Koumare,
Bharta Rakshati yauvane,
Rakshanti Sthavire Putra,
Na Stree Svatantra marhti.

It is English rendering which reads as follows:

Protected by father as wards
And by husband when married
In old age protects the son
The women shouldn't be free.[49]

It is also against the concept of *Kuldeepak*, meaning son. The novelist with the help of the protagonist, her sister and her daughter conveys the massage that a daughter or a woman may also be *Deepika* or *Kuldeepika*. She rejects the age-old concept of *Deepah* or *Kuldepah*, which only a male child can be: as in *Amritvardhan*:

दीपाः स्थितं वस्तु विभावयन्ति,
कुलप्रदीपास्तु भवन्ति केचितं।
चिर व्यतीतानपि पूर्वजान्ये,
प्रकाष्ठायन्ति स्वगुण प्रकर्जातं।।[50]

(Lamps illuminate only those objects that are placed over there some offsprings highlight their family. However, only a few transgress the good deeds of their ancestors and out of their-own virtues illumine themselves).

Or Jayasee's comment in *Chitrarekha*:

राज पाट धान का हैं, जग मँह पूत पियार।
जो दीपक घर नाहीं, जानहुँ जग अंधियार।।[51]

(Power pelf riches nothing like son, without he [him] the world pitch dark).

What the novelist wants to urge one and all that, daughters are born just like boys to human beings:

अंगादंगात्संभवति पुत्र्वद् दुहिता नष्टणाम्।।

(Like the son, daughter too is born of the same organs of man).

Why should then daughters be deprived of their right of equality? They deserve the same respect and must be treated equally. She is optimistic about it that sooner or later womankind will attain the glory she is capable of and will achieve her due honour and respect in the family and society, house and heart.

Eventually, the novel ends with an optimistic suggestion for the womankind through the protagonist that 'let us not lose hope,' because it is a universal truth that, "Tine heart, tine all",[52] (Here, tine means lose). (If you will lose heart, you will lase all). She also desires to change the prevalent view, "Man dreams of fame, while woman wakes to love",[53] as the blurb says, Aasha Rani "'Sweetheart of Millions' makes one fatal career-move: She falls in love that destroys everything she attained after seven long years of exploitation".[54] The extract reiterates the notion of caution to women. Asha Rani's life is an account of the survival and success along with a consuming love, which is passionate.

NOTES

1. Shobhaa De. *Selective Memory: Stories From My Life* (New Delhi: Penguin Books India Private Limited, 1998), p. 331.
2. *Ibid.*
3. *Ibid.*, pp. 331-32.
4. *Ibid.*, p. 332.
5. *Ibid.*
6. Alessandro Monti, "Shakti Unleashed in Muppyland: Shobhaa De and the Making of Modern India" in *The Fiction of Shobhaa De*, ed. by Dodiya (New Delhi: Prestige Books, 2000), pp. 28-29.
7. C.P. Surendran, "Just Another De", *The Illustrated Weekly of India*, November 6, 1992.
8. *Ibid.*
9. Interview with Yashodhara Dalmia, *The Times of India*, April 29, 1979.
10. "Tender, Beautiful and Erotic: Lesbianism in Shobhaa De's *Starry Nights*", Prabhat Kumar Pandey, in *Indian Women Novelists*, Set-III: Vol. I. by Dr. R.K. Dhawan (New Delhi: Prestige Books, 1995), p. 127.
11. "Towards Masala Fiction—Shobhaa De's Starry Nights", by V.M. Madge, in *The Journal of Indian Writing in English* Vol. 26, No. 1, (Gulbarga: Gulbarga University) ed. G.S. Balarama Gupta, Dept. of English. p. 30.

12. Shobhaa De, *Starry Nights* (New Delhi: Penguin Books Private Limited, 1991), p. 157. All further references to the novel will be incorporated in the text.
13. Gail Lewis and Merl Storr, *Feminist Review* (Autum, 1996), p. 54.
14. A Woman More Sinned than Sinning: A Study of Starry Nights by Sandhyarani Dash, *The Fiction of Shobhaa De: Critical Study* ed. Jaydipsinh Dodiya (New Delhi: Prestige Books, 2000), p. 168.
15. *Ibid.*, p. 167.
16. *Ibid.*, p. 168.
17. Search of Identity in *Starry Nights* by Nisha Trivedi, *Shobhaa De: Critical Study,* ed. Jaydipsinh Dodiya (New Delhi: Prestige Books, 2000), p. 182.
18. Geeta Barua, "Rise and Fall of a Star: A Study of Starry Nights", in *The Fiction of Shobhaa De: Critical Study* ed. Jaydipsinh Dodiya (New Delhi: Prestige Books), p. 176.
19. Nisha Trivedi, "Search for Identity in Starry Nights"; in Jaydipsinh Dodiya's *The Fiction of Shobhaa De: Critical Study*, p. 182.
20. Sudhir Kumar, "Artist as Vamp: A Feminist Approach to Starry Nights", Jaydipsinh Dodiya, ed. *The Fiction of Sobha De: Critical Study* (New Delhi: Prestige Books, 2000), p. 193.
21. M.P. Singh, "Feminist Campaign and the Indian Context", March 8, 2001, "Meet on Feminist Campaign" Published in *Hindustan Times*, Lucknow Edition, March 9, 2001.
22. Geeta Barua, "Rise and Fall of a Star: A Study of Starry Nights", Jayadipsinh Dodiya, ed. *The Fiction of Shobha De: Critical Study* (New Delhi: Prestige Books, 2000), p. 176.
23. Sudhir Kumar, "Artist as Vamp: A Feminist Approach to Starry Nights" (Dodiya, *The Fiction of Sobha De: Critical Study*), p. 197.
24. Sandra M. Gilbert and Susan Gubar, "The Mirror and the Vamp: Reflections on Feminist Criticism", in *The Future of Literary Theory*, ed. Ralph Cohen (New York: Routledge), p. 154.
25. Anita Desai, "Secret Connivance", *Times Literary Supplement*, 14th Sept., 1990, p. 972.
26. *Ibid.*
27. *Ibid.*
28. Shobhaa De, *Selective Memory: Stories From My Life* (New Delhi: Penguin Books India (P) Ltd., 1998), p. 332.
29. A.G. Khan, "Shobhaa De Vatsyayani" in R.S. Pathak's *Indian Fiction of the Nineties* (New Delhi: Creative Books Ltd., 1997), p. 47.
30. Ira Pande, *Literature of the Baby-log*, Seminar, No. 384, 1991, p. 37.
31. Sunil Sethi, "De in *De Out*", Seminar No. 384, 1991, p. 37.
32. S. Swarup, *Feature in Femina* (May 8, 1993), p. 9.

33. V.M. Madge, "Shobhaa De's *Starry Nights*", *Critical Essays* on *India Writing in English*, Edited by A.S. Ratnam (New Delhi: Harman Publication House, 1999), p. 31.
34. J.M. Waghmare, in "Foreword" of *Critical Essays on Indian Women Writing in English* (Bangalore, 1998), p. 12.
35. *Ibid.*
36. *Ibid.*, p. 11.
37. R.K. Dhawan, *Indian Women Writers* (New Delhi: Prestige Books Ltd., 1995), p. 14.
38. *Ibid.*
39. *Ibid.*, p. 15.
40. Jeremy Hawthorn, *Studying the Novel: An Introduction* (New Delhi: Universal Book Stall, 1992), p. 82.
41. Rosalind Miles, *Women Writers and the Conquest of the Novel* (London and New York: Routledge and Kegan Paul, 1987), p. 5.
42. Alfred C. Kinsey et al., *Sexual Behaviour in the Human Female* (New York: Pocket Books, 1965), pp. 448-49.
43. Quoted by Nancy Friday, *Innocent Love* (Publisher's name and place is not given, 1980), p. 78.
44. Sheikh Nafzavi, *The Glory of the Perfumed Garden* (London: Granada, 1978), p. 30. (quoted by P.K. Pandey).
45. Simone De Beauvoir, *The Second Sex* (London: The New English Library, 1966), p. 155.
46. Shere Hits, *The Hits Report: A Nation-wide Study* of the Female Sexuality (New York: Dell, 1987), p. 409. (Quoted by P.K. Pandey, "Tender, Beautiful and Erotic: Lesbianism in Starry Nights" in Dodiya's *The Fiction of Sobha De: Critical Study*, New Delhi: Prestige Books, 2000), pp. 206-07.
47. P.K. Pandey, "Tender, Beautiful and Erotic: Lesbianism in *Starry Nights*", Dodiya, *The Fiction of Shobha De: Critical Study* (New Delhi: Prestige Books, 2000), p. 207.
48. Sandhyarani Dash, "A Woman more Sinned than Sinning: A Study of *Starry Nights*", Jaydipsinh Dodiya, *The Fiction of Shobha De: Critical Study* (New Delhi: Prestige Books, 2000), p. 172.
49. *Manusmriti*. IX. pp. 2-3.
50. *Amritvardhan* (Vallbhadev Krit *Subhasitawali*), p. 258.
51. Jayasee, *Chitrarekha*. p. 25.
52. Rosaline Fergussion, *The Penguin Dictionary of Proverbs* (London: Bloomsburg Books, 1991), p. 125.
53. Alfred Tennyson, *The Idylls of the King*.
54. Back side of the jacket of the book.

4

Sisters: Unity and Sanity, Corridors of Power

The third novel of Shobhaa De, *Sisters* (1992) is dedicated to her parents, Indira and Govind Rajadhyaksha, her brother Ashok and her sisters, Mandakini and Kunda—for tolerating her. This novel has also been misinterpreted and misjudged by the critics. A.G. Khan in his article "*Shobhaa De 'Vatsyayani'*" regards her "entire acrobatics as an attempt to reduce 'fiction' to 'fucktion.' She has no literary pretensions. She sells chat masala with abundance of violence, stunt film action".[1] He fails "to capture the feminine sensibility".[2] While in Neena Arora's eyes, in *Sisters*, Shobhaa De neither "focuses her attention on the aristocrats of high social circles nor on the stars or starlets of the Bombay [Mumbai] film industry, but on the "richie-rich" intriguing corporate world of business tycoons"[3], because in Shobhaa De's "world, all men have lust for only two things—money and women—and all the women chase after men and money. All relationships centre around sex and all the scenes revolve around sexual encounters".[4] According to E. Satyanarayana, "unlike its predecessors, *Sisters* for the first time deals with the psychic conflict in its liberated woman-protagonist who is caught between a 'personal self' and a 'societal self'".[5] In nutshell, we can say the "theme of self-assertion is central to Shobhaa De's third novel *Sisters*".[6]

Yamuna Prasad considers Shobhaa De "a realist"[7] and treats *Sisters* as a worthwhile novel because it "is a mirror of the messy life and moral chaos of the urban women. Significantly, the novelist uses images of 'vultures' and 'sharks' for the corrupt business tycoons and 'mouse' and 'fish' for their women victims".[8] He further says, "*Sisters* is a novel of suspense and conspiracy, crime and punishment",[9] along with it, it is "a realistic novel with some serious issues about urban women with the expansion of business empire",[10] in it "the contrast between [the] two sisters is the most important aspect of the growth of the plot of the novel";[11] but Yamuna Prasad's opinions are also not all correct though he tries his best to estimate the importance of the novel with some facts.

Bijay Kumar Das misconcludes when he writes about *Sisters*, "The theme of the novel makes an interesting reading"[12] because in his opinion "Shobhaa De has been successful in depicting the story of two upper class young business women in Modern India within the ambit of the art of fiction"[13] in this novel. He further says, "Shobhaa De dives deep into the hearts of liberated upper class women in the contemporary society and depicts the characters as they are, not as they should have been [and charges of], she is not concerned with the traditional concept of morality and purity in love";[14] but this is rather paradoxical to his own comment on the novel: "Things and events depicted in the novel might not have happened to him/her, but he/she invents them camouflaging them as real to elicit reader's total participation. Shobhaa De precisely does that in her novels. Social concern is the main thrust of all her novels".[15] Therefore, in the opinion of B.K. Das, this novel is simply an interesting story, which portrays the characters of liberated upper class Indian urban women in the contemporary society, as they are, but not as they should have been. But, it is only partially true because the novelist through the under-current of the novel asks her readers "What should be and what should not be?" by portraying the Pathetic or admirable picture of women in her novel.

However, we can not ignore Shobhaa De's own observations, "She said she never wrote, any junk she wrote popular fiction"[16] "Having been provoked by the pervasive 'hot sex' sequences in her novels, critics have completely ignored Shobhaa De, a writer with feminist leanings".[17]

The story of *Sisters* is inspired by a single, riveting visual, which the novelist saw in the foyer of the Taj Mahal Hotel and noticed "Young, beautiful and chic, the woman walked with supreme confidence".[18] The novelist discovers that, she is the daughter of a successful businessman and has just returned from the states after acquiring a degree in business management from a prestigious school and joined her family firm as a senior vice-president. She has succeeded in 'making her presence felt in the board room'[19] with her talent. "This woman represented the new face, the changing face of India—glamorous, capable, on top of her life, career oriented, ambitious and successful [to the writer, who even though knew nothing about her, but treats her as] a mental image of the central character to fix on"[20] as Mallika/Mikki Hiralal in *Sisters*.

In the novel, the character Mikki is young, beautiful glamorous and on the top of it, capable with supreme confidence, who not only makes her presence felt by others especially men but she also represents the new and changing face of India. However, behind her success is her union with her half sister Alisha, an illegitimate child of her father from others womb, who assists her sincerely. Their fortune changes drastically from victim to victor after their union. The title of the novel in itself symbolizes and demands for integrity, mutual co-operation and mutual understanding among women for their own betterment and development. It seems to support slogans of Women's Movement such as, "Support each other and save ourselves",[21] "Women support other women".[22]

The title of the novel stresses on the point of woman's 'unity' and 'integrity.' More than this, the two line comment on the novel by the publisher also conveys the same essence to us via its under current, "They were beautiful, wealthy and sought after. They were sisters and they were at war".[23] The novelist provides 'tolerance' as a master key to women to overcome their personal weaknesses like envy and anger for one another, so that they may unite for their emancipation. This is well reflected in the following comment on the novel:

> When her parents die in an air crash, Mikki Hiralal suddenly finds herself the owner of the sprawling Hiralal industrial empire. Abandoning her studies in the United States, she returns to Bombay, only to find her father's business affairs in a mess. Almost bankrupt, beset on all sides by creditors, takeover, tycoons and unreliable associates, Mikki realizes there is only person she can turn to for help—the beautiful Alisha, her father's illegitimate daughter. There is only one hitch: Alisha hates Mikki.[24]

Thus, unity is the main theme of *Sisters*, which womankind may get through by getting victory over their feelings of hatred and envy with patience, tolerance, and mutual understanding. The view justifies that, "Sobha De's novels are different from the novel written by other women writers. Her themes and language are more contemporary than those of other writers".[25] But, critics like S.P. Swain still hold the misconception that, "Shobhaa De views women as nothing but sex, a mean to satisfy masculine lust",[26] ignoring the fact that, "there [is] always a man in the picture. A man using, abusing and finally discarding a woman".[27]

There are enough evidences not only to prove and support that through this novel, the novelist demands for the unity among women, but also to get rid of unwanted arguments and allegations as the protagonist says to her half sister in the novel, "We only have each other",[28] who realises this fact after too prolonged but true sacrifice, service, devotion along with the prudent, patience of job shown by the protagonist for Alisha, due to which "the two sisters held each other close and cried the last years away" (161) because they are "innocents" (161) and "the man responsible for it was their father who is dead". (162) Thus, they are ready and strong enough to face the world and their "great future—with or without men". (222) Alladia Uma's statement applies to this novel:

> Women's bonding indeed is a significant theme in Women's writing. A sisterhood of women to overcome the oppressive atmosphere through mutual support. A sisterhood of women to provide stability. A sisterhood of women to show the existence of a base of common concerns, a reiteration of the existence of a history, a tradition [sic].[29]

Besides, *Sisters* also expresses the novelist's feeling that, the "fortunate girls [are those], who determine their own futures".[30] Keeping in view the authority of decision making or self-determination, which is expressed by the novelist in the end, it is partially incorrect to say that, "*Sisters* has an open ending or unending like E.M. Forester's *A Passage to India* ending on the note 'Not yet, Not yet'".[31] It ends with a note of anticipation about women's emancipation and empowerment through unity and mutual understanding among them, so that they may lead and live *a life of an empress*.

The novel starts with an unfulfilled dream of a fifteen-year-old girl who belongs to a very rich and prestigious family of an industrialist. She knows nothing about sorrow and she does not weep or cry when woken and made aware of her parents death in an air mishap. She asks her servants to bring her a cup of coffee and in the meantime, she goes through the *Times of India*, which has two columns with a photograph of her father on the front page along with headline, "Industrialist and wife die in air mishap". (3) His short biography is written with complete terseness along with messages, from the Presidents of many business clubs and associations. Simultaneously, two lines from the Chief Minister and the Governor expressing that his death is "'A great loss'. 'A serve blow', 'His place can never be taken'"(3) which proves that Seth Hiralal has died as an "undisputed tycoon of tycoons", (3) who started his career as "a small-time merchant of scarp".(3) But, Mikki wryly thinks over her own condition, "Survived by his only child, a daughter, Mallika, studying at Present in the U.S.", (3) and a "single [woman] can be exploited far better than their male counterparts. Or their married Sisters",[32] more than this she knows it very well that "Her father had been quite a man [and] quite a bastard too". (3)

While a few miles away from Mikki's bungalow, in a small suburb of Bombay, Alisha, the daughter of Bachchoo [Hira Lal] and his concubine, mocks at this piece of news, "Survived by his only child. And what about me? What am I? A puppy? A kitten? A pet?" (3) Because nobody thinks of them, she concludes, "Life was not fair" for them, for which she curses everyone including her father. So, Patriarchy and its followers isolated both the sisters from each other in the name of social norms. Mikki is made too lonely, and weak to face the world and her own responsibilities, while Alisha's isolation from society makes her insolent and jealous of her own sister. So, owing to a male dominated society and system, both the sisters are not only separated but also become hostile to each other, which is fuelled by men and society, not acknowledging the "open secret"(5) of Seth Hiralal, deliberately. This turns the "*Shanti Kutir*" the house of Hiralal into "*Ashanti Kutir*".

Ramankaka and other uncles of Mikki, who stopped Alisha from attending the funeral forcibly, further separate both the sisters. This surprises Mikki, as she guesses about the girl "We could be sisters". (10) Ramankaka uncomfortably answers her query about the girls, "The girl you saw is your father's daughter from another woman, a long-time mistress. The girl's name is Alisha. She was born four months after you". (12) At this news, she feels betrayed because "her father now seemed a total stranger who'd led a sneaky double life", (12) but it consoles her for loss of her parents as she has "a sister? A half-sister?" (12) It suddenly occurred to Mikki that she is not alone and that she has a sister, a younger sister. She decides that, "she [is] not going to let her go to claim the only blood relative she [has] left". (13) Alisha is deliberately kept away from Mikky by Ramankaka to weaken her position to justify his and ironically about remark himself, which he uttered before Mikki, "the world is cruel Place. There are enough vultures waiting to pounce on you, I don't want anybody to take advantage of your present state of mind". (11) In order to reduce her into a living puppet, he cautions her against signing "anything given by anyone without checking with [him] first". (11) He tries to misguide Mikki about her father's dubious nature, especially about his affairs with Leelaben and his daughter Alisha, "Your father didn't want me to. He saw no reason for you to know about his other life". (12) He further diverts her from her father's death and ugly past to protect himself and his own evil designs, by his consolatory remark, "Baby, all that is in the past. The chapter is closed. Your father is dead, and with it, his other life and other attachments. You have to think ahead, plan ahead". (12) He not only wants to close the matter but also tries to keep Mikki alone and aloof from Alisha, to make her an easy prey, because "a single [woman] can be exploited far better",[33] Shobhaa De is however cautioning women to be "Beware. And be smart. The Daddy of today can easily turn into the monster of tomorrow, even if he isn't villainous. Once his protective umbrella is gone, baby, you're on your own. If you don't watch out, you're dead meat".[34]

Owing to the improper behaviour of Ramankaka towards and the role of Seth Hiralal in the life of Alisha and her mother, envy breeds in the heart of Alisha for her sister Mikki. Her dissatisfaction with patriarchy is well expressed in her statements like; "Nobody had thought of us",(3) "What about me? What am I? A kitten? A Pet?"(3) Which eventually leads her to this conclusion, "Life [is] not fair".(5) Her anger is further increased by the inhuman behaviour of Ramankaka and of others who stopped Alisha to participate in the funeral of her father as they did not like to see her as a heir to Seth Hiralal's Property.

Ramankaka tries to divert Mikki's attention from her father's death and his affairs and also the issue of Alisha, just to get advantage over Mikki and control over Hiralal group of Industries. In the first opportunity which he finds in privacy, he advises Mikki, "*Beti,* there are many things we have to discuss. I have a lot to tell you, we need to talk about your future and the future of your father's industries",(10) He makes determined efforts to keep Mikki away from Alisha as he easily forsees that their unity would ultimately destabilise his position in the company. "Don't be nervous. And don't commit yourself to anything. If there's something you don't understand, just look at me".(12)

The death of her parents, double role of her father and troubled condition of Hiralal Group of Industries due to debts, losses, low profits, paucity of funds, etc.; puzzle her "I'm broke. Flat broke". (22) Mikki feels betrayed due to her fathers "double life" (12) and ponders over the role and character of her father in her and her mother's life. Seeing the silver-framed photograph of her own along with her mother, "How ironic it was that her father should've spent a major portion of his days with both of them observing him, while his loyalties remained elsewhere—with two other women whose existence she had just discovered". (17) The novelist through the reaction of Mikki, insists on loyalty and fidelity from men in their respective roles, responsibilities and character. Later, to improve her condition, Mikki sees Alisha and asks her with her moist eyes "I want us to be friends, Alisha. I'm reaching out to you as someone who is a part of my life, whether you like it or not. You can't just walk away. We are sisters—nothing can change that"; (26) but Alisha replies coldly, "Yes, I do see we are sisters. You have all the money, all the status our father's name, his home, everything. And I have nothing. That is the difference". (26) Upon it, Mikki promises Alisha to change each and everything to her desire if a chance is given to her (Mikki). She also urges Alisha "not [to] fight" (26) because they "need each other". (26) But, the envious Alisha says "I don't need you, baby. If you need me, it will be on my terms. And when I decide I need you". (26) To Mikki's repeated persuasions, Alisha turns deaf ears, "We may not be rich like you but we have self-respect. We value our independence" (16) Mikki feels very lonely.

Owing to the lack of company, courage, funds and some reliable assistant, she [Mikki] is left completely alone. Her condition is very well reflected in Anjanaben's comment. "Mallika is alone young. She needs people. She needs a husband. The girl is like a mouse with vultures all around just waiting to pounce on her". (27) It shows that the virgins are the most vulnerable beings in the male dominated society. Thus, Mikki is nothing but a "poor thing" (27) in the eyes of men and women. In the meantime, as per direction and plan of Anjanaben, Shanay returns from United States, because, he is the most suitable person for Mikki, and through marriage "he will take over the Hiralal Industries". (27)

Shanay has spotless character "of 24 carat gold" (40) and is far better than other boys of his age group and is a cause of envy "in the eye of other women" (40) and the best part of him is that he is very obedient to his parents. Anjanaben has now only one wish to fulfill, a wish for a happy, harmonious, healthy home. She says: "He will marry the girl I find for him and live with us in our humble flat. She will take over the kitchen and both my husband and I will retire, attend *kirtans* and look after our grandchildren. What more can we ask of God? What more can He give us"? (41) Here, the novelist emphasises on marriage, sweet and harmonious homely life, respect for traditional culture and a joint family system full of gratitude to God. She also stresses on the importance of mutual understanding, respect and cooperation. Shobhaa De beautifully puts the old people's feeling through Anjanaben, "We may not have wealth but we have health and a son who will take care of us in the old age". (41) But with the passage of time and situation, Anjanaben changes her opinion. She becomes an opportunist and preys on Mikki. Here, the novelist asks women to be firm in their opinion and character. They must cooperate and help a helpless and needy woman like Mikki. Thus, she emphasizes on unity among women. Though Mikki is burdened with responsibilities after her father's death, but no one takes her seriously in her own office, simply because she is a girl, and that too an inexperienced one. Her staff feels irksome, due to her ultra modern dress, so to improve her appearance and status Mrs. D'Souza advises her to opt for "Indian clothes", (29) as men are accustomed to it. Owing to patriarchal culture and system a woman is not free enough to choose and wear a dress of her choice. The novelist, therefore, demands freedom for the womankind to choose their life-style.

Being a daughter each and everybody expects her and her future to be simply "an obedient daughter-in-law in some prominent family". (30) This is why neither her father had taken her "into his confidence" (30) nor anybody "takes [her] seriously". (30) So, Mikki becomes an isolated being, socially. Ramankaka tries to keep her away from business and other economical affairs and that is why, he indirectly asks her to live an inactive life, because being a woman whatever act she will do will end in futility, "Why waste time with solicitors and accountants? What will they tell you? Nothing. They will give you a cup of tea, compliment you on your nice dress and send you home". (30) After this un-encouraging comment he tries to take all the affairs of her company in his hand by showing his pseudo-faith. "Leave these serious matters to me. Trust me. I will guard your interests like a father. But you will make things difficult for yourself if you do things without consulting me". (30) So, Ramankaka once again tries to isolate Mikki socially, economically and legally through psychological pressure and threat, to grab all the properties from her.

Though Mikki is not aware of Ramankaka's treacherous design, she openly declares her intention to "change just about everything" (30) and will readily face all the patriarchal "prejudices" (30) from men like Ramankaka, to resurrect her father's companies, responsibilities and liabilities, till all the things and acts are not completed on her "terms". (31) She also gives a warning that if her employees will not assist her, then she will "sack them". (31) Thus, she starts playing like a businesswoman, which terrifies even Ramankaka, whose tone changes "Mikki! sorry, Madam, you are your father's daughter. I'm willing to extend the same sort of cooperation to you as I did to your father". (31) This respect and recognition she gets when she asserts herself; "My genes are the same as my father's even if my gender isn't. I will learn whatever I have to and I will hire whoever I think fit". (31) But, after noticing a change in Ramankaka's attitude, she expresses her gratitude for his service and presence; "The corporate world is full of sharks, Ramankaka. I'm so glad that I have you on my side". (31) The novelist here asks women to face the world boldly, take care of their rights, power and monetary affairs like that of Mikki who asks for "facts and figure". (31) They should also take the help of men to tackle other men or problems caused by them.

In the meantime Shanay, who has joined Mikki's Hiralal Group of Industries, finds out that he is working in her concern "not just for Mikki's sake, but his own" (42) because he realizes suddenly that he is back in love with Mikki. However, he is not very optimistic and knows that his love for his beautiful cousin will be "doomed". (42) He says to his mother Anjanaben "Stop dreaming, Mummy", (42) when she expresses her earnest desire to him, "All my hopes are pinned on you—on your future. Today she trusts you, depends on you. Don't be a fool. This is your opportunity to better your own life, and ours. If you marry Mikki"; (41) but after knowing his negative, rational, clear, honest reply, she curses him for being her son, who due to "a little freedom" (41) forgets his "parents and his duties" (41) towards them. The novelist, through the portrayal of Shanay appreciates men who are plain, pure, perfect, polished, devoted to their assigned work, non-opportunists who give respect to womankind and help them in need, and not for men like Ramankaka, who opt for the policy of divide and rule. Shobhaa De speaks for the policy of "Unite and rule".

Shanay who is always on Mikki's side, informs her that her father's plane crash was not an accident, but "a case of sabotage". (43) She asks Shanay to "get to the bottom of" (43) the case. Here, Shanay suspects Ramankaka of starting "all these stories". (43) When he comes to know through Mikki that entire case was personally handled by Ramankaka, with her comment that "I'm sure Ramankaka will cooperate", (44) Shanay gets confirmed about his hand in the Killing of Mikki's father, "That is my biggest fear. Will he?" (44) Later, Shanay discloses one more sensational piece of news to Mikki, about "major irregularities in several departments", (77) and that Hiralal Industries is heading towards catastrophe for which he holds Ramankaka responsible. But, Mikki is not ready to accept it because she trusts Ramankaka and thinks that, "without him [her companies] would've gone down the drain".

(77) Shanay says to her very clearly "that old man is cheating you", (77) but Mikki irrationally holds Shanay's mother and "the generation gap" (77) responsible for his hostile behaviour towards Ramankaka. He gives proof to Mikki of Ramankaka's fiddling acts, which are almost everywhere. "He has converted the losses cleverly to his own advantage and indulged in many *benaami* transactions. The money has been grabbed by him, he managed to take it out of the country in various *havala* deals". (78) Eventually, he concludes from the evidence given by the night watchman that Ramanbhai "has destroyed all the papers. The day after [Mikki's] father died, Ramanbhai came to the office late in the night to shred a lot of stuff". (78) Mikki is partially convinced that these genuine evidences can't be ignored and Hiralal Industries is going to face a "Big trouble". (78) She requires "funds" (78) to overcome it, for which she thinks she can "tap Navin" (78) because, banks will not look at her and market's interest rates will be very high for her. But, in her folly she forgives Ramankaka considering his old age. Here the novelist asks women never to neglect any serious and suspicious figure, facts, action or information like Mikki, who has to suffer for it in the course of time.

While Mikki engages herself in the "Operation Salvage" (45) to save "Hiralal Industries before some shark swallow [it] up", (45) Ramanbhai plays a treacherous act against her by visiting Alisha at her home, with flowers and sweets. Alisha's mother Leelaben openly criticises Ramanbhai as "a dangerous man" (46) who can betray her [Alisha] one-day as he did to Bachchoo or Seth Hiralal and now with Mallika Hiralal. She also informs Alisha that he handles "all the money affairs in [Hiralal] companies", (47) so he knows about each "*naya paisa*" (47) Alisha assures her mother, "I don't wish to fool him. I just don't want him to fool me, that's all". (47) Later, he discloses some secrets to Alisha that Hiralal Industries is on the verge of "bankruptcy" (48) but it will be no problem for her as she will inherit "a substantial figure" (48) from the trust fund set up by her father, to which she can have full access when she'll turn twenty and in comparison to her half-sister, Mallika who has "virtually nothing to her name other than her mother's jewellery and certain other fixed assets such as properties, which are likely to be attacked shortly" (48-49) to pay off debts. In the end he puts up his proposal to Alisha that, "with the help of other interested investors, you can gain effective control over the companies" (49), and he'll "run the business side" (49) till she is not ready. Here, he tries to find out some ways to exploit Alisha and squeeze her money out "for the take-over" (49) of Hiralal Industries, with the help of "backers standing by" (49); but he finds Alisha a smart girl, "harder, sharper, with the instincts of an alley cat". (48) Though, Ramankaka here tries to exploit both the sisters by dividing them and increasing their gulf of envy, but he finds it little difficult to exploit Alisha, because she is not alone and that she is very alert.

Alisha is not surprised by Ramanbhai's visit but she feels shocked "to find her mother in Ramanbhai's arms, as she rested her head against his chest, her body heaving". (47) She is revolted "This man, whom her mother had just a short while ago dismissed as a servant. Seeing their intimacy, she also wondered how many times they'd slept together"(48). Here, the novelist criticizes the women of easy virtue because they not only degrade themselves in their own eyes and in the eyes of the world but also in the eyes of their progeny, who feel ashamed and insulted. More than this, they won't get any ideal notion to live a moral life. But, the worst thing of an easy virtue woman is that, she becomes a commodity of physical pleasure. Here, Shobhaa De suggests women not to surrender before men but to have moral force to command respect in society.

In one night, Mikki receives two offers of marriage, one from Mr. Binny Malhotra, a total stranger, who is well aware of Mikki's poor financial condition. The second person is Navin, who puts forth his proposal in a boyish way. "I love you, Mikki, and I was going to ask you to marry me" (53) because he thinks that she needs him due to her loneliness. But she is not yet ready for marriage, though she knows that she is "Young, known and desirable" (49).

Binny Malhotra invites Mikki to his residence. Mikki, who neither knows him intimately nor finds any "evidence" (55) to prove his marital status like, "a photograph, a feminine touch in sight—children, bicycles, doll, torn comics, or sneakers in the hall", (55) comes to know everything about the man who is "a shark, ready to snap up the first fish in the ocean", (57) when he puts forth his business proposals before Mikki in the garb of help. "I'm prepared to take on Hiralal Industries with all its current liabilities on two conditions. The first—that you marry me. The second—that you relinquish complete rights in all your father's affairs to me—and that includes properties and any other assets my lawyers will come up with". (56) After knowing the sinister design of Binny Malhotra, which may make Mikki a vulnerable victim in every walk of life—economical, legal, political and social, she immediately rejects his proposal. "Thank you for the interest shown—but no, Hiralal Industries in not on the market and neither am I, even if the bidder is quoting the highest price". (56)

In the meantime, Amy an elderly woman gives a few words of advice to Mikki regarding marriage, because without man, a woman is incomplete, as marriage brings in identity, belongingness, self-esteem, affection and care. "You need a man in your life". (58) Here, the novelist suggests that man is an integral part of woman's life, but not the man who treats woman as a dignified domestic servant, like Binny Malhotra, who does it in the later part of the novel, with Mikki.

Navin's mother Sudhaben sends her marriage proposal to Mikki through her nearest relative Anjanaben, who criticizes her son Shanay for his weak nature and therefore, its advantage has been taken by Navin. Anjanaben views Navin and his family worthless because they have "no morals. No values" (59). Because of envy she conveys the message with some twist and proposes her son's marriage with her.

> You know this boy. His family is good, quite good. Not as good as yours, but they have money. The boy, I'm told, is a little wayward, but that is to be expected in rich families. Take my Shanay—steady as a rock. We

may not have money, but we have values, culture, traditions. These things are important (61).

Here, the novelist stresses on values, culture and traditions, because only these qualities and the relationship based on them may make a society more civilized and worth living. Before putting her proposal, Anjanaben likes to emotionally blackmail Mikki first by commenting on her lonely but too busy life. "Girls are busy outside, everything gets neglected inside", (60) and secondly by conveying to Mikki that, she has asked her son to come back from abroad, when her parents passed away just for the sake of Mikki, because she thought, Mikki needs them or "some one. Shanay is an obedient" (60) and then she puts her son's marriage proposal, "Anyway, now I can only look forward to his marriage. What more does a mother want besides a good *bahu* in the house? Someone who will make her son happy. If you know of any young girl, just like yourself, you let me know" (60-61). The novelist asks us to respect a woman and provide her enough freedom so that she may take her decisions, because she is more aware of the needs, conditions, and demands of family, its members and to some extent the society itself.

Anjanaben wants to take advantage of Mikki's puzzled condition through her vague talk, but Mikki within no time understands that she wants her to marry Shanay and not Navin. Without any delay, Mikki clears the misconception that she cannot marry with Shanay, even though she likes and trusts him, but does not "love" (61) him. More than this, she has apprehension that either "he would fail as husband or may be, [she] would fail him as a wife" (61 & 62).

Mikki agrees to marry Navin, not for love, but because she is "looking for a husband, marriage, not an affair", (62) who may be "well off" (62) to help her in the Hiralal Industries, though she feels sad at the way Navin sends his mother to propose to Mikki, and that too through an aunt. She considers it foolish since they were frank with each other. But the novelist gives her approval to this indirect approach, "Not unromantic, correct. That's the way it's done if you believe in an old-fashioned, conventional arrangement. And I think all that is very important to Navin's family". (62) Here, two views of the novelist come very clearly before us: One, a husband must be supportive to his wife and second, one must opt for the traditional way of marriage.

The novelist has questioned a few activities because they not only restrict the freedom of a woman, but also bring dishonour and degrade her like premarital sex. Navin enters into Mikki's bedroom in her absence and "Sprawled out on her silk coverlet, his arms behind his head, his shoes resting on the bed" (63) but, before Mikki can react, he commands her, "Baby, don't start bossing me around so soon. There's enough time to make me a hen-packed husband", (63) due to which she cools down in no time. Next, he tries to molest her, before their engagement, but when she opposes it furiously, then Navin declares to her; "This was just a test. I'd heard you were quite a fast babe. I'm happy to see you like this. That's what I'd expected from my future wife. I don't like *chaalu* women. So, Mikki you've passed with flying colours". (63) But the novelist doesn't agree with these patriarchal views.

Ramankaka tries to separate Mikki from the company of Shanay, because he acquaints her with intrinsic information about company's records and financial bungling done by Ramankaka. For this specific purpose, Ramankaka diployes two goons, who on the night of the engagement ceremony of Mikki with Navin, stop the car of Mikki and ask her to pay them six lakhs of rupees "six lakhs, or you're dead", (65) for Shanay owes the amount to them, or they'll be "forced to do something [she] won't like". (64) Owing to her incautious womanly nature, and without going in depth, she suspects Shanay of taking the loan. She scolds him and asks "Ramanbhai to monitor Shanay's schedules and projects more closely. And she'd take away some of the key areas of responsibility from him". (67) This is what Ramanbhai wants.

Behind the curtain Ramanbhai meets Leelaben to get the power of attorney to manage her [Alisha's] affairs, to control her interests, [and] to see Mikki privately". (72) He assures her that he will convince Mikki to sell her companies to Alisha "to keep Hiralal Industries in the family" (72) and also win over her fiancé Navin, because he knows that "nobody in this world is beyond temptation". (72) So he spindly time in "manoeuvring skills, manipulation, persuasion" (71) to grab the Hiralal Industries, by dividing both the sisters by filling in the feeling of envy and contempt in their hearts for each other through his deceits. Leelaben knows Ramanbhai is "a canny, ruthless businessman", (72) who dissuades Seth Hiralal "from divorcing his wife and marrying her when their affair had been at its peak". (72) She warns Alisha against him and is sure that, "if anybody could deal with Ramanbhai, it [is] her daughter". (72) Alisha assures her mother that "We women of the world have our instincts" (72) but she does not become a source of trouble for Mikki at the instigation of Ramanbhai.

Mikki asks for some financial help from Navin, keeping in view that the partners should stand behind each other in the hour of need. She meets Sudhaben along with executives for it, but Sudhaben does nothing except giving verbal sympathy "*Bachchi Hai*.... We must encourage her, now she has joined the business community" (81) while Navin expresses his helplessness. She fails "miserably in her mission" (81) and feels humiliated. Mikki is left to herself, though Shanay gives her moral support. Finally, she calls off her engagement with Navin without any explanation.

Ultimately, she falls a victim to Mr. Binny Malhotra, who has "money, power and access to anybody in the government" (69) except "acceptability in society". (69) Mikki knows that "he's rogue. Much older. Not [her] type at all", (62) but, for Mikki, he is the only hope to help her "to shoot to the top" (83) in the business world. She ties up with Malhotra while keeping the option open for divorce in case of "a disastrous marriage". (83) She decides to take a risk. Shanay regrets it "O Mikki—why did you have to make such a big sacrifice? Your life is more important than the fate of Hiralal Industries. I cannot work here any longer". (88 & 89)

Soon after this decision, Mikki has to face many problems. The most perturbed person is Ramankaka who accuses her for handing over the Hiralal companies, his "life's work" (89) to Binny Malhotra on his conditions and terms. He accuses her of being irresponsible to his year long loyalty and hard-work and threatens her, "You are making a big, big mistake, my dear. And you shall pay for it". (89)

Anjanaben opposes her marriage to Binny because he neither belongs to their community nor possesses good reputation. Mikki makes it clear to Anjanaben, that she knows what she is doing. Then asks her, "Where was my community when the Navin fiasco took place? Nobody bothered to call me or meet me after the engagement broke off. And you know, how badly that family behaved?" (92) Here, dignity is the prime issue in the eyes of the novelist because, a life without it is even worse than hell. One must not compromise one's dignity at any cost.

Just before the auspicious moment of her marriage, Mikki finds herself placed in a "situation in which she [was] at Binny's mercy, stripped clean of all her assets, her business, her properties—just about every conceivable possession. She'd traded in all that for everlasting love. And now that she'd been short-changed, cheated, a sense of panic convulsed her. It was too late since the marriage *mahurat* had already begun. [She found herself totally] trapped, scared and terribly alone". (98-99) She also comes to know that Binny is a rude and ruthless person and has a concubine "Urmi". (98) In this pathetic condition, she pines for "her sister Alisha" (99) with the hope that she will understand her and help her, because she is "the closest person left for in the world". (99) She earnestly requests her for help. "We share the same blood. We had the same father. I need you help me, help me", (99) but Alisha remains unmoved and taunts her:

> So, you beat me to it once again. Bitch! And now crying on the phone. I am the one who inherited a trust. You inherited debts and just as I was about to get everything, you sold it off to a stranger, an outsider, a vulture who will devour you and spit out the bones. Serve you right. Go ahead and marry him, or don't. But leave me alone". (99)

Mikki finds herself between the devil and the deep blue sea after listening to the outbursts of Alisha.

After marriage, Mr. Binny Malhotra keeps her away from "all the arrangements" (107) of home and industries, and treats her like his fulltime slave. He says, "Princess, your job is to look beautiful". (107) "You won't be doing nothing. Looking beautiful is serious business. Women work hard at it. And full time". (109) He has not "married a business tycoon. One in the family is enough" (109) as he needs a wife who stays at home and looks after him. He is not ready to work with Mikki, in the company. "No. Our women stay at home and make sure the place is perfectly run. They fulfil their husband's every need and look good when their men get home in the evening. No office-going. No business meetings. And you'd better get used to it". (109) She is reduced to be just the wife: "You are Binny Malhotra's wife. And you'd better start behaving like her. In our family, women are trained to obey their husbands, you will never question me or complain. You don't have the right. I will not tolerate it". (116) He thinks that she has to fulfil only certain "social duties and obligations" (116) in parties etc., and "butter [his] toast". (116) But, the novelist is opposed to all the above patriarchal trends used by men. But, Mikki expects what every woman wants from her husband: "I wanted some one with whom I could share my life. Is that such an impossible expectation?" (117) Mikki now realizes why her parents shared countless breakfasts "like characters in a silent film" (116) in her childhood. Thus, things have not changed.

Amy, who feels and expresses great sympathy for Mikki, consoles her "Don't be naïve. All marriages turn like this. Perhaps not quite so quickly. But certainly after a year or so. You have married a man of the world. Be realist". (116-117) She tells her that men like Binny are too busy in their work, so she should not expect "romance" (116) from him but men "are in search of sex". (117) Therefore, she asks her to "be patient" (117) and "enjoy it". (117) She also asks her not to saddle her life "with the responsibility of a child", (117) but wait till "the marriage settles down". (117) She tells Amy that Binny is against her pregnancy and threatens of either an abortion or divorce. Mikki is too frightened because she cannot go anywhere, as she has nothing left in her name. She is further terrified to learn that, "Binny already has a family. He is the father of two children, a boy and a girl—Nitya and Urvashi". (119) Upon Mikki's wailing over her miserable condition, finally even Amy wails for Mikki, "This is no position for a girl like you to find herself in. No money, no husband, no baby I wish you well. I'm there whenever you need me". (119) Mikki gets into this mess because Binny treats her as a commodity, and wants her "to remain firm and tight for his pleasure". (119) The novelist criticizes men like Binny as "a low down bastard" (119) because they disgrace entire womankind through their indecent acts and takes advantage of her beloved's weakness and love, like Binny. In spite of Amy's suggestion to fix Binny, Mikki regretfully utters not to take any legal action against her husband: "Amy. I don't want to fix him. Trouble is, I love the man. Call me a doormat, a slave, a victim, anything. But, I feel hopeless and helpless. It is as if I've forgotten what pride is or ever was. He can, and does, trample all over me". (119) Amy remains helpless to help her in any way, but here the novelist asks womankind to overcome this specific weakness, due to which they are freely exploited by men, and asks them to opt for the policy of "tit for tat".

Owing to total submission and pain Mikki expresses her view that in love there is no place for pride and she feels content "to share the same roof" (124) with her husband, "at least in the eyes of the world". (124) Moreover, with a sad smile she admires him "like a God", (124) without caring "who he sleeps with" (124) simply because, finally "he comes home to" (124) her. On the basis of it, the novelist through the words of Amy pronounces judgment on women of Mikki types as "legitimate prostitute", (124) who are visited by their respective husbands only at the time of their personal need. This is why the novelist generalizes herself through Mikki that an Indian woman lives a life similar to that of a prostitute. "Amy, all I know is, I satisfy him; he satisfies me. I don't care how that makes me look. Beside, all wives are prostitutes to some extent. Weren't you? Don't you use your body to reward or punish? What's the big difference?" (124) But, the under current of it is that, the novelist wants women to change their submissive and age old mentality, to create a new world which is fit for women. In a way the novelist give the same message as has been said by Manu in *Manusmriti*:

अरक्षिता गष्टहे रुद्रा पुरुराप्तकारिभिः।
आत्मानमात्मना यास्तु रक्षेयुस्ताः सुरक्षिता।।[35]

(Even such women folk who are kept under constant vigile by trustworthy men are not safe; only those are secure who can defend themselves by their own virtues).

On the other hand, Alisha becomes a rich-bitch, enjoys the company of many friends, and starts living a luxurious life. However, she ignores her mother to the extent that she becomes another victim of "loneliness". (129) Leelaben was already suffering "a great blow" (129) after the death of her [Alisha] father Hiralal. Though she does not mention her loneliness before Alisha, but she confesses it to the doctor. The doctor informs Alisha that her mother needs her "time and love". (129) Though physically she is all right, but not emotionally, therefore "she require reassurance and understanding" (129) from her own daughter, as she is feeling "extremely rejected and unloved". (129) She faces too much stress, which is disturbing her mental balance and is getting expressed through physical symptoms.

Binny Malhotra goes abroad leaving Mikki alone at home. Ramankaka phones Mikki during his absence and tries hard not only to convince her that he has been trying to impress Alisha to buy out Hiralal Industries with good intentions, because "Alisha...was the one person [she] could sell to, and still keep the company in the family" (136) as in his eyes "Hiralal Industries has always been more important than anything else". (136) He also sympathizes with her and informs her that her life is in "danger", (137) her own husband, is "planning to kill" (138) her. He narrates a touching story just to convince her and win her favour. He tries to black-mail her emotionally, for this he asks Mikki to have faith in him, because "material things do not matter to [him after he lost his] only son years ago in a car accident near

Bangalore.' (139) He assures her that after his death he has dedicated his life to Hiralal Industries and to Mikki. He is more loyal to Mikki because he thinks that she needs a father as much as he needs a child. The novelist has shown that women are easily emotionally blackmailed by men to win their favour and advises women to be emotionally and rationally strong enough to judge things critically.

Binny returns from abroad "in a foul mood", (139) and wants to live alone because he is not "used to sharing his room with anybody and that her presence in it distracted him", (139) which reminds Mikki that her parents also occupied separate rooms. Mikki's sensuous hunger is neglected by Binny, whom she has "missed physically" (140) for long time. Therefore, to grab his attention she is "willing to compromise her own life if it meant he'd notice her, listen to her, acknowledge her existence". (140)

Two days after his return from abroad, Binny finds Mikki in his kitchen baking something special for his birthday, in Lucio's company, who is a friend of her; but Binny scornfully and suspiciously asks her, "I couldn't trust you. Get out of my house this minute. It's over. I don't want to pollute my house. Out! And take that pansy boyfriend of yours with you". (141) He doesn't pay heed to Mikki's earnest request and ardent love, "Binny, why? Why are you doing this? What I have done? I love only you. I'm innocent...I can't live without you". (141) But, he sneers at her "women like you don't die so easily. Now get out". (141) The novelist criticizes men for their barbaric, exploitative, opportunistic behaviour, but she also appreciates men like Shanay who assist a woman in the time of distress. "Don't worry. I'll be by your side always", (144) for which Mikki thanks him. Here, the novelist want's to convey the same thing that has been said in *Manusmriti*:

अन्योन्यस्य अव्यभिचारो भवेदामरणान्तिकः।

एज्नः धार्मः समासेन ज्ञेयः स्त्रीपुंसयोः परः।।[36]

(Meaning thereby: Life long faithfulness to each other by both the spouses is in essence the highest virtue of a man and a woman/couple).

With the loss of economic power, Mikki loses her social status, and her faith in legal action. The novelist criticises the mute, meek, forgiving nature of women because it gives encouragement to moral wreck like Binny. The novelist herself seems to cherish the view that it is not through legal and constitutional action but penance, sacrifice and service that woman can attain to her pristine glory. That's why through the protagonist she states, "A lot of people did, but the problem was I loved the man...and I still do". (143) While, Amy retorts to it angrily, "stop that, Mikki! Don't you have any pride left?" (143) Through Mikki, the novelist wants to take such things to a higher moral plane where the emancipated intelligent woman tries to counter the crudities and atrocities with sane and tolerant attitude and wages relentless struggle to solve the issue through enlightened public opinion.

Binny puts forward a "divorce petition" (144) against Mikki with "seventeen charges including adultery. But, what got her was the one that said her marriage to Binny remained unconsummated and therefore the marriage annulled". (144) Bhawana asks Mikki to "move back into your own house, do not give up your claim to your father's place", (146) because such an initiative is taken by a man when he wants "a quick and inexpensive way out of a marriage". (144) Here, the novelist sardonically taunts at the mean nature of men against women and loopholes in the legal system. She also simultaneously shows the importance of money and parental support in a woman's life, to face the world, without which "her life could have been a lot worse". (147) The novelist also asks for united family structure.

"The concept of female camaraderie is strictly for the birds, believe the class which alleges that the fair sex is anything but fair and is 'more competitive, manipulative, cattier and nastier to each other than one would generally like to believe'".[37] The same quality we observe in the reaction of Alisha at the pathetic condition of Mikki, who knew that her marriage is over and thinks; "serves the bitch right. Miss High and Mighty deserved to be pulled down. Now let's see what she does and where she goes". (149) So, instead of helping her half-sister, she rejoices. The absence of Mikki in Binny's "palatial home" (149) creates a vacuum in Alisha's life because it deprives her the thrill of joy in seeing tormented Mikki through her bathroom's large window. Alisha feels "cheated, as if the entire exercise of getting this place had become futile without Mikki to torment her. Bitterly, she thought 'Once again I've been defeated by her'". (149)

Alisha gets attached to Dr. Kurien, but "after learning that Dr. Kurien is a devoted family man, she feels disappointed and takes up with Navin again", (148) but doesn't forget all about Dr. Kurien. Leelaben, far from enjoying her daughter's newfound riches, found herself completely alone and sank into depression, which eventually resulted in her death on account of "a massive cerebral haemorrhage". (151) Alisha blames the doctor and not to herself for the death of her mother. She remains unmoved by the death of her mother, which is reflected through her sexual relationship with Navin in the bed, while "people are waiting for her downstairs at her mother's *uthamana*". (154) When she comes to know that Mallika has come to her to express her "condolences" (153) her behaviour is very rude, "Get up! You are not welcome in my house, Miss Hiralal. Or do you still call yourself Mrs. Malhotra?" (154) Mikki craves for union with her sister, but she is unable to concretise it, due to envy and misunderstanding of Alisha. But Mikki doesn't mind it at all even in her desperate, deserted, lonesome and insecure condition of her life, due to lack of "a man around" (155) her.

Next day she receives a phone call from Dr. Kurien, who informs Mikki about Alisha's condition that her sister has tried to kill herself. "She slashed her wrist in bathroom earlier today. She's at my nursing home, in the ICU", (156) and gives her the address. When Mikki is on the way to the hospital, she sincerely prays "for her sister's life and, in a way, her own". (156) For two days and nights, Mikki does not leave the nursing home as Alisha hovered precariously between life and death. Alisha is fighting "to live" (158) and from her inner heart "grew a certainty that this was one battle she would win". (158) Mikki determines to win over her sister by her service, sacrifice and selfless love for her under any condition and at any rate. "I have to make sure, it never happens again. Ever. I'm going to look after her from now on. Let her protest and fight. I won't listen to her. She needs me. And I need her too", (159) because till now they were "depressed, distracted, desperately lonely" (159) which made them feel "weak, low and defenceless". (159) They easily become victim of men, worthless men like Navin, only on account of their weakness. The importance of unity is realised by Mikki at present, while Alisha also realizes the same thing after a few days later, which eventually unites them and "the two sisters held each other close and cried the lost years away". (161) She pleads for trust:

> Look, Alisha, let's learn to trust each other. You need me now...just as I need you...I can understand your anger. But let it be in the past where it belongs, the man responsible for it—my father and yours, is dead. Forget what happened, I'm prepared to blank out everything and start everything from scratch. (161)

Owing to the determined efforts of Mikki, "Alisha's animosity almost completely gone as a result of Mikki's determined effort to break it down, the sisters now spent their time catching up with each other's lives" (162) at home, after Alisha is discharged from the Nursing Home.

After their union, Mikki gets enough moral courage to protect herself and her sister against exploitation by men, as she does with Navin after calling him up; "I never want you to call or try and see either of us again. Do you understand? You're nothing but a low down S.O.B. Stay out of our lives permanently. You could have killed my sister!" (165) It was Sapana, P.A. to Alisha who was instrumental in bringing her closer to Navin. She was responsible for introducing Navin and Alisha to each other in a "house warming party". (165) Sapana admits her guilt and also tells them that she had planned the same thing for Mikki. She apologizes to her for this act, which ultimately led to the tragic incident, which takes place in Alisha's life.

Sapana later discloses the reason for planning "revenge" (166) against Alisha. She holds Hiralal responsible for her vengeance who after giving her a job in "one of his divisions", (165) "ruined" (165) her life after the abortion which was performed by a "quack" (165) and later knocked her out. She joined Alisha, but as soon as she came to know that she was daughter of Hiralal, she started plotting against her. Sapana's hatred for Alisha changes into love with the passage of time, "but by then it was already too late for her to save Alisha from the clutch of Navin. She also tells Mikki that, "Ramanbhai knew everything" (166) and "suspect[s] he was blackmailing Seth Hiralal". (166) She also informs Mikki that he met her recently "to know if the child was alive, if someone else could stake their claims to the Hiralal legacy [and tries to lure Sapana by regretting]. You know, you could have used the child to get you something out of Hiralal", (166) so that she may disclose her all the secrets from her heart. With this information, Mikki comes to know the "newer and blacker aspect of" (166) her father's personality, who "had been a real bastard" (166) in her eyes. This makes her to brood over her "poor Mummy for the first time in her life" (166) and also the poor sister.

Though after their union, both the sisters are "left in the lurch" (179) by their "trusted employees", (179) yet with the help of their new zeal for life and hard work, they overcome the situation. Mikki gets poetic justice when Mr. Binny Malhotra along with his concubine and illegitimate children die in a "car accident while driving from Bangalore to Ooty in a head on collision with a truck". (169) This reflects the novelist's anti-adultery view, which even Nature doesn't approve of, which is immoral, unethical and against true human nature. Although, Mr. Malhotra remained disloyal to Mikki through out his little life, yet Mikki shows her fidelity to him even after his death by overseeing "all arrangements for the funeral", (169) and by doing this, she spoils the plans of the executives, who want to dismiss her from her legal access and right to Binny's property.

Mikki, who really loves her younger half-sister Alisha, wants to give her a good amount of share in her now well established company "to make her feel loved and wanted. One of the family" (178) because Mikki owes her that much as well as "that girl has suffered, suffered more than any one will" (178) due to uncertainty in her life, so "Mikki wants to make up for it". (178) This provokes Ramanbhai into leaving her with a demand to give him "a stake in the business—a share holding". (178) Soon after it, he hatches a plot against Mikki to kill her, but it eventually results in his confession of his crimes, "I had you all killed like flies. And nobody found out. Nobody will now. Bahadur Singh behind a truck is a death machine after Malhotra's death, this Shanay business came up. Whatever I did after that, I was forced to do". (208-09) He also discloses her the weaknesses of Alisha "many boyfriends, ruining her life with liquor, sex and even drugs" (210) due to which finally "she'll kill herself". (211) But, this ill man is overpowered by Mikki's silent-cum-true lover Shanay, while the Policemen "grabbed hold of Ramanbhai" (213) and saved (both Shanay and) Mikki.

Eventually, their integrity has given a new light, life and meaning to them, which is expressed by the novelist as a new dawn of freedom, honour, honesty, status and equality in most dignified manner. "The sunlight came pouring into the room through the enormous bay windows of Mikki's—and Alisha's—beautiful home, bathing the two sisters in its golden glow", (217) which will lead them "to great future", (222) "with men" (222) married to them respectively, who may care and share life with them in equal proportion and affection. Thus, the novelist hopes that the unity, *sanity*, mutual-understanding and co-operation of womankind will make their future favourable and bright for each and every woman.

Through the comments of different characters in the novel, the novelist stresses on marriage, conjugal love, need of mutual understanding between spouses, and her emphasis on stern and staunch anti-adultery attitude of life. Leelaben recalls the remark of her mother on her concubine status after the death of Seth Hiralal "Leela you will have everything in life, but not domestic happiness", (5) which is the most precious thing in human life and for entire humanity. That is why, Leelaben in later phase of her life asks her daughter Alisha to "get married into a decent family. Be a gentleman's wife. Have nice children.

What else can a mother want for a daughter". (102) She harshly criticises her for her uncertain liaisons with "muslim" (102) or other fellows. We come to know the same sort of anti-adultery attitude through the comment of Dr. Kurien on the proposal of Alisha to divorce his wife to marry her. "For woman like you—men are like playing things. Today, you want to break-up my marriage. Tomorrow you'll get bored and move on to some other man. Where will that leave me?" (164) He later condemns himself for his adulterous act. He confesses to Mikki that be has committed "a mortal sin" (199) and has realized that "adultery [is] a sin". (199) "It was wrong. The love was wrong. We were sinners". (199) Seth Hiralal, who raped Bahadur Singh's wife "paid it with his life for it". (207)

Married life is a must in the eyes of the novelist, that is why Alisha tells Mikki about their marriage, "Eventually, you are going to remarry. And I hope not to remain spinster forever. I'd like kids; lots of them". (167) The same thing is suggested by Amy to both the sisters. "What the two of you need are the husbands. Good solid husband to manage you and your money". (195) It is further stressed in the dialogues between Alisha and Mikki. Alisha says, "To us and to a great future—with or without men. Mikki corrects it, 'No, no make that with. Yes, all the way". (222) Then Alisha adds, "I had marriage in mind" (222) to which Mikki replies "so did I" (222) because it does not "ruin" (222) a woman's life.

The novelist considers money and religion as a means for the betterment of human beings and humanity but not as a goal. Ramanbhai, the main villain in the novel says to Mikki, "What did money get you? A widow before twenty-third birthday. And dead before the twenty-fifth". (208) Similarly, Mikki's warning to Alisha to get out of the trauma of Dr. Kurien, "Religion is not a tool or trap to get a man. Be responsible for once in your life", (189) expresses her rational attitude to life and attaches utmost importance to the greatest human institution i.e. marriage.

NOTES

1. A.G. Khan, "Shobhaa De *'Vatsyayani'*" (Veena Noble Das & R.K. Dhawan's *"Fiction of the Nineties":* (New Writing)", (New Delhi: Prestige Books; 1994) p. 47.
2. *Ibid.*, p. 49.
3. Neena Arora, "An Analytical Study of *Sisters"* (Jaydipsinh Dodiya's, *"The Fiction of Shobhaa De: Critical Studies"*, New Delhi: Prestige Books (2000), pp. 216-17.
4. *Ibid.*, p. 216
5. E. Satyanarayana, "The Dialectics of Self-Assertion: The Liberated Woman in *'Sisters' (Ibid)* p. 211.
6. *Ibid.*, p. 211.
7. Yamuna Prasad, "Shobhaa De's *'Sisters':* Not a Junk but a Novel", Amar Nath Prasad, *Indian Women Novelists in English* (New Delhi: Atlantic Publishers and Distributors, 2001) p. 103.
8. *Ibid.*, p.103.
9. *Ibid.*, p. 104.
10. *Ibid.*, p. 107.
11. *Ibid.*, p. 105.
12. Bijay Kumar Das, "Shobhaa De's *Sisters*: An Appraisal" in his book *Critical Essays on Post-Colonial Literature* (New Delhi: Atlantic Publishers & Distributors, 2001) p. 91.
13. *Ibid.,* p. 91.
14. *Ibid.,* p. 93.
15. *Ibid.,* p. 91.
16. C.P. Surendran quotes Shobhaa De's statement in *The Illustrated Weekly of India*, Oct. 31—Nov. 6, 1992. Vol. CXII, 44, p. 34.
17. E. Satyanarayana, "The Dialectics of self-Assertion: The Liberated Woman in *'Sisters'*" (Jaydipsinh Dodiya's, *The Fiction of Shobhaa De,* New Delhi: Prestige Books), p. 211.
18. Shobhaa De, *Selective Memory: Stories From My life,* (New Delhi: Penguin Books India (P) Ltd., 1998) p. 333.
19. *Ibid.*, p. 333.
20. *Ibid.*, p. 333
21. Neera Desai and Vibhuti Pate, *Indian Women: Change and Challenge in the International Decade 1975-85* (Bombay: Popular Prakashan Pvt. Ltd., 1985) p. 84.
22. *Ibid.*
23. Shobhaa De, *Sisters* (New Delhi: Penguin Books India (P) Ltd., 1992). Back side of the jacket of the book.
24. *Ibid.*

25. Veen Nobel Dass and R.K. Dhawan",*Fiction of the Nineties: An Introduction*" (New Writing) New Delhi: Prestige Books, 1994) p. 16.
26. Dr. S.P. Swain, "Shobhaa De's *Socialite Evenings*—A Feminist Study" (Manmohan K. Bhatnagar, New Delhi: Atlantic Publishers and Distributors, 1999) p. 137.
27. Shobhaa De's *Starry Nights* (New Delhi: Penguin Books India (P) Ltd., 1991). A statement by the character and protagonist of the novel, Aasha Rani, p. 157.
28. Shobhaa De's "*Sisters*" (New Delhi: Penguin Books India (P) Ltd., 1992) p. 153. All further references to the novel will be incorporated in the text.
29. Alladia Uma, "Is there Anything Beyond?" (A.S. Rantam, "*Critical Essays on India Women Writing in English*", New Delhi: Harman Publication House, 1999) p. 25.
30. Shobhaa De, "A Fate Like Radha's"(*The Week*, July 16, 2000) p. 11.
31. Yamuna Prasad, "Shobhaa De's *Sisters:* Not a junk but a Novel" (Amar Nath Prasad, *Indian Women Novelists in English,* New Delhi: Atlantic Publishers & Distributors, pp. 110-11.
32. Shobhaa De, "Corporates Prefer Singletons", *The Week*, November 19, 2000. p. 10.
33. *Ibid.*
34. Shobhaa De, "A Fate Like Radha's" (*The Week,* July 16, 2000) p. 11.
35. *Manusmriti*, 6:12.
36. *Ibid.*
37. "Camaraderie among women is a myth?" by Manjari Mishra, Times News Work, Lucknow (*Times of India*, New Delhi edition, 11th March 2000) p. 10.

5

Strange Obsession: Rise and Shine

The *Strange Obsession* (1992), the fourth novel by Shobhaa De is a psychological novel, in which the novelist has dealt with an obsession. Critics like Neelam Tikka and Gajendra Kumar opine that the novel deals with the philosophy of lesbianism and its practice. This novel acquired popularity for depicting lesbian relationship. The entire story of the novel revolves around the life and lustful relationship of two youthful girls, Amrita Aggarwal and Meenakshi Iyengar (Minx or Meenu). But it is not only this much.

The novelist has her own opinion regarding the novel. It is different from all her previous novels. She writes:

> For the past twenty-five years, I have been at the receiving end of a woman's obsessive attention. While this person is not the psychotic Minx of the book (or not that I know of), she is equally cunning and complex. I tried to get under the skin of such an individual whose each breath revolves around the existence of another in a manner so compulsive, it's terrifying. The book developed into a thriller at some point, with Minx meeting a fiery end. In real life, the woman who inspired Minx is still around. Still stalking, still obsessed... She no longer affects me, the old anger has disappeared. I received her daily blank calls with far more equanimity than I used to ten years ago. When *Strange Obsession* was announced, she wrote me a long letter, fearing exposure and threatening suicide. (The *Stardust gang* treated her like Casper the Friendly Ghost). The secret is

> safe. And will remain so till one of us dies and even after.[1]

Thus, this novel too is based on the realities of life. There are references to lesbianism in many Hindu scriptures and erotica some of which are quoted below:

> अंतः पुरगताः काष्चित् स्त्रियाष्चाप्राप्तभाण्डकाः।
> भगे ह्यन्योन्य विष्ठवासात्कुर्वन्ति मुखचापलम्।।[2]

(Deprived of copulation women of *haram* perform on each other *auparishtik* (cunnilingus).

> यदि पुंसां गतिर्ब्रह्मन् कथंचिन्नो पपद्यते।
> अप्यन्योन्यं प्रवर्तन्ते न हि तिज़्ठन्ति भर्तज़ु।।

(O Learned One! If women don't have a man and the husband too, is away, they indulge in intercourse among themselves employing artificial means). *The Mahabharat,* "Anushasan Parva", 37: 22.

> Some women of the *harem*
> When they are amorous,
> Do the acts of mouth congress
> On the *yonis* of one another.
> Vatsyayan, *Kamasutra*, xiv

And the prime theme of the novel is *freedom from obsession*. It is expressed in the last line of the novel, "Amrita was free at last".[3] The protagonist confirms it with some hesitation, when she confesses harsh realities, before Meenakshi Iyengar's father. "Your daughter and I shared an unnatural relationship. She forced me into it, blackmailed me, tortured me, scared me and then, I began to enjoy it. To response. I became dependent on her, till I met my husband who saved me from her clutches". (204)

In Shobhaa De's previous novel *Starry Nights* lesbianism was an expression of women's liberty, while in this novel it is an obsession. A sequence of obsessive thought that finally entraps the protagonist into a strange obsession, through convulsive-obsessions. The blurb on the back cover of the book illustrates it:

> *Strange Obsession* is the story of the gorgeous young super-model Amrita Aggarwal. Within months of her arrival in Bombay, she is the envy of its beautiful people. Then, one day, she attracts the attentions of a mysterious woman called Minx. As the months pass and the demands of her unwelcome suitor grow, Amrita's life turns nightmarish. An unforgettable novel of sexual obsession and its calamitous consequences.[4]

It is Minx who is first obsessed, due to her intimacy with her father. Her father accepts, "My daughter is the severely disturbed child of a disturbed mother. She suffers from delusions. I tried hard, too hard, to be both mother and father to her. To protect her". (203) Because "My wife has been institutionalized for the past ten years. This news would kill her". (202) Therefore, in the absence of her mother and her motherly affection, she gets the share of "love and care from her father. She loves him so much that her love changes to obsession. She gets badly spoilt because of [it] and her whole personality changes".[5] And to achieve her goal, she becomes a sly, clever and strong-headed girl. Her father allows her to do any rational or irrational act, without any serious consideration; for instance, we may refer to the case of Parthasarthi, whom Minx wants to destroy. Her father accepts thoughtfully, "I was always afraid of her, scared of her rage, unsure of what she might do if I reacted. She was crying. And I remembered the little girl without friends who used to crave her mother's company. I felt sorry and would've done anything she wanted me to". (204)

Owing to this, Minx longs for physical proximity with her father, as she wants to fulfil and compensate the loss of motherly love with father's overall caressing and protective attitude. But, because of her mental sickness and obsession, she tells a lie before Amrita that her father makes her feel that it is her duty to satisfy his lust in absence of her mother. "He made me feel it was my duty. 'If your mother doesn't, you have to'". (45) This is why Neelam Tikkha writes, "she feels it to be her moral duty to satisfy him",[6] which is nothing but expression of her obsession. Mr. Iyengar, father of Minx laments over it,

"My little Meenu how could she have told such loathsome lies about her own father? I curse the day her mother gave birth to her". (203) She tells so because she is 'the severely disturbed child of a disturbed mother. She suffers from delusions, she tells lies and she makes up stories". (203) "Her transformation into a lesbian is due to this Electra complex".[7] She expresses it when she says "My father raped me", (45) and in a symbolic way, she expresses her faith in it. "He made me feel it was my duty. 'If your mother doesn't, you have to'. I believed him. I thought that's how it was in other people's home too. That was my one big mistake". (45)

But, it is mainly because of the mother's psychological maladies that Meenakshi Iyengar becomes such a neglected and spoilt child. Poor father does not perpetrate any physical excesses upon her. His only fault is that he couldn't compensate for the love and concern of the mother. Even her father accepts it, "Is this the price I must pay for neglecting her when she needed me?" (203) Due to this "she develops hatred for her own father and every man. She becomes a lesbian and forcefully falls on an upcoming model—Amrita".[8] That's why she is "trying to make friends with" (47) her.

Amrita's fondness for Minx starts soon after her first chance encounter with Minx, where Minx helps and supports her. She is assisted by Minx in an unfamiliar city and in the nick of time. She feels, when Minx looks at her, a little obsessive. "Let alone a woman [Minx], no man had ever looked at her the way Minx just had. And no previous compliment had affected her in the same manner". (6) This is the beginning of the strange obsession for the protagonist in the new city of Bombay, where human sentiments are hard to find as people are awfully busy about themselves and there is hardly any time 'to see and stare.' Karan's dialogue reveals it, "I'm here to shoot you. Not to flatter you. You're doing a job and getting paid for it. Same as me to me, a model is a model—a subject for my camera. Nothing more". (10-11)

Karan tells Amrita about Minx, "that female is bananas". (18) He also tells her about a model of Chandigarh, who was also very often accompanied by Minx, much as she does with her at present, till one day she suddenly disappeared for good. These pieces of information given by Karan, make Amrita wide alert against Minx. But, Minx starts tightening her noose on Amrita by giving her presents, sometimes "a frozen heart" (21) while at others "silk undies". (22) She tells Amrita plainly, "You can't get rid of me that easily", (21) when she wants to avoid her. She confides in Amrita, "You have became a part of me. You live right here in my body. I can feel your presence inside me all the time. Today it's a helpless, dumb animal's heart in your fridge...tomorrow it could be mine. Don't play with my life, Amrita. You'll regret it...". (23)

Minx wants to develop a closer relationship with Amrita, while "Amrita wanted to get as far away from Minx as she could". (23) She firmly put it to Minx that, "We can never be friends. You are weird. Abnormal". (22) At this, Minx reveals to her, her real self, "Abnormal? What are you talking about? You think I'm a bloody lesbian, don't you? but I'm in love with you. I love you. I adore you. It is not sexual. I don't wish to go to bed with you. All I want is to be around you. That's all". (22) Upon it, Amrita contemptuously replies to her, "Forget it: We can never be friends or lovers or anything, whatever you're after, you won't get it". (22-23) Thus it is very clear that both have different likings. Amrita likes men, while Minx fancies women. Here, "Minx knows what she is. She, consciously or subconsciously, identifies herself in negation. She is extremely passionate for Amrita and sometimes becomes violent".[9]

Lesbianism is not only Minx's newly acquired obsession, it also expresses her acute feminist attitude too, as observed by Robyn R. Warhol, who says:

> A person of the female sex who is erotically attracted primarily to persons of her own sex (who may not refer to herself as lesbian, another term whose definition is under debate within feminism), might be either strongly feminine or strongly masculine in her gendered self-presentation, or most likely—her gender identity would, like most homosexual persons, be made up of a complicated combination of gender 'differences.'[10]

Gajendra Kumar, therefore, is correct up to some extent when he writes that, "Lesbianism is a psychological perversion, an obsession and something like eccentricity. It should be part of feminism".[11] But, he is not fully correct, because the undercurrent of the novel and behaviour of the protagonist is against it. Amrita wants to free herself from the obsessive clutch and trap of Minx. "I'm scared to death of her, Karan. I feel she could harm me someday. I can't go anywhere without the creepy sensation that she is close by somewhere, watching me. It's a horrible position to be in". (24) Amrita's fierce reply to Minx "Don't you dare touch me" (29) for her deep and only desire "I want you to be mine" (28) is anti-lesbian and anti-obsessive. So, lesbianism and obsession can't be mentioned as the aspects of 'Feminism.' This view is supported in the novel when we are acquainted with "Rover (Ranjit Grover) the rogue. Right now, he was the property of a sprightly divorcee, Sangita Singh, a much-travelled, much-loved woman of the world". (32)

Minx hates men. That is why she condemns Rovers for having permissive sex with Amrita. She says before Amrita, "He screwed you. That man is an animal. He fucks anything that moves". (34) Owing to this hatred, she beats him savagely and takes Amrita to her "Gynae" (35) "to be medically examined [by] a blood check", (35) so that, she may be certain that Amrita is free from any "sort of bugs" (35) being distributed by Rover through sex. Here, in a way, Minx treats Amrita as her own property. It can be further illustrated by Minx's obsessive nature, due to which inspite of Amrita's complaint "You are the one who is sick", (35) and protest "You have no right to intrude into my life like this. No right to talk to my family. No right to interfere"; (36) she thinks and says to Amrita "You are stuck with me, I love you. I have to protect you. It's my duty". (36) This raises a question about the need for protection of women, "Why do they need protection in society?" Minx indirectly gives its answer, "The Sickons in the world are people like you. Bloody sex-starved nymphos, ready to fuck the first man they can lay their hands on. I have no such problems. I'm pure and clean". (35-36) This raises another question, "Why does a woman surrender before a man or a woman?" A woman surrenders because circumstances are created which compel her to do so, as in the novel Amrita does before Minx.

The novelist criticises the patriarchal view about women in society. Amrita recalls her friends telling her about Rover in the restaurant, "He treats his women like dirt. He'll use you and discard you. S.S. will chew you up". (38) While Rover himself arrogantly says to her, "Nobody wins me, lady". (38) This shows the novelist's feminist concern about the status of womankind in the male dominated society, which is very deplorable. She holds women to be responsible for their deprived condition. "'Women are women's worst enemies,' I'm not sure who coined it (probably a very shrewd man who was certain gullible female would promptly fall for it, and predictably they have!), but it has acquired the sort of popularity, acceptance that borders on disgust. And to think that more and more women seem to be exploiting its cheap appeal!"[12] The novelist through her above comment seems to disagree with the idea that women are worst enemy of their own kind. Even if, the weaker sex has any weakness, she may find a solution, which lies in the female solidarity. As the novelist writes:

> "Female solidarity need not be a myth, something that women merely dream about. We have our natural affinities and polarities. It is only a matter of harnessing our *shakti* and putting it to good use, to ensure a more beautiful, creative and productive world for ourselves".[13]

Minx has "extremes" (42) of nature and dominates over Amrita who tolerates her but with contempt. "OK, Minx. You win. But this doesn't look like normal behaviour to me". (42) She rejects Minx's love because it is polluted with lesbian lust. "You say 'I love you' to me as if it's perfectly natural for one woman to say it to another. I think it's abnormal. You are abnormal, don't like women". (42) Here, the novelist rejects lesbianism. Simultaneously, she considers heterosexuality as natural. She expresses it through the inquisitive reply of Minx.

"Why does it make you sick? Because I belong to the same sex? Is that my only sin? but what about that animal Rover's love? Because they are men. And it is normal". (44) Here, the novelist suggests women not to surrender before any man, simply because he is a man.

Inorder to win the sympathy of Amrita, Minx tries to blackmail her emotionally by narrating to her a fictitious story about her own abuse as a child. She tells her that, 'at the age of thirteen, she was raped by her own father.' Although she wins Amrita's sympathy by appealing to her emotions through her false story, yet on the other hand "Amrita had made up her mind for a new place to stay", (48) so that she may get rid of Minx and her obsessions. Finally, she favours "the idea of sharing Sheila's Versova flat". (49) Amrita is convinced that Minx is making her life miserable. She tells Sheila that, "one of the reasons I want to move out is her. In fact, it's the main reason". (51)

The novelist gives paramount importance to marriage in a woman's life. She puts it through the words of the protagonist who says to Sheila "two years from now, I'll be married". (51) But, Sheila feels sorry for her because of Minx. "What she did to Rover nobody wants to mess around with that female. Not even Karan. And he was really keen on you". (51) She puts it before Amrita in a straightforward way, "But with that crazy woman in your life, how can you think of marriage?" (51) Later, Amrita accepts the reality hopelessly, "I can't seem to get rid of her, she is not one of those harmless fans. I don't know, this one is demented". (55)

Minx is such a demented and maniac creature that she disfigures Lola with acid burns simply because Lola, a model, managed to take away one of Amrita's assignments. Minx herself informs Amrita about it. "What Lola did to you. Don't worry. It has been taken care of. Lola won't pose for another photograph or of another show again. I've seen to it". (59-60) She burnt her with acid and harmed her generative organ with some corrosive instrument. Lola is getting treatment in a hospital. But she doesn't actually die. Minx does so just to "make [Amrita] happy". (60) Amrita's strong rebukes to Minx do not deter Minx from her obsessional character. "No matter how far you go to win me. I'll never like you, never love". (62) And in frustration she says, "I hate the sight of you. Go and kill whoever you want. I'll hate you more despise you, spit on you, why don't you kill yourself instead?" (62) Minx shows a liking for this remark of Amrita, "Will this make you happy? I'll kill myself. I'll give you my life. What more can I give you?" (63) This reply of Minx makes Amrita even more "Sick". (63)

Minx is a sadist. Her remark about herself, "I'm a Gemini. We do things in extremes" (42) justifies her misdeeds on Lola. Because, even Doctor's opinion agrees with it when he tells Karan about the pathetic condition of Lola. "It wasn't just an acid attack—the poor girl was carved up nicely. Her insides were mined with a switch-blade shoved through her vagina. Only a sadist would mutilate an innocent young girl like that. Her chances are permanently destroyed". (68) Minx's sadistic nature is further proved when we learn about her life-style, when Karan goes to see her. He finds her as always "dressed in black, and alone". (69) Owing to the differences and enmities among womankind, entire womankind is defamed. Karan vehemently criticizes Amrita for the deeds of Minx. Through the words of Karan, "Sad to think a woman could do such a thing to another woman, isn't it?" (68) The novelist tells women to live a self-regulated life, and at the same time asks them not to indulge in any such activity, to fulfil their anti-social ambitions, "If this is what ambition does a person, it's better to remain in the slow track. You have become a cold-blooded, ruthless bitch. Even worse. May be, Minx is responsible for doing this to you. But she doesn't control your life or own you. Or does she?" (65-66)

Amrita, who has achieved her ambition to become "India's highest-paid model in a remarkably short time that even her rivals marvelled at her meteoric rise", (66) is now "sunk into a deep depression after Lola's 'accident'". (71) Karan suggests Amrita "to get out of Bombay" (75) to overcome depression and to protect herself from Minx. Minx further tries to possess Amrita by filling her hairline parting with her blood. While

Smearing Amrita's head Minx says, "with this blood, I pledge my life to you in the presence of these two witnesses". (76)

Amrita leaves Bombay for Delhi to get rid of Minx. In the flight, she meets Parthasarthy (Partha), an editor of a news-magazine 'weekend,' and a sort of friendship develops between them.

Gajendra Kumar is not conclusive when he writes that, "*Strange Obsession* does not deal with the struggle for power and feminism".[14] Shobhaa De herself writes, "I write with a great deal of empathy towards women. Without waving the feminist flag, I feel very strongly about the woman's situation".[15] "I had always been gravitating towards women. I was a woman's woman".[16] Regarding the struggle for power and woman's emancipation, she says, "Eventually, every relationship is a power struggle either on overt or subliminal level. The very concept of the sexes locked in eternal battle is negative and destructive".[17] This statement of Shobhaa De may provide the key to understanding the overall concept of man-woman relationship as highlighted by her in her different writings. Shobhaa De stands for synthesis not schism, for unity not discord, for love not antagonism. Differences of opinion or viewpoint may always be there but the underlying stream of love and concern must always wash away the ferns of dichotomy and disbelief. It is here that Shobhaa De joins hands with some of the eminent thinkers of our times and it is also here that she can be deemed as a true spokesperson of Indian culture. While one of her interviewers writes, "One has to concede the fact, that the relationship between men, women and society is not of differences alone but of access to power".[18] There are many examples to verify the above comment of the novelist and her critics, but we'll take only two. First, when Minx asks Karan to "collaborate" (70) with her on Amrita's issue, she threatens him by saying, "The point is: who is double crossing whom?" (79) Second, when Amrita finds, her husband's hanky and a pool of blood and listens to the muffled voice of Rakesh in the tape sent by Minx. She is astonished to think, "Could she have successfully overpowered some one so much bigger or stronger?" (185-86) The remark that this novel does not deal with the struggle for power and feminism is, therefore, off the mark.

Amrita's father is quite appreciative of Minx. But, Amrita does not like to talk about her even though Minx has done a good job for her in Bombay, "she packed everything carefully" (85) in her absence. Then Amrita realizes that, "There was no place for her to go in Bombay. And no one to turn to except Minx". (85) Even in such a delicate situation, Amrita remains reluctant to tell her family about the strange development in her life. Just because she doesn't "want them to discover the ugly truth about Minx, Lola or even Sheila. This was something she wanted to sort out on her own. But it was not going to be easy". (86) At this time, she began to trust Karan implicitly, who sends some mixed signals to her in Delhi.

In Delhi, Amrita meets Partha at Valentino, where she is dumbstruck to see Minx, "My God can't you leave me alone?" (89) She snubs her, "Rubbish nothing you do is a coincidence. You're spying on me making me miserable. What do you get out of torturing me like this?" (89) "Amrita feels like an interloper" (89) when Minx and Partha are too busy in talk. Minx warns Partha that she is "a fixer, remember? I make it my business to know everything about every one". (91)

For the first time, Amrita has "a feeling of sympathy for the wretched woman before her", (93) when Minx shows her reduced breast to her. At the same time, she says she "got the feeling you [Amrita] didn't like them—that their huge size put you off. I didn't like them either. May be, I blamed then for whatever was happening between me and my father". (93)

A man or a woman in himself or herself constitutes his/her best friend or worst enemy; the only thing that matters is self-control. Lesbian lust is based on woman's inordinate desire for erotic pleasure. Erotic pleasure among growing boys and girls may at best be only condoned, not eulogized or appreciated. Because, Woman's Lib demands from women more and more self control and not a free and unrestrained play. Otherwise, they will become victim like Amrita, who realises it after her lesbian affair with Minx. "Somehow, somewhere deep down inside her, Amrita knew she was trapped. There was no escaping from Minx now. And that was what made her recoil and cringe. No escape. Her future was inextricably linked with the other woman's. The whole thing had gone exactly as Minx would've wanted it to". (95) Minx tightens her grip over to her, "after last night, darling, no explanations are necessary. You belong to me and I belong to you, it's that simple". (96) She further pacifies Amrita saying, "Don't worry, You'll get used to it. How do you think couples stay married for years and years living out of each other's pocket?" (97) But, she is not ready to leave Amrita alone in any condition. "I go where you go. That's the way it's going to be from now". (99) So, Amrita loses her freedom due to her lack of self-control. Therefore, the novelist wants to say here that whosoever wants to remain free, must be a master of his own self. This is why Lord Krishna in the *Bhagvadgita* has issued solemn warning to all mankind with regard to unbridled passions: "Even as a charioteer checks his restive steed, so do thou, if thou art wise, check the passion, which if it runs wild, will hurry thee away". And Lord Buddha perhaps has given utterance to all time truth when in *Dhammapad* he says, "Neither father, nor mother nor the kindred one can confer greater benefits than does your own well-directed mind".

Amrita had never felt so trapped before. She doesn't express it even to her brother when he asked her, "I have never seen you like this. Are you all right?" (101) He expressed his anxiety for her. "Amrita is capable of looking after herself since we had full faith in her. What is worrying me is the change I see. Amrita was never like this". (101) She expresses her helplessness first before Parthasarthy and then before Karan. "I feel so helpless, there is no way she is going to leave me". (102) Karan proposes to her to "get married" (103) with him, but she doesn't agree because Minx "wouldn't let" (103) her. More than this, she doesn't like to put Karan's life "to risk". (103) Later "Amrita had realized what a terrible mistake had been committed. There was no way she could undo it now. No way she could reverse what had transpired between Minx and her. Silently, she cursed herself for surrendering to Minx's advances". (105-106) But, she knows that, "she would have to live with that one big regret for the rest of her life and pay for the temporary suspension of her senses two nights before, perhaps forever. Amrita had resolved never to succumb again, Minx cajoling". (106) But she fails in it and for which she suffers in her life, till she is able to overcome this weakness of hers.

After her second lesbian encounter with Minx, "Amrita was more determined to get away from Minx". (109) Seeing Amrita disinterested in her, Minx says with scorn "I'll become a man, just to satisfy you". (110) She is planning to "undergo a sex-change operation". (110) She wants to do it for the sake of Amrita, because, she thinks that Amrita wants "a prick to enter" (110) her. Therefore, she determines, "I'll go out and get one. Money can buy you anything. I've always said. Even a bloody dick". (110) At this, Amrita raises a humanitarian question, especially related to motherhood without which a woman's life is meaningless in this world. "You may be able to get some quack to stitch on a plastic dick. But will that make me pregnant? Will you be able to fill my womb with a child?" (110) Thus the protagonist conveys the novelist's views about the importance of motherhood here. Later, she rethinks and reassures herself, "This morning's love-making was crazy, crazy, Crazy. Never again, she promised herself". (110) These utterances of Amrita may be regarded as the novelist's suggestion to women that fulfilment of life demands progeny through natural means and not wasting oneself through self-indulgence.

Amrita meets Partha for an "urgent help" (111) from him. She tells him that Minx "is dangerous, and I'm scared or her". (112) She is not worried about herself, but "the other people around" (113) her. Amrita conceals the fact that "she had slept twice with Minx, even though to a direct question of Partha, 'Have you slept with her?' She lies and says 'No'". While Partha diagnoses Minx not as a "lesbo but as an alternative sexuality". (113) And asks her to take Minx to some psychiatrist.

Minx wins the favour of Amrita's parents, as Mrs. Aggrawal says, "Darling, it is all sorted out now. Your father and I are feeling so relieved. Meenakshi has promised to take good care of you. I know you'll be well looked after by her". (116) Minx once again assures Mrs. Aggrawal, "She is in the best hands with me. I know exactly what she needs even before she herself does. Auntie, give me your blessings. After all, you are like my mother. What is the difference between Amrita and me". (117) But, the irony and deception contained in Minx's words is realized only by Amrita, who is fed up with the dubious nature of Minx and questions her propriety to dupe her mother, "How dare you deceive my poor mother?" (117) She further says to her, "You are a manipulative bitch and I hate you. [and warns her] But you can't get away with this for long wait and see!" (117)

On the other hand, Minx warns Amrita to remain aloof from Partha. "Remember, one false move and the man is dead. I'll carve up his balls and present them to you on a platter". (118) She cajoles Amrita for not being grateful to her as she saved her "from these vultures". (118) Upon which Amrita replies with contempt, "I'm not going to spend the rest of my life being controlled by a pervert. I'd rather die than live with you". (118) The protagonist wants to get out of Minx's lesbian obsession. Minx proves herself a lesbian when she advises Amrita against Partha, a male, and wants her to be her partner. "If I were you I wouldn't go gabbing to the strangers with shady past. And if I were you, again, I'd stay miles away from men with possessive wives". (118) Because as Mr. Iyengar informs Amrita, "Meenakshi was mortally afraid of being exposed, she thought Partha was going to, strip her naked in the public, that is when she decided to use her own means and methods" (204) which results in "Partha's road accident". (123)

Amrita returns to Mumbai in the company of Minx. She lives with her in her apartment, where she feels "suffocated. And spied on like a prisoner and longs for her independence". (122) In this miserable and pathetic condition of Amrita, "Karan wanted to pull Amrita out from the hell-hole she had landed herself in". (119) But, he is helpless to help her, because Amrita is under strict observation by Minx. Later Amrita realises that Minx is "capable of anything and everything", (124) and this frightens her even more.

In Mumbai, Minx enslaves Amrita for shooting pornographic pictures of her. "Right now, you are my slave, let me feast my eyes on you". (128) "I want to remember every bit of you—every pore, every mole, each little hair", (128) she says as the camera panned over her body recording each detail. And after shooting, she was seen to "leap off and rush into her bathroom". (129) In the bathroom, Amrita finds Minx "watching the just shot tape on the small screen—replaying certain portions over and over again—trapped in a fantasy of her own, mouth repeating Amrita's name". (129) "Six months later, Amrita thought to herself how easily she had fallen into a pattern. Nothing seemed strange to her, not even Minx's wild swings in mood, or her pathological need to possess her". (30) It shows here that Amrita is thoroughly obsessed and trapped by Minx. Amrita likes Minx "when she was like enthusiastic, preening and childishly smug. It was other Minx who scared her. That Minx made only an occasional appearance these days". (132) Minx wants to see Amrita as "the highest-paid model in India, a rich woman". (131) She gives Amrita "ten thousand rupees as 'pocket money'", (131) she also purchases a property on the outskirts of Pune, referring to it longingly as "our retirement home". (131)

The lesbian relationship between Amrita and Minx becomes so notorious that for all practical purposes, they are "treated like a couple [and] no body dared ask Amrita to dance". (133) Even Karan is careful to keep distance, of her", (133) he roughly replies to her, "Forget it, kid. I value my life". (133) Upon which Minx mocks at Amrita's attempts, "Sad! Sad! No saviour for you. What a pity you seem doomed to spend your life trapped with a witch". (134) But, an anxious mother speculates about the grim condition of her daughter and expresses her anxiety during "their frequent phone conversations. 'Baby, you don't sound like yourself at all. What's wrong?'" (136) Though, "Amrita evaded her questions with excuses, but she didn't entirely convince Mrs. Aggarwal". (136)

Mrs. Aggarwal has full faith in her daughter, that's why she defends her staunchly against her brothers. "Not my girl, she's a good child. She'll marry the man Papa and I find her". (136) After seeing Rakesh Bhatia, Mrs. Aggarwal dreams about him as her "son-in-law". (137) He is a young businessman of Indian origin settled in USA along with his mother and two sisters. He is in India in the search of investment opportunities, for which he meets Mr. Aggarwal and along with him he visits his home. Owing to his handsome personality, refined behaviour and polished life style, Mrs. Aggarwal is flattered and fascinated by him.

Mrs. Aggarwal's fascination for Rakesh Bhatia compels her to ask him to meet her daughter. She informs her daughter about him, "Darling, I've found a boy for you". (139) But, Amrita who is already captivated and obsessed with the idea, that she is being watched, regrets her mother's proposal for her marriage. "Mummy, I'm not looking for a husband. When did I tell you to get married?" (139) At this, Mrs. Aggarwal raises an issue about Amrita's "future". (139) Amrita thinks upon it and says bitterly, "My future has already been decided for me". (139) This shows her helpless condition in which her soul is suffocating and wants to get out of it. But to her mother she says, "It's sweet of you, Mummy, but I don't think I'm ready for marriage yet" (139) due to the fear of Minx. She takes full precaution against Minx and ended her conversation with some safeguards and notes. She says to her mother, "Tell me his name and don't give him this number. You call me and let me have the Bombay address and I'll phone him". (139) This puzzles her mother.

Now, Amrita wants to "Rise and Shine" (105) out of her shackles, caused by Minx's obsession. She thinks, "this was the opportunity she'd been waiting for, dreaming about". (140) Amrita considers Rakesh as an instrument of her "escape" (140) and freedom from the bondage of Minx's oppression, tyranny and injustice. She wants to outplay Minx with the help of Rakesh, because he is an American citizen. Owing to this, she presumes, "Minx's tricks would not work with the police in New York, and finally, she would be free. After that, she would divorce him start another life. A life without Minx". (140) Amrita's eyes started "shining brightly in the dark" (140) with new hope for her freedom.

Amrita meets Rakesh at the "Rangoli" (140) restaurant. They pass nearly two hours. At the time of departure, she remembers about the "Croissant", she has to purchase for Minx. Rakesh guesses the nervousness of Amrita and teases her. But, he somehow comprehends the miserable condition of her when he says, "Your frightened little girl, I was only kidding. But whoever it is who's making you this nervous—I envy him". (144) Later she goes to Oberoi Towers across the road along with Rakesh to purchase the croissant. At the time of making payment, she feels the presence of Minx, which makes her "cold [and] shaky". (145)

Here in the Oberoi Towers, Rakesh has his first brief encounter with Minx over the issue of Amrita. But, Minx wins the game. With the help of a "snub-nosed pistol" (145) in her hand, she says to him "Take a look at what's in my hand, lover boy. Try any funny stuff and she's dead. You too". (145) And without delay "three of them walked swiftly out of the arcade", (146) but later on Rakesh informs about Amrita's pathetic condition to her parents.

Amrita's condition described through such expressions as 'cold,' 'shaky' and 'pathetic' leads, us to infer that any unsocial, inhuman and unnatural act, which lesbianism definitely is, makes us guilty conscious and drives away our self-confidence and fearlessness. The novelist also suggests indirectly that the modern Indian girls in their enthusiasm and recklessness want to adopt Western habits and mores but all such habits and mores can't bring them the peace of mind and happiness. The modern Indian girl has to develop her discretion so as to be able to distinguish between real and deceptive, fake and genuine, deleterious and healthy. Lesbianism, which is just a form of self-indulgence, dissipation and destruction, is an anathema to votaries of Indian culture, and for that matter, to the novelist herself. The novel ends on a happy note when the protagonist enters into matrimony and gets rid of the octopus grip of Minx's lesbianism.

Minx's traumatic moves start on Amrita as soon as they reach their residence. First, Minx with the help of a lighted match singes "the tip of her [eye] lashes" (147) and then sets it to her "pubic hair", (147) due to which "the room soon filled with the acrid smell of burnt hair", (147) while Amrita "drew up her knees and cried out in pain". (147) Minx's most surprising action at this juncture on Amrita is that she forces "her [Amrita's] legs apart" (147) without any warning and inserts something in her at which Amrita experiences "a sharp, searing pain as something hard and long was shoved into her. "'Enjoy, enjoy, enjoy,' Minx laughed pushing the object in and out. 'Think of him. That's how it would have felt, come on, show me how much you like it, I got it specially for you.'" (147) And, "the last thing Amrita recalled before passing out was Minx on top of her, head thrown back and laughing maniacally". (147) She welcomes the approaching blackness: "'I want to die,' she sighed before closing her eyes". (147) Thus the protagonist is so gripped by the convulsive obsession of Minx that she hopes for her liberation only after her death. She feels completely "sapped and defeated". (148)

Here, the novelist has provided a graphic description of erotic pleasure with unnatural sex escapades. The novelist has also given the net result of such escapades as the passive partner in the sex orgy here 'wants to die' and she feels completely 'sapped and defeated.' The pertinent point involved here is, has nature provided man with the propensity of sex only to indulge in it for titillation and erotic pleasure or has this godly gift any higher and nobler purpose? Questions like this abound in Shobhaa De's *Strange Obsession*, and she leaves it to the intelligent readers to find out an answer.

Three days later, when Amrita regains her consciousness, she finds herself "very weak" (148) and alone. In the meantime her mother has come there to nurse her. She repents for her error, when she says to Amrita, "What has she done to you?" (148) "You silly, foolish girl, why didn't you tell me what was happening? Why did I have to hear it from Rakesh?" (149) Later, Karan, Billoo and Mrs. Aggarwal rescued Amrita from cruel grip of Minx. "Amrita and her mother were safely airborne when Karan met the crazy Minx running blindly out of the parking lot". (151) In frustration Minx shouts, "He kidnapped my woman. He helped her escape. She is gone. I will kill him. I will kill myself". (151) And she is true to her words when Karan informs Amrita on the phone, "last night. Minx tried to kill herself". (153) Here, it is the novelist's grim warning to the society at large that sex-obsessed maniacs like Minx must not be allowed to have their way and thrive. The novelist is also hinting at the need and efficacy of a happy homely life, which is a *sine-qua-non* for maintaining social harmony and functioning as a check against aberration and social disintegration. If Mr. Iyengar had taken proper care of his only child Minx, especially after her mother being institutionalised, there was every chance that Minx would not have become a deviant and a social liability. Man must not aim to have progeny so long as he doesn't ensure their proper nurture and growth to prevent them to become a social liability, for in the society, nobody will like Minx as a social being.

The long suicidal note of Minx brings panic for Amrita and her family. She considers it as her "destiny", (153) like other frustrated and worn out Indian women. But at this crucial moment in the life of Amrita, she has "one hundred percent" (154) support of her family, when her father says with determination, "She has gone through hell if more is to follow it is our duty to support her". (154) Amrita, does not want to live a dependent, desolate and indiscreet life. It is for this reason, that she tells her mother in a resentful voice, "Please don't treat me like some hard-up woman nobody will look at. Why is everybody so desperate? I want to work. Make my life again". (155) She represents the novelist's view. She wants that society must change its negative, obsolete and deleterious views about women and provide them the fullest scope for the development of their personality, so as to enable them to overcome the traumas and dark perils of their lives with their own positive, creative and sterling qualities and carve out a niche for themselves in society.

"Amrita had not been able to overcome her shame and guilt quite as easily...wondering how she had allowed herself to fall into such an obvious trap". (157) While, Rakesh "didn't wish to discuss her past", (157) [she must be] hatching a plot. A plot that would affect Rakesh—not her". (157) She raises the issue with him on the morning of her engagement, upon which he says, "don't worry", (157) "the nightmare is over". (160) The reply of Rakesh boosts her morale and for the first time "Amrita felt unconditionally confident about the step she was going to take shortly. Rakesh would make a wonderful husband". (161) But "the trauma of what she had experienced—the guilt that refused to go away—had instilled a new fear in her mind. She was certain, she had gone off sex permanently". (158)

Here, Amrita's fears are not false. The inscrutable power of sex that nature has conferred upon man for progeny and perpetuation of the race, when abused and taxed beyond measure gets either extinct or defective. Homosexuality, lesbian relationships, sex with animals and pets, sex orgies in any form or manner, sap human energies and it is now common knowledge that the dreaded disease of AIDS originated with unnatural sex between man and animal. Examples galore can be cited where even inordinate use of contraceptives has ended in infertility of women, rendering their desire for progeny only a distant dream. Drugs, sedatives, artificial devices and even tobacco strain the human system and have the same deleterious effect. Therefore, through Amrita, the novelist has issued a solemn warning that it is our duty to guard our boys and girls against physical and mental excesses or else, their development is likely to suffer and their personalities may become stunted and lop-sided.

In the absence of Amrita, Minx becomes "a psychotic despot". (166) She resembles "a ghost: her hair dishevelled, her clothes grubby and torn, her expression ravaged, her words crazed". (162) She is unable to "live without", (162) Amrita. Even though, she tried her best to get Amrita out of her system. She says to Karan "I've tried to get her out of my system. I've stopped at nothing—hypnosis, psycho-analysis, shock-therapy, tranquillizers, even a witch doctor. Nothing works. I want her so badly; I'm in physical pain. (163) It shows Minx's obsession about Amrita. While Minx's condition justifies the novelist's comment, "I believe a woman looks what she feels".[19]

During a simple marriage ceremony, Amrita introduces Karan to Rakesh as her "best friend. He saved my life in more ways than one". (167) This justifies the modern view of Feminism, which evolved at the Beijing conference on women that "Days of bra-burning feminism are over".[20] Because "women have realized they can't do it alone and they don't want to do it alone. After all, what is the point of having men who are filled with resentment or with low esteem".[21] Thus, the role of men is put as an agenda on Women's emancipation. In the same manner Shobhaa De, the novelist, demands men's equal participation and co-operation to the cause of women's liberation.

Amrita has "done the right thing with the right man by marrying Rakesh". (169) Here, the novelist seems to give due importance to marriage, because it brings fulfilment in the life of a woman in the same ways as Malvika Sanghvi writes about Shobhaa De, "Marriage has added a richness and fulfilment to her world view".[22]

In the Oberoi Hotel, Minx moans on the other side of the room booked for Rakesh and Amrita. But, Rakesh assures Amrita for her safety. "Don't worry darling, you are here with me forever, safe and secure". (72) These words of consolation marked by genuine love and concern for Amrita and that too, from a man who only a couple of hours before was a mere stranger, evokes feelings of gratitude in Amrita for Rakesh and her sentiments find expression in spontaneous pearl drops of tears from Amrita's bewitching eyes. "Tears of love, regret and relief" (172) The free and open conjugal life, love and romance between Amrita and Rakesh, which takes place even in the car (176) gives expression to De's view, "that sex is no longer the most dreaded and despised three-letter word in India, there is enough cause to celebrate".[23] They travelled by car from Delhi and reached Nainital late in the evening and stayed in an "isolated wooden colonial bungalow". (177)

The next morning Rakesh goes alone for the morning walk, but does not return even after "nearly two hours since he left the house. He had told [the *mali* and Ram Swarup] he'd be back in fifteen minutes". (179) This makes Amrita anxious for Rakesh, and in anxiety, she raises her doubts about his safety whether or not "any thieves, or *daakus*?" (179) Is he abducted? But the *mali* denies it, "No, no memsaab, all that goes on in the cities, we people are honest and god-fearing. No, it is not a human who can hurt you in these areas, but wild animals?" (179)

Amrita along with the *mali* goes out in search of her husband. They meet Ram Swarup half a mile down the forest path. The *mali* spots something flapping in the under bush. He sends Ram Swarup to investigate. Amrita recognises it as "Rakesh's scarf, the one his mother had knitted for him". (180) Soon the mali traces "fresh blood" (180) and shows it to Amrita. She is horrified to see "a small pool of blood on a large stone covered with blood". (180) The mali consoles Amrita, "let us not lose hope", (181) and takes charge of the situation and "led them away from the spot". (181) He also suggested to "phone the police *chowki*". (181) But, except Amrita "nobody seemed particularly worried". (181)

Even the police are unable to solve the mystery and come to some conclusion. The remark of the District Superintendent of Police only expresses his perplexity when he says, "We believe it is not as simple as it appears, it is possible your husband has been abducted". (183) But, "in her heart, Amrita already knew the answer—the one that was eluding the police. A move was certain...but in the early hours of dawn. The time of day preferred by her tormentor". (183-84) That's why she is "not afraid" (183) even though "she was alone in a strange place with strange men for the first time in her life". (183) She also knows that "to win this round, she had to be smarter than her adversary and keep her cool. [Because] one false move and Rakesh would be dead". (183) That's why she vows to herself that, "she wouldn't allow that to happen even if it meant losing her own life". (184) Thus, with the example of the protagonist, the novelist not only highlights the loyal and devoted nature of womankind, but she also demands that both men and women should be loyal and devoted to one another. They must be ever ready to make sacrifice for the good and welfare of each others.

The next day, Amrita receives a packet containing "Rakesh's ring and a cassette [with] no label". (185) The cassette has a recorded speech in it, in which Minx says, "Farewell, my darling, my life, my precious one. Remember one thing, whatever I am doing is all for you; only for you". (185) This message of Minx shows that she is still obsessed with her. Another instance we get when she says to Rakesh. "Pity I don't like men or I'd have gone for you rather than that scrumptious wife of yours". (191) "Amrita was mine and will remain mine". (191)

After listening to Minx's message and the "muffled sound off" (186) Rakesh, Amrita comes to know that Minx was in the same vicinity and concludes that Minx had kidnapped Rakesh". (186) For a while, Amrita is surprised to think "Could she have successfully overpowered someone so much bigger or stronger?" (185-6) But, within no time she comes to think that "there is no gang, it is just one woman—one single woman". (187) But, she is neither understood nor assisted by police as the inspector says to her "Madam, I have understood what I wanted to. The time to understand is now yours. You are under arrest as of now". (187-8) He does so because Amrita herself accepts that, "This woman is not a stranger. She is known to me". (187)

On the other hand Minx is waiting for Amrita's arrival, when she says to Rakesh in the log cabin "We might be here for, let's—a day, a month, a year, may be forever. That depends on how badly your wife wants you". (190) While Rakesh realizes that how much "it was important to her [Amrita] to unload her dark secrets in an affort to free herself from the overwhelming sense of guilt". (192)

Amrita goes out on her own to find Rakesh, with the faith that he is "safe and that Minx would not be able to touch him". (193) After seeing her, Minx praises her, "marriage suits you". (194) Minx wants to make love with her, but can't as she notices some change in Amrita. Minx says in frustration to her, "you smell different. You smell of a man, your man. He is all over you. Every where I can't touch you ever again". (195) Later, she forces Rakesh and Amrita to dance and play with each other a naked and erotic dance as "the performance of their lives", (197) so that Minx can shoot "the best porn film ever made". (197) She is able to do all these things with the help of her pistol. "Remember, I'm the one with the gun. I want to see some great action in this dump". (196)

Minx's love for Amrita changes to hatred of the same degree, when she says to Rakesh "you have seen how well she fucks women. I get the feeling she's even better with men. Amrita seems to love it. And what Amrita loves, I want to destroy". (197) This justifies Minx's own remark "I'm a Gemini. We do things in extremes". (42) Here, this extreme is the major cause of the obsession. Through Minx, the novelist shows the most intense hatred and love of womankind.

At the climax of the scene, Minx becomes a maniac. She "threw down the video camera, flung down the gun and dances around them ecstatically, yelling and screaming obscenities. Exhausted by the effort Amrita lay on Rakesh's chest". (199) And "neither of them noticed that Minx had strewn around them [while moving] frantically around the room chanting a mantra of some sort". (199) After hugging both of them she says, "This is heaven, I couldn't have dreamt of a better end to your love story. Darling, you've made me so happy. I could die right now. They heard the small sharp click of a cigarette lighter and then they smelt the smoke". (199) Rakesh drags Amrita out of the cabin, while Minx keeps on laughing, singing and dancing in the cabin. After throwing some "gunny sacks" (200) on Amrita to cover her body, he enters into the cabin to save and pull out Minx. The villagers rescue them from the fire "alive". (201) Mr. Iyengar consoles Amrita on this tragic accident, when he says "They're alive both of them. They look far worse than they are, don't worry, we'll be able to fix them up as good as new". (201)

Mr. Iyengar suggests Amrita that "Your husband needs a strong woman to sit by his side, not a wreck, which is what you'll end up being if you don't listen me". (201) About Minx, he says, "My daughter is tough. She is not one to give up. Your husband seems a strong person too. The doctors are optimistic". (201) He expresses his gratitude to Amrita and her husband for saving his daughter's life, "if he [Rakesh] had not gone in after her, she'd have been dead today". (201)

When Amrita accuses him of using, abusing and exploiting her daughter, he regrets and relapses in remorse for Minx's sickness and her pathetic condition. "My daughter is the severely disturbed child of a disturbed mother. She suffers from delusions, she tells lies, she makes up stories. I tried too hard, to be both, mother and father to her. To protect her. But today I realize, I've failed". (203) For in his busy career he "couldn't pay her the attention she needed" (203) due to which Minx watched the blue films in her school days. Thus lack of mother's care and watching the blue films cause perversion in her character. The novelist has shown the importance of a woman's role especially that of a mother for the individual, family, society and future of humanity, which cannot be denied. Shobhaa De seems to be a votary of the traditional view about women and Indian culture expressed in the following lines:

पवित्रा मङ्गला नारी नृणामर्धाङ्ग भागिनी।

नारीम् विना पतिः पुत्रः परिवारः तथाक्षमः।।

Woman is auspicious and without her, man and family is incomplete. In our scriptures there are many instances of this, for example:

स्त्रीजु प्रीतिर्विष्ठोज़ेरा प्रीज़्वपत्यं प्रतिज़्ठतम्।

धार्माथौं स्त्रीजु लक्ष्मीज़्य स्त्रीजु लोकाः प्रतिज़्ठिताः।।[24]

(Love resides in women alone. They contain progeny. Dharma, money and fortune too are in them. In them only is established this world).

Without housewife, even wealth is useless as observed by Panditraj Jagannath in *Bhaminivilas*:

हरिणीप्रेक्ष्णा यत्र गृहणी न विलोक्यते।

सेवितं सर्वसम्पदभिरपि तभ्द्वनं वनं।।[25]

(The house without doe-eyed woman, inspite of wealth, is like forest).

The great power possessed by woman is described thus:

Both sun and moon fear potent sway,
And tides no power on earth can stay,
Brahmins and priests almighty are,
But womankind is mightier for.[26]

Amrita too narrates her story to Mr. Iyengar as to how she had shared an unnatural relationship with Minx, who forced her into it. First she blackmailed her, then tortured and scared her, which she in later phase "began to enjoy". (204) She became so dependent on her that she "thought we'd spend our life together till I met my husband. It was he who saved me from her clutches". (204) Mr Iyengar assures her that "You and your husband will never be bothered again. That is my promise to you, your secrets are safe with me. I have destroyed them—every single scrap of paper, film, photographs and recording". (205) Further, he tells and consoles Amrita for her freedom and safety. "You have nothing to fear, now or in future. I give you my word. Meenakshi will not be allowed to come anywhere near you again as long as I live". (205)

Amrita feels "free at last" from all sorts of obsessions and traps when she goes through a piece of news printed in the *Hindustan Times*. It is a "terse, crisp, to the point" (208) announcement about the death of Minx, on the top of the page. "Iyengar [Meenakshi] passed away on 7th August in Bombay under tragic circumstances. No condolences please". (208) She "reread it a dozen times" (208) to confirm it and to overcome her fear from which she is suffering, "Amrita was free at last". (208) Through this novel, the novelist suggests women to lead a completely free and un-obsessed life. Amrita feels "safe and protected; the dark didn't frighten her any more". (206) She expresses it when she croons softly to her unborn baby "we are at home". (207)

Here we get a glimpse of the traditional Indian view of the novelist, which is so well expressed by Manu, who suggests that man and woman must work together in their life:

प्रजनार्थ स्त्रियः सष्ठ्रटा सन्तानार्थ च मानवाः।

तस्मात्साधारणो धार्मः श्रुतोपत्न्यासहोदितः।। (9:95)[27]

(Women are created for procreation and men for sowing the seed. Therefore, both of them should discharge all duties together. So, say *Vedas*).

NOTES

1. Shobhaa De, *Selective Memory: Stories From My life*, (New Delhi: Penguin Books India Private Ltd, 1998) pp. 333-34.
2. Quoted in *Kamakunj*, p. 167.
3. Shobhaa De, *Strange Obsession* (New Delhi: Penguin Books India Pvt. Ltd. 1992), p. 208. All further references to the novel will be incorporated in the text.
4. *Ibid.*, The back side of the jacket of the novel.
5. Neelam Tikkha, "Lesbian Relationships in Strange Obsession", in Jaydipsinh Dodiya, *The Fiction of Shobhaa De: Critical Study* (New Delhi: Prestige Books, 2000), p. 222.
6. *Ibid.*
7. *Ibid.*, p. 223.
8. *Ibid.*
9. Gajendra Kumar, "*Strange Obsession:* A Critical Study", (Jaydipsinh Dodiya, *The Fiction of Shobhaa De: Critical Study*, New Delhi: Prestige Books, 2000) p. 229.
10. "Feminism", in *The Oxford Companion to Women's Writing in the United States* (New York: Oxford University Press, 1995) p. 310.
11. Gajendra Kumar, "*Strange Obsession:* A Critical Study", (Dodiya's *The Fiction of Shobhaa De: Critical Study*, New Delhi: Prestige Books, 2000) p. 231.
12. Shobhaa De, "Women are my best friends", (Shobhaa De, *Shooting from the Hip*, New Delhi: UBS Publishers Distributors Ltd., 1995) p. 114.
13. *Ibid.*, p. 116.
14. Gajendra Kumar, "*Strange Obsession:* A Critical Study" (Jaydipsinh Dodiya, *The Fiction of Shobhaa De: Critical Study*, New Delhi: Prestige Books, 2000), p. 228.
15. *The Hindustan Times*, 12 February 1995, p. 3.

16. Malvika Sanghvi, "The Word Factory", *The Times of India*, 28th January, 2001, p. 1.

17. Shobhaa De, *Shooting from the Hip: Selected Writings* (New Delhi: UBS Publication, 1995), pp. 111-13.

18. *Life Style*, a Saturday magazine of *The Statesman*, 18th July, 1998, p. 2.

19. An interview to Nandini Guha, *Life Style* "*The Statesman*" Saturday, August 1, 1998, p. 3. [Commented by Shobhaa De].

20. Anita Katyal, "Days of bra-burning feminism are over", *The Times of India*, New Delhi, Thursday, June 8, 2000, p. 16. Commented by Angela King, special adviser to the UN secretary general on gender issue and advancement of women. Published under the title of.

21. *Ibid.*

22. Malvika Sanghvi, "The Word Factory", *The Times of India*, New Delhi, 28th January, 2001, p. 2.

23. Khushwant Singh and Shobhaa De, ed., *Uncertain Liaisons: Sex, Strife and Togetherness in Urban India*, (New Delhi: Viking/Penguin India, 1993) pp. xxi, 208.

24. Vijay Bahadur Singh (ed.), *Kamakunj*, (Varanasi: Mahashakti Sahitya Mandir, 1933) p. 385.

25. *Ibid.*, p. 229.

26. *Jatak Book*, quoted in P.K. Agrawala, *The Unknown Kamasutras* (Varanasi: Book Asia, 1983), p. 176.

27. Prakash Priyadashi and Rajiv Tiwari edited *Manusmriti*, (Delhi: Manoj Pocket Books, 2002) p. 289.

6

Sultry Days: Hypocrisy a Curse

Sultry Days (1994), the fifth novel by Shobhaa De is dedicated to her children: "For my children—Ranadip, Radhika, Aditya, Avantika, Arundhati—finally, a book by me that they can read".[1] This dedication astonishes us, which is also endorsed by the comment on the blurb of the novel, "Ms De Shocks Indian and much of its literary set like no other writer today".[2]

About this novel, Shobhaa De says, "it is a simple tale of doomed love, simply because it took me back to my college days and to the edges of the pseudo-arty intellectual world I flirted with briefly before beating a hasty retreat".[3] Through this novel, she criticizes the "self-styled bohemians [who want to] change the world but not their smelly underwear; the dirty old man of Mumbai, turds; the corporate ladies, the pseudo-intellectuals, pariahs and parasites who feed off the rich while spitting on their 'capitalist values'".[4]

The novel presents two protagonists: "God [or Dev], the male protagonist,—a composite made up of several types"[5] whom the novelist considers as one of her "better-etched characters [but she regrets because] he wasn't for real",[6] while the female protagonist is Nisha or "Nasha' as he, Deb, dubs her".[7]

Nisha falls in love with God, a parasite, on account of his peculiar and passionate qualities. Owing to his too ambitious a nature, inharmonious and loveless life, God deviates into the world of money and materialism very well brought out in the following comment:

> On a sultry, rainy Bombay day Nisha, an impressionable teenager, meets God in the college canteen and falls in love with his ragged, bearded looks and crude, streetwise manners. God patronizingly accepts her into his 'group' and it is in this way that their long and passionate romance begins. God's driving ambition leads him into the unreal world of pseudo poetry, art for hire and compromised journalism while Nisha lands a job in advertising. Sycophants, court jesters, whores, dirty old men, fixers, pretty boys and party girls drift in and out of their lives (and interrupt their romance!) as their careers take off with dizzying speed. And then, abruptly and harrowingly, everything about their lives goes wrong.[8]

This happens because of God's false or so-called pseudo-life-style, which forces him to think that he is "smart and clever. Staying ahead in the race. A race to nowhere and nothing. And the loser often ended up dead".[9] Nisha also notices this and searches her own identity and aim through God and his works: "If God had changed, so had I [Nisha]. I [Nisha] missed me too. The old me". (860) And because of hypocritical and artificial life God at the end of the novel "Died like a dog [but not] like a God". (873)

The extract given above confirms the study of critics like Sharad Srivastava, who maintains that through this novel, Shobhaa De returns to the mainstream i.e. 'new woman' is absolutely correct. Nisha loves Dev, due to his being a mixture of opposites, but a pleasing personality, and in the process of seeing God's pseudo-commitments, she discovers her own commitments. Indira Bhatt remarks that Shobhaa De, through this novel, only portrays the modern life-style of neo-rich, is not convincing. The novel critically scrutinizes the modern human life, which is full of vanity, vacuity, hypocrisy, and unreal unnatural with surfeit of ambition, desire for luxuries and over-expectations. These have condemned man to lead a sub-human life much to the chagrin and discomfort of one and all. The writer, therefore, is dead against all cant and hypocrisy and is in favour of a refined and pious life. Her stark and simple message is communicated at the end of the novel through the lives of both the protagonists.

Nisha develops affectionate bonds with God in the college canteen. In fact she develops a kind of "infatuation [for him, which simultaneously] attracted and repelled" her. (705) God actually fell short of her expectations: "His hair, matted locks, full of lice-nests and other creepy crawlies. One hand of his invariably engaged in scratching. He was most revolting". (705) Even though be lives a good life because of his frank views regarding life, like "I am what I am—take it or leave it" (707) and "Opposites attract". (708) All his expenses are met with by his colleagues like God's temple, his attitude towards girls is too pragmatic—"use them and leave them". (708) Thus he is simply a "taker". (709)

This crude God has some good qualities also. He "works as a freelance reporter and does other stuff correcting proofs, galleys" (709) to pay his fees. More than this, he receives a "scholarship from Columbia". (709) He is also "fluent in German, can understand French and [can] read Spanish". (709) He is also a bit radical in nature, which he expresses through his anger upon his own father, "If you choose ideals, why did you have a family?" (709) He says so as he experienced pangs of poverty, because it is universally accepted that only money keeps the machinery of life running smoothly and maintains harmony among otherwise warring sections of society. Ideals on the other hand serve as food only for thought and try to rationalise seemingly absurd situations. The novelist means to say, therefore, that our daily life must be guided by practical wisdom trying to strike a balance between materialism and spiritualism and God and Mammon. The same thing is uttered by God that, "he wasn't interested in wealth [and insists that] money was only a means to an end". (715)

Pramod Kumar Singh misjudges Nisha's love and affection for her lover God, "The love and obsession of 'Nisha' to her lover 'God' was quite strange and unusual. Usually, when a gal (girl) is seen in love with someone, she cannot tolerate any third one coming between her lover and her".[10] But, Nisha remains calm and shows no sign of envy towards Bijli, a prostitute, when she comes to know about her that she is everything for God: "Mother, sister, lover, daughter".[11] It is money and power that makes God "feel powerful, [more than this] Bijli was a person to God [because] she had feelings [for him, and] she was the one 'woman' who understood him, [along with it she remains] faithful"[12] to him till he has affair with her. This feminist sense and insistence on loyalty has been neglected by Pramod Kumar Singh, due to which he has misjudged and misinterpreted the novel and its characters, as "a tale of strange obsession".[13]

Nisha likes God because he is the only one who finds her "frown [is] cute" (706) and he is not "like the other boys. He [has] character". (711) That's why Nisha says, "I would die without him. I'd go mad with grief". (711) She adores him like a real God, not due to reasons as mentioned above, but because he inculcated a sense of belongingness in her. Nisha says, "God had expensive test in most things. I loved buying things for God. It gave me a sense of belongingness...gifts...he takes entirely for granted". (714)

Nisha's own comment shows in what high esteem she held God, "Till I met God, my father had been the most important man in my life. He worked for a multinational which sold a range of useless products". (717) Here, the novelist criticises multinational companies, their workers and products. But, the main point of criticism by her is the worthlessness of man, who is faithless in love. God, who is loved by Nisha, gradually turns into a parasite. This is justified by his attachment with Nisha, who takes up a job with a "mediocre agency" (711) straight after college, and Dev "In any case, all he ever calls him "a parasite and a sponger".[14]

In the beginning, God is not "interested in money [because it is] only a means to an end" (715) for him. He is "ruthless and candid" (718) in his opinion about every one, not sparing his own parents. He shows a complete disregard for his parents, "They screwed and made you by accident. Does that mean you should be grateful to them forever? I only hope they were having fun while making me". (718) In his eyes every woman's real need is "a good screw". (717) Here, Indira Bhatt is correct up to some extent that, "Shobhaa De chooses to depict the modern life-style of the nouveau rich people with their physicality given full swing"[15] because the novelist "caters to the western critic's image of the land of Vatsyayan"[16] and "portrays the world of sexually infatuated people".[17] So that the western critics and readers may "wonder about the sex-starved Indians".[18] Even Pramod Kumar Singh has misjudged Shobhaa De's novels, when he writes, "Sex and sensation is one of the favourite themes of Shobhaa De. While depicting sex, usual or abnormal, she never hesitates to go up to an extreme she can talk about anything: homosexuals, prostitutes, extramarital relations, adultery, *gandus* (homosexual) etc".[19] But, this is not wholly correct, as the novelist here not only portrays the modern life-style, but also denounces it and feels sad for the deviant youths who indulge in such things in the name of modernity. Indians are becoming more and more consumerist in nature, and losing their spiritual and cultural qualities.

God enters the literary circle through proof checking and becomes the assistant editor of *Plume*, an art magazine. A fortnightly magazine's editor Nandan Kapoor, who promises God to establish him in the field of journalism, promotes his career. "Do me a great cover story and I'll make you in one stroke". (747) This gives a speedy upward turn to his career and life, but the contact of Yashwantbhai Dawani [a politician with muscle] led him astray and he slips into gloom and is doomed. He becomes Yashwantbhai's chief "minder and henchman", (826) but in fact, it is "the beginning of the death of the rebel and the visionary in him. [It happened so because], as God gets more and more the taste of 'power' and 'money,' his commitments appear to be pseudo-commitments".[20] Nisha too notices that, "God had changed" (777) because for him even "time is money". (833) The changed God's real God is 'Money and Luxury' provided by Yashwantbhai and God in turn is helping him in consolidating "his image within the party", (777) because Yashwantbhai is well aware that "the right mentions in the right papers" (777) will consolidate his image within the party.

God feels flattered by the words of Yashwantbhai Dawani, such as, "I think you are the best reviewer in town". (777) These words have hypnotic effect upon God as he belonged to an ordinary and lowly family. He has deep faith in money and the material world of give and take, because he knows fully well that 'money begets money' and 'money makes the mare go.' At the same time, he is also conscious that money is the source of power. This is why he tells Nisha, "You don't understand power. Today, that's all that counts, Power. And we who wield the pen, have it". (780) He ignores her warning and suggestion that, "same pen can become a jack-knife. Ask your father", (780) and tells her about his motive, "you-scratch-my-back-I-scratch-yours? Two-way traffic, baby. And I need him. Not now. But I'll some day, and then ask him to pay up when the time comes". (781) Therefore, God not, only engages himself with Yashwantbhai, but also with many "VIP's in the town, interviewing culture-vultures [who woo fame, fortune and success through him] in the high-life of the city". (778) Thus, he sells his soul to the system and becomes a part of it.

Nisha notices that God has changed and has become more or less "like everybody else". (777) This makes him behave like "a mortal, like all the other journalists in town, a bum who shamelessly sold his pieces for a few pegs of Scotch and a five-star evening". (777) Here, the novelist, through God vehemently criticises those petty minded, selfish journalists, who escape from their responsibilities towards the nation and its citizens. They not only lose their spiritual identity and behave like "a bhadwa", (781) in the hope that "these people will lick [their] chappals for publicity"; (780) forgetting that they'll readily spit on them if they "ever lose" (780) their job, becoming a "laughing stock". (786) It is, therefore permissible up to some extent that, God "scoffs at everyone. But as the years go by, he is corrupted by [lures of luxuries] that money can buy and becomes the chief confident of a corrupt businessman-politician Yashwantbhai Dawani",[21] who is ruthless in his dealing and extracting money as donation from businessmen and industrialists.

God gradually attains the status of representing "the elite coterie of 'opinion makers'". (796) His special talent lies in "dropping the right names at the right time". (796) So, he starts living and behaving like a "capitalist" (803) and does not wish to be noticed by anyone, not even by Nisha. Thus, he mixes "business and pleasure", (811) which in practical life hardly go together.

God is "heartbroken" (818) for the first time, when Firoze "a lesbian", (816) wins Kiki from him. In frustration, he utters venomous words for beloved Kiki: "One bitch is as good as another". (818) This scurrilous remark amounts to blasphemy against the whole womankind. The irony is that, while commenting on a woman or womankind, a man forgets all the norms and morals and becomes oblivious of his own vicious life. This leads to creating a vicious atmosphere where the moral law is put to jeopardy and calumny holds sway. The novelist here thus gives a note of warning and urges upon man to eschew slandering woman, as woman has been much exploited and forced to pander to man's wishes.

Owing to the force of circumstances, God begins to treat Nisha "like a sexless person". (818) This studied negligence on the part of God forces Nisha to negotiate with Iqbal to have a flirtation with him, though she does it with some hesitation. She says to Iqbal, "Let's not. I really don't want to, if you don't mind". (820) But, she gets warm for sex due to Iqbal's persuasion and also because of her ardent desire to have it with a painter of Iqbal's eminence. Iqbal on his part is important. Despite his overpowering passion, he fails to commit intercourse. He looks pathetic "with his jaw open and eyes shut in pseudo-orgasmic bliss". (821) Nisha is stricken with remorse, for it was her own desire for sex, which took her to Iqbal. When the hollowness of the entire experience dawned upon her, her conscience pricked her all the more. Everything including nude and sexual pictures looked sexless to Nisha, "there was nothing even remotely erotic about them, "there was nothing even remotely erotic about them anymore". (821)

It is pertinent to remark here that through this episode, the novelist highlights a trend in the modern urban society, which is unfortunately becoming common i.e. offering sex to high and mighty in society by female having inferior motives to fulfil. Nisha, though not a flaming beauty is gorgeous nonetheless, offers herself to Iqbal, the famous painter and artist and notorious as a womanizer, just to gain a place in his art gallery and thus become noteworthy in the eyes of high society. The second feature which is equally deplorable is the lust and sex-appetite on the part of the so called high and respectable in society who, though sexually weak and impotent, are ever keen to enter into sexual relationship with a posh woman, if not a noted beauty. The novelist is dead against this sexual anarchy in society and deprecates this tendency since it is eating very vitals of our social fabric.

Nisha apprises God about her affair with Iqbal, but the changed God remains unperturbed and indifferent. He seems to have controlled his passions and emotions. This was quite unlikely departure from God's behaviour hitherto-fare and naturally. Nisha feels highly "disappointed". (821) His nasty and "tepid reaction" (821) has caused the feeling of "contempt" (821) in her. It also proves that "exactly how far [they'd] drifted apart. [They] were no longer immersed in the minutiae of one another's lives". (821) If one has become a "Capitalist Kutta" (852) then another a "Jhooti bitch". (852)

God sells away Bijli, his motorbike, which had been nicknamed by him as his personal prostitute or keep, because he doesn't "need her anymore". (821) More than this, he acquires a "car [of] a friend's", (821) which shows that he has progressed a step forward in the direction of money making. But, this is high time when God feels acutely the need for a spouse who could meet his physical needs and prove a courteous and caring wife. With this end in view, he proposes to Nisha and asks her if she was prepared to marry him. Nisha downright rejects the proposal as she has now come to know god as a "deranged-or the world's biggest egoist". (822)

Here, the novelist asserts that in men's world, a woman is "practically insignificant [and remains merely a part of man's] property".[22] This problem of an inferior status up to some extent "arise(s) from [a woman's] sexuality that has been repressed by patriarchal culture, especially in traditional societies like ours",[23] where due to stark ignorance a woman is merely treated as a thing of carnal pleasure. That's why Nisha rejects God's offer. The novelist suggests women to value their self-respect more than anything else and raise themselves so as never to submit before man's autocratic and irrational demands.

God finds a much-wanted diversion in Pramila, a divorcee and much older woman. He calls her a "ghatan. A Nagpure girl". (823) She possessed everything a woman can ask for, "a husband with a 'solid' job, security, lovely children, a moped of her own and all the time in the world to pursue her interests"; (822-23) but she feels suffocated with "boredom and frustration" (823) because her husband, Vilas proves to be a boring husband, as he is engrossed in his engineering job at the PWD office, and doesn't pay attention to his family and wife. Consequently, this diverts her attention from hearth, home and husband to writing poetry of "intense, erotic and enraged" (823) type in the Marathi language, so as to collect enough amount of money "to catch a train to Bombay and never [to] return". (823) This is one glaring example of how a happy home is ruined by the utter negligence and apathy of the husband, who is hard-working bread-winner and the epitome of family's honour to the outside world, but is useless to his wife. Little wonder if such apathy leads to disaster. Thus, due to a husband's negligence, Bombay claimed "another victim or trophy". (823) The novelist emphasizes that it is the bonds of love; concern and care that make a family a cohesive and closely-knit unit and not the pomp luxuries that may embellish the exteriors, but cannot compensate the lack of warmth and genuine concern.

A few months later, Vilas receives Pramila's letter, who sends it after getting a job in a "Marathi Fortnightly". (823) The letter contained her enquiry about the children and the husband, but with no postal address, which only worsened the relationship between the couple.

Pramila returns home from Bombay on a specific mission to get "a divorce and to take children"; (823) but Vilas still loves Pramila, and does not wish to give her divorce. Finally, the matter is settled after ten days when Vilas's mother screams, "Take the girls. The son is ours. He bears our name". (823) Here, the patriarchal system of society and the love lost between husband and wife comes in for some criticism by the novelists as conjugal ties are not the children's play to be snapped at will, nor the children as commodity to be bartered at the pleasure of the parents. Such inharmonious attitude only harms the social fabric beyond repair and breeds revengeful attitude in the minds of children who later become liabilities and social hazards.

In Bombay, God comes in contact with Pramila through Yashwantbhai, who lures her and says that he needs a woman like her in politics for raising "women's issues" (824) and she is the right person. By this she'll not only get a "good job [and] pay", (824) can also look after her "daughter's education, everything". (824) More than this, she may be 'protected' from the bad characters of the city, because they can molest and usurp "a single [and] helpless woman". (824) Thus Yashwantbhai blackmails Pramila for working for him in politics in the name of her and her daughter's security and safety. He gets success in his mission as "Pramila got the point. Very quickly". (824)

R.S. Pathak's remark about the image of man in Shobhaa De is valid: "The image of man that emerges from Shobhaa De's novel is generally negative. A male character is almost invariably portrayed as seducer, exploiter, wife-beater, rapist, torturer or a cruel and callous husband".[24] This remark may have some apparent cogency but is far from conclusive. Although here 'Pramila' has been depicted as a hapless solitary woman, but her own role in ruining her family life was no less significant. Leaving the safe precincts of her home at Nagpur and a caring husband and affectionate children, she sneaks to Bombay, an unknown city in search of pelf, power and pastime, more appealing and entertaining. There the human shark in the form of Yashwantbhai not only exploits her sexually but also leaves her as a moral and spiritual wreck. The novelist warns womankind as such abject conditions of life are their own creations, which can be obviated only through discretion and strength of character.

God tried to help Pramila by publishing her interview in a newly launched city magazine with the title "Woman of substance". (824) This is indicative that there are occasions in life when a man is not averse to helping a woman selflessly. God even becomes so affectionate and caring about Shruti, Pramila's young daughter, who after so many months of isolation and boredom, feels immensely relieved after finding a man around her. Shruti develops "phobia and immense fear" at the age of seven due to her lonesome condition, as she waits all alone for the arrival of her mother till late in the night. This makes God visit Shruti not only "on weakend" (825) but also on days when Pramila is out to attend some "distress calls from various women while ignoring the distressed victim she'd left behind at home". (825) He even purchases a T.V. set to lessen Shruti's monotony and boredom. More than this, he proposes to marry Pramila who declines the offer for two reasons. Firstly, God's personality did not impress her and secondly, and more importantly, she is "worried about Yashwantbhai's reaction", (825) who is so kind and generous to her that he drops her home "after a late night conference". (825) Pramila was sure that Yashwantbhai's involvement in her would deter God from having any idea of marrying her.

Now, God has become "Yashwantbhai's chief minder and henchman", (825) who rewards him with "cooking gas, telephone and a brand new Maruti" (825) for his services. But, God's sheepishness and embarrassment due to his new acquisitions soon wear off and is replaced by a "devil-may-care cockiness". (826) He says, "I deserve all this damn it". (826) He becomes insensitive on account of greed, not worrying about his own future. On the other hand Nisha is too worried for his future and safety, and she feels "severely disturbed by

[God's] drift"; (826) which seems to her a "dangerous game". (826)

Yashwantbhai deploys God as mediator between himself and Dharam Khanna, whose goons are creating hurdles for Yashwantbhai and his industry. God comes to know of the 'Marital and financial' troubles in Dharam Khanna and his wife Ruki's lives, for which he offers his services to act "as leverage". (826) Their relationship is like that of modern Bombay metropolitans, whose lives under the sinister influence of liquor has become so wretched and despicable that the bonds of mutual love and respect between a wife and husband are all but lost and what remains is a mockery of relationship which is merely a routine in practice. Children of such families also become social liability. The novelist, therefore, issues a timely warning to all right thinking adults to save themselves and their progeny against the scourge of drink.

Dharam Khanna marries Ruki, a glamorous woman, after his wife deserts him due to his impotence but luckily, for both Ruki and Khanna, none of them had any issue from their previous marriage. Sex-dissatisfaction drives Ruki to have sexual liaison with Stash, a black American agent of CIA. God's ingenuity enabled him to have some pictures of Stash and Ruki when they are "cavorting in the swimming pool". These objectionable photos would defame the Khannas while Stash would lose his job. Yashwantbhai is highly pleased with this service by God and rewards him with "a mini-factory of his own".

While God barters away his soul for lucre, Nisha acts discreetly and instead of cringing before some moneyed devil, opts for an honest and self-respecting job of supplying "Basmati rice and chick peas to Gulfies". (839) She also thwarts Iqbal's sinister and lustful moves. But, she has the premonition that "The Pramilla chapter" (836) would some day cost dearly to God and thereby to her as well.

Iqbal, the eminent artist with sex-mania, wants to organise a fair of prostitutes under the title *Rundiyon Ka Mela* (844) and he arranges wide publicity so that prostitutes of every hue and colour from far and near might congregate in Bombay and provide lustful pleasure to onlookers. Tarantula, the editor and publisher of a sexy magazine, publicised the proposed fair, with a title "Salaam Prostitute" (844) along with Iqbal's interview and titillating and lewd photographs which put to shame all decent and self-respecting people. "Exposed breasts" (844) the symbol of the fair, was all the more humiliating for the decent gentry of Bombay. As members of this oldest profession of the world converged in Bombay, it was a gala feast for the voluptuous and the sex-maniacs. Sobriety and decency beat a hasty retreat. The novelist here exhorts woman not to be a party to man's exploitative and humiliating devices but to rise above sex and erotica as life is an opportunity which has to offer far better things than mere sex and self-indulgence.

The novelist is further critical of women's hankering for power and craving for money, which eventually is also a source of power. Woman wants to subjugate man, not through divine virtues of love, service and sacrifice but by pandering to his wishes and by compromising her virginity with his lustful manoeuvres and in return getting money from him. Further, media also comes in for sharp criticism by the novelist. Media today has become a handmaiden of the rich and the powerful. Journalists can be exploited for petty gains and in doing so they flagrantly violate their code of conduct. What Tarantula says to Nisha to achieve success in this sordid world is suggestive of the fact that to what depths these so called guardians of public law and morality can stoop to meet their ends. "Compromise, darling, [says Tarantula to Nisha], is not a dirty word in my dictionary. To get and stay there you need two things in your armoury, talent oodles of it, and guts". (846) The words Tarantula uses to express her motive, namely, 'seduce' 'climb down' 'compromise' are horrible in their implications and terrifying in comprehension. These things however have been used by the novelist to depict life in Bombay or in all the cosmopolitan towns, where Mammon is the only God known to people and where the "nouveau rich"[25] are dictating the life style to commoners. The novelist however, does not negate the importance of "money"[26] but life, she maintains, is far more valuable.

It is a considered and valuable opinion of the novelist that people, by and large, have a tendency to be impressed by appearance, pomp and show and not by the genuine qualities. She cites the example of Rita Hayworth whose opinion about Mahesh, though perfunctory is nonetheless important for the flimsy and the unwary. "He smells good [she says]. He looks good. He must be good". (848) But in fact, the situation is quite contrary. He has affair with Kiki. His arrogance, unconventional appearance and the promise of violent sex made him irresistible and attractive to wardwomen, "compared to the wimpy money bags married to those screechy socialites, God was quite a man". (849) Thus, gradually with the help of his artificial life-style, God becomes "a status symbol" (849) as Tarantula concludes. It was not money which made God a favourite amongst sex-starved women, rather, the absence of their husbands who often left them and went out on errands, oblivious of either sex desires of their partners or their need for any other object domestic or otherwise.

Iqbal's son Parthiv is an ambitious young man, a journalist and partner of Amar, a big shot among elite circle of Bombay. Parthiv wants to start a new "futuristic journalism in India" (853) an ambitious venture and to make it a success he directs his officials to adopt every method regardless of scruples to increase subscribers to boost the publication; and to resort to all other tactics prevalent in the journalistic world including dirty tricks of the American Media to defeat their magazine's contenders.

One of the competitors of Parthiv happens to be "Femme" (846) of Tarantula against whom they do not hesitate the least in hitting below the belt and adopt the "usual garbage that men employ to assassinate a woman's character". (855) Tarantula, a lady of high susceptibilities can't put up with such insolence and she goes underground but keeps in touch with God and a few other trusted friends. God who still had some godly streaks left in him comes to Tarantula's help at such a crucial moment in her life. Yashwantbhai, in conformity with his demoniac character, scolds and stops God to help her by saying, "let her go to hell. You have nothing to lose by". (854) "*Saali ko marne dey...tera kya jaata hai* (let she bitch die...what do you have at stake)?" (854) This is how anti-social elements revel in human indignity and privation although apparently they show off and swear that they are amongst the greatest benefactors of mankind.

This game of calumny, ill-will and character assassination reaches its high peak when Amer and Parthiv in their news magazine *Samachar* printed Tarantula's mother's interview under the caption "My Daughter Disowned Me". (855) This was a fatal blow to Tarantula's dignity as a woman and her prestige in society. This interview affected her so adversely that for a time being, her spirit was all numb "she lost her fighting spirit" (856) as if she won't be able to *paise* her head. The most ironical and perhaps the most telling remark in this interview was, "I hope she'll find God (irony!) and make her peace. Tell her, I forgive her". (855-56) For Tarantula, there was nothing left to hide any more: "She threw in the towel. And came crawling to Yashwantbhai". (856) Lady Tarantula's pathetic condition is a grim reminder to all well-meaning men and women never to treat their kith and kin, especially the parents, in a despicable and dastardly way both on humanitarian and pragmatic grounds because the nearest ones when turned awry will expose one to one's very bones and provide utmost advantage to one's adversaries.

God was quite aware that Parthiv and Amar could be penalised as both of them were guilty of a massive tax evasion in a shady newsprint deals. But, he failed to report these secrets to Yashwantbhai and thus became suspect in his eyes. Elections being round the corner, God became oblivious of these matters. He expected that Yashwantbhai would make him also a candidate in the elections and like others he would also win the elections.

God's father is also a contender in the election against a candidate fielded by Yashwantbhai. He is banking upon his good work among factory workers and is confident that they will vote for him *en masse*. God on the other hand is busy with his pre-occupations. Either he got complacent or was oblivious of the ferocity of Yashwantbhai's sinister methods to eliminate his adversaries who come in the way of his sordid interests. God leaked a few "confidential papers and dropped several hints" (856) about Yashwantbhai in Amar's office. He misses the signals and fails to report matters to Yashwantbhai "thereby becoming suspect" (856) in his eyes.

Yashwantbhai relied upon God to utilise his contacts to get favourable and positive reports written about him. But it was no longer as simple as before, chiefly because Yashwantbhai stopped being liberal in the supply of money and liquor to reporters. However, Yashwantbhai discovered it a bit too late that all was not well with the media as especially, two top persons in the newspaper world who mattered most were drifting away from him. This was extremely bad, especially for God.

Publication of ugly stories about Yashwantbhai's underworld connections infuriated him beyond measure. He snarled at God, "Can you explain to me, you nincompoop, what is going on? It's your job to fix these things. Kill the stories or kill them. That is if you aren't on their payroll yourself". (857) It was just a matter of time before destiny willed him to be eliminated, God did try to move fast but it was already too late.

Nisha knew pretty well that God was eventually going to harm himself by aligning himself with Yashwantbhai, but the difficulty was that God himself did not find any harm in working for Yashwantbhai. Nisha in the meanwhile busied herself with writing out press material. Nisha gets an alluring offer from Amar and Parthiv to write light profiles for three months. Nisha writes a profile of Yashwantbhai, which irks God. He storms into her house and says, "Nisha! *Yeh tuney kya kiya? Kyon kiya*, [huh why the hell did you do this?"] (859) This was soon after God's father had tough time with Yashwantbhai's goons. God issued a warning to Nisha that Yashwantbhai would certainly retaliate; he is not a man to forget easily. Nisha tries to argue with God but he tells her solemnly, "I am here to warn you as a friend—be careful". (860) "Was that some sort of a good-bye", (860) Nisha wondered. God looked quite weary and for the first time Nisha felt quite defeated. When Nisha requested him to play his flute, he merely said, "it broke" (860) and left.

Nisha often thought of God especially about the time six years ago, when they had first met each other. A lot of change had overtaken both of them since then. Nisha continued her writing and they received coverage in the city's journals and magazines. But in the meanwhile, what God had predicted about Yashwantbhai started coming true concerning Nisha, "It started with threatening calls at home which my mother answered and hastily passed to my father if he was around". (864) God advised Nisha to hire some bodyguards but she didn't agree with the idea of having scruffy fellows around. He even offered to send some of his chaps but Nisha said a polite 'no.' At that time probably God was not aware of the real target.

The fatal moment, not quite unexpected, came at last and came with all its fury. God had been shot at. Nisha and her mother rushed to the intensive care unit of the Nair hospital. "The fatal bullet had entered his stomach and lodged itself in his spinal cord". (867) God's father was there at the unit threatening Yashwantbhai and his henchmen of dire consequences. It took about ten days for God to recover enough to be shifted to the general ward. News about God did appear in the local newspapers, but any reference to Yashwantbhai was conspicuously missing. "God suffered a relapse four days later". (869) God's father and Nisha by turn remain by his side. For Nisha it was just like a scene in the movies. She was "longing to hold this impossible man in [her] arms and whisper to him, 'Dear God, be mine'". (871) Nisha had soft feeling for God throughout but destiny didn't want them to be united in wedlock. When God breathed his last, neither his father nor Nisha happened to be by his side. "God had probably picked the time to die with care—defiant and alone". (873) God's silent passing away forces us to think about the uncertainty of life. Nisha says, "Died like a dog, or like a God. If you prefer to reverse the letters like I do". (873)

God's character as depicted by the novelist is a grim reminder to all modern youths who are animated by high ideals, are social and egalitarian in outlook, have a commendable level of education, though by no means liberal, yet enough to enable them to have a foothold in the modern competitive life which can also enable them earn a fairly good income sufficient for an honest and self-dependent life, if not an opulent one. God was well read, had a flair for knowledge, and was good enough never to disown the poor and bend his knees before insolents people. He was straightforward, called a spade a spade, could never tolerate hypocrisy and yearned for social reform and well being and a heart which pulsated with sympathy and concern for the teeming millions of the Bombay metropolis. It would not be wrong to say that God symbolised a tragedy of high intentions self-defeated. The inordinate desire for wealth and power somehow came to dominate his psyche and what was worse, amassing of wealth with unscrupulous means was no more abominable for him, which he formerly considered so despicable.

In his unscrupulous pursuit of power and pelf, God sought help and patronage of Yashwantbhai, himself a human shark who disdained nothing in the realisation of his sordid ends. God's judgement became still more blurred and his tragedy still more grievous when he cultivated friendship and patronage of Yashwantbhai's adversary also. God on his part didn't take any extra care not to disclose his liaison with Yashwantbhai's antagonist. In the cutthroat competitive life of the modern world, torn asunder by mutual strife and dissension an adversary's friend and well-wisher easily becomes an eyesore and Yashwantbhai lost no time in coming to conclusion, rightly or wrongly that by aligning himself with his adversary, God had virtually stabbed him in the back, had become a traitor, and his elimination would be just the right step to avenge treachery.

Sultry Days presents a vivid picture of society, which in its details is a kaleidoscopic presentation. R.S. Pathak's remark that "Sultry Days fails to unfold a cogent, unified picture of life",[27] therefore, seems to be wide off the mark as he fails to catch the spirit of the work and appreciate its cogency in the context of the present social milieu. He is also not correct that the image of man that "emerges from Shobhaa De's novel is generally negative. A male character is almost invariably portrayed as seducer, exploiter, wife-beater, rapist, torturer or a cruel and callous husband".[28] But this statement is not corroborated by facts in the novel. For instance, God never even thinks of exploiting anyone although at times his female admirers offered him money, personal service and their bodies as well. Yashwantbhai and other exploits Pramila, due to blunders she has already committed. This apart, the novelist uses "homosexuals and lesbians"[29] just to provide a glimpse of the moral and social degradation becoming a cancer to society and thereby asks the pertinent question: "Where are we proceeding to in the name of modernization, progress and civilization?"

R.S. Pathak is right, "The novelist seems to be happier when presenting female character. It is their plight that she is chiefly concerned with". In *Sultry Days* male characters like God, Yashwantbhai, Kamlesh, Kawla, Lucio, Anil Bhandari, Mr. Bindiya and Vilas are perfect in themselves and in their respective roles.

The institution of marriage, which serves for the social needs like love, security, and children, is according to R.S. Pathak, "breaking up"[30] due to sexual promiscuity and women's economic independence. Now, nobody considers it any longer that marriages are "made in Heaven".[31] Simultaneously, "fidelity in married life is replaced by sexual freedom"[32] and lastly, he says "Marriage is not regarded as essential in *Sultry Days*".[33]

The above charges are fallacious when put against the backdrop of social facts. Not only because, "History proves that marriage is essential to the well-being of human society, and that celibacy brings ruin upon states";[34] but also because modern marriages are breaking due to change in the viewpoint of modern generation. They pay too much attention to "money", (833) "business and pleasure", (811) culture-vulture in the high-life of the city" (778) "priority [to] success", (760) addiction to "workaholism" (792) for more and more "power" (780) to get entry into "five star" (748) hotels with lop-sided "character" (793) and selling their "soul [s] to the system", (794) forgetting their "duties" (727) towards children, family and society, and saying, "Who knows about marriage-*sharriage*, *yaar*. I'm as happy as I'm", (725) due to it "opposites [are] attract [ed]" (708) towards each other to satisfy their sensual desires, thus, helping in bringing abnormalities in society and deterioration of pious institution of marriage.

Instances galore can be cited in the novel where through many characters, the novelist holds the institution of marriage in high esteem and accords it all importance. But, marriage must be shared on terms of equality. Sujata, the sex queen says, "This is my life. I want to live it my way" (727) and about her family and succession of male and female lovers, who parade under the nose of her family, she says, "I could easily have left and gone away. I receive marriage proposals all the time—But no. My place is in my home". (727-728) Nisha's mother bothers a lot over collapse of her "marriage". (744) Even Nisha says that, "My mother was cracking up. It was the uncertainty that was killing her". (754) Finally, as concerned the matter of Pratimaben she confronts Kamlesh Verma with her decision:

> I've had enough of your bullying and hypocrisy. I've kept quiet for far too long. You can go to hell with your pompous talk and empty boasts. I'm sick of living this false life. It is my turn now. I'll go along with Pratimaben with anything I choose to do. She makes me fell like someone. So you can go to hell with your lectures and your Sindhi girl friends—you don't henceforth, I'll make the decisions about my life. And the first one is that I'm taking a job. (813)

Virginia Woolf's remark is quite appropriate, "Imaginatively, she is of the highest importance. Practically, she is completely insignificant [and] the property of her husband".[35] Before, being liberated from her husband's hypocrites Nisha's mother was simply, "a passive, obliging receptacle for [Nisha's father's] semen as and when 'he' felt the urge to discharge in her body".[36] Under such circumstances, therefore, the marital bed to them is hardly different from "a cold battlefield with two unhappy people lying stiffly side by side, year after year, dreaming different dreams and yearning for a closeness, comfort and satisfaction that eludes them completely".[37]

This being the reason, the novelist wants to tell the same thing through Nisha's mother which she has already discussed in *Shooting From the Hip*: "It is time they [women] are made aware of their own potential and power. *Shakti* needs to be harnessed, directed and explored for the furtherance of over all human development.' [so that] Men will have to come to terms with woman power".[38]

While, Sujata, the sex queen's remark, "men are adorable beasts" (773) and Kiki's "I like women, I like men too, but women more" (816) and Mona's confirmist one that "No men. No future" (861) have their relative values God's own demand and desire before Nisha, "I need someone to cook and everything. These *maids-shaids* are hassle, *yaar*. I need my own woman. If you want, I'm a *seedha-saadha* fellow. Give me my *daal-roti*, a warm bed, twice-a-week *maalish* and a daily screw" (822) is practical and down to earth. Even Nisha's own desire for marriage which she expresses at different times "It was I who wore my heart on my sleeve. God had only to say the word, and I would be his. His what? Slave, side-kick, girl. It hardly mattered". (711) "On the day he spoke to me about finding someone else, my heart sank by the second listening to him. What was he saying? I would die without him. I'd go mad with grief". (711)

For "a sense of belongingness", (714) Nisha is attracted towards God, not bothering about his worthless condition, who has "no future, nothing. No looks. No money. Nothing"; (714) but, she "loves him" (715) simply. She also does not bother about her mother's threat to her.

She indirectly proposes to God, "Couldn't you wait till you got married?" (725) She further hints to him by saying, "You'd expect your wife to be untouched. No?" (725) She takes her last step to entrap God by making "Bi-monthly disappearances" (758) with him. And then by directly asking him "Are you asking me to marry you?" (767) Requesting him discreetly, "God please. P-L-E-A-S-E. I know you asked me to marry you. Why do you feel so ashamed now? Every body gets married. Even communists and poets". (758)

It's the obstinate nature of God who declines the proposal of marriage for his quest for ambition, money, power and status, because for him "Nothing for free, remember. Not even love". (772) He dies a dog's death without experiencing the importance of love, family, marriage, humanity, etc. This grim realisation dawns upon him at the last moment of his life. His life remains balanced till he is in the company of a woman, Bijli, who is "everything [for him, a] mother, sister, lover, daughter" (725) and who remains faithful to him.

Nisha longs for God throughout her life "Dear God, be mine". (871) She has to part from her lover in the hospital because of her father's untimely cardiac trouble and she feels remorse for it. Thus, we can say that, R.S. Pathak's two comments, "Marriage is not regarded as essential in the fictional world of Shobhaa De"[39] and "Marriage is not regarded as essential in *Sultry Days*"[40] are not correct. The novelist is in favour of marriage especially the one, which commands complete understanding and agreement between the spouses. Only such marriages, according to her, may bring harmony and contribute to the development of society.

Thus, through this novel, the novelist asks us to opt for truthful, simple, harmonious, human life. She also expresses her views for the welfare of womankind by asking to provide them respect, status and equal share in power. Further, she asks for matrimonial norms to be followed equally by men and women for the ethical uplifnment of society. At the same time she suggests to us to earn money and other material things through right means and as help for living a better life and for achieving noble ideals. She also advises us never to leave our

Swadharma; i.e., pristine nature and remain attached to our roots.

NOTES

1. Shobhaa De, *Sultry Days* (New Delhi: Penguin Books India (P) Ltd., 1994), p. V.
2. *Ibid.*, The jacket of the novel, this quotation has been taken from *The New York Times*.
3. Shobhaa De, *Selected Memory: Stories From My Life* (New Delhi: Penguin Books India (P) Ltd., 1998), p. 336.
4. *Ibid.*
5. *Ibid.*
6. *Ibid.*, p. 336.
7. *Ibid.*
8. Shobhaa De, *Sultry Days* (New Delhi: Penguin Books India (P) Ltd., 1994). Back side of the jacket of the novel.
9. Shobhaa De, *The Shobhaa De' Omnibus* (New Delhi: Viking/Penguin Books India (P) Ltd., 1995), p. 860. All further references to the novel will be incorporated in the text.
10. Pramod Kumar Singh, "Shobhaa De's *Sultry Days*: A Tale of *Strange Obsessions*", Pramod Kumar Singh; *Indian Fiction in English* (New Delhi: Atlantic Publishers and Distributors, 2001), p. 114.
11. Shobhaa De, *Sultry Days* (New Delhi: Penguin Books India (P) Ltd, 1994), p. 28.
12. *Ibid.*
13. Pramod Kumar Singh, "Shobhaa De's *Sultry Days*: A Tale of *Strange Obsessions*", Pramod Kumar Singh, *Indian Fiction in English* (New Delhi: Atlantic Publishers and Distributors, 2001), p. 113.
14. Shobhaa De's "*Sultry Days* and Gita Mehta's *A River Sutra:* A Study in Orientalism", Dodiya's, *Fiction of Shobhaa De: Critical Study* (New Delhi: Prestige Books, 2000), p. 98.
15. *Ibid.*
16. *Ibid.*, p. 106.
17. *Ibid.*
18. *Ibid.*, p. 107.
19. P.K. Singh, "Shobhaa De's *Sultry Days:* A Tale of *Strange Obsessions*" in Pramod Kumar Singh, ed., *Indian Fiction in English* (New Delhi: Atlantic Publishers and Distributors, 2001), p. 115.
20. Sharad Shrivastava, "Return of Shobhaa De to the Mainstream 'New Woman'", Jayadipsinh Dodiya, ed., *The Fiction of Shobhaa De: Critical Study* (New Delhi: Prestige Books, 2000), p. 234.

21. R.S. Pathak, "Shobhaa De from *Starry Nights* to *Sultry Days*", Jaydipsinh Dodiya, *The Fiction of Shobhaa De: Critical Study* (New Delhi: Prestige Books, 2000), p. 71.
22. Virginia Woolf, *A Room of One's Own* (New York: Harcourt, Brace and World, 1929), pp. 45-46.
23. R.S. Pathak, Sobha De, "From *Starry Nights* to *Sultry Days*", Jaydipsinh Dodiya, ed., *The Fiction of Shobhaa De: Critical Study* (New Delhi: Prestige Books, 2000), p. 70.
24. *Ibid.*, p. 73.
25. Indira Bhatt, "Shobhaa De's *Sultry Days* and Gita Mehta's *A River Sutra:* A Study in Orientalism" (Dodiya's *The Fiction of Shobhaa De: Critical Study*), p. 98.
26. R.S. Pathak, "Feminist concerns in Shobhaa De's Work: A Study In Attitudes" (Jaydipsinh Dodiya), p. 39.
27. R.S. Pathak, "Shobhaa De from *Starry Nights* to *Sultry Days*", Jaydipsingh Dodiya's, ed., "*The Fiction of Shobhaa De: Critical Study*" (New Delhi: Prestige Books,), p. 72.
28. *Ibid.*, p. 73.
29. *Ibid.*, p. 76.
30. *Ibid.*, p. 80.
31. *Ibid.*
32. *Ibid.*
33. *Ibid.*
34. Alexander Walker, "*Women: Physiologically considered as to Mind, Morals, Marriage, Matrimonial slavery, in fidelity and Divorce*" (Delhi: Mittal, 1987), p. 80.
35. Virginia Woolf, *A Room of One's Own* (New York: Harcourt, Brace and World, 1992), pp. 45-46.
36. Shobhaa De, "Sex in the Time of Stress", in Khushwant Singh & Shobhaa De, ed., *Uncertain Liaisons: Sex, Strife and Togetherness in Urban India* (New Delhi: Viking/Penguin India, 1993), p. 4.
37. *Ibid.*
38. Shobhaa De, *Shooting From the Hip: Selected Writings* (New Delhi: UBS Publication, 1994), pp. 112-13.
39. R.S. Pathak, "Feminist concerns in Shobhaa De's Work: A Study In Attitudes", Jaydipsinh Dodiya, *The Fiction of Shobhaa De: Critical Study* (New Delhi: Prestige Books, 2000), p. 40.
40. R.S. Pathak, "Shobhaa De from *Starry Nights* to *Sultry Days*" (The Fiction of Shobhaa De), p. 80.

7

Snapshots: The Oriental vs the Occidental

Snapshots (1995) is the sixth and psychologically, the most powerful novel of Shobhaa De. Owing to its intricate plot, it has been misinterpreted and misjudged by various critics. Urbashi Barat considers it as a mosaic work of Shobhaa De. Madhumalati Adhikari feels that it is a postcolonial text through which the novelist tries to present a picture of powerful-cum-emancipated new woman. R.S. Pathak is of the view that the novel presents the mundane picture of urban Indian women's lives, crazy for power equation with men in the society, but, B.K. Das considers it an "amoral"[1] and pornographic work because "life is presented [in it] as it is, not as it should be"[2] specially about women of "the upper-class society in the metropolis"[3] of India.

The real concern of this novel is not simply the revelation of the dark secrets of private lives of six women, which lay buried deep in the past until their reunion after a decade and a half or more when they left Santa Maria High School of Bombay. The novelist has attempted to focus in this novel on Indian feminine and humanitarian view of life by presenting a sharp comparison between the oriental (Indian) life-style and ideals and the occidental (Western) life-style to which they were template after their separation from the school.

She portrays the individual and social evils not to imitate or confute and contradict, but to eradicate and eliminate them from our lives and society, with a view to elevating the humanitarian standards. In this novel her target is the western materialistic hypocrisy and its blind imitation by Indians who boast upon it. She writes:

> *Snapshots* had an unexpected start. I was invited to an old girl's lunch by a former classmate. It was in honour of a London based lady who'd been in school with us. The smug woman from London, dressed in a dreadful, synthetic 'suit' and speaking in an affected accent, had been the most obnoxious of the lot with her blatant boasting and even more blatant show of certificates and citations. In my half-awake state I thought of the book. The character fell into place. The story revolved around the pictures, a group of old school friends bring to a similar lunch. The book was born in that ghastly, *nouveau riche* drawing room crammed with over-dressed, competitive women.[4]

In the novel, Swati is protagonist "of *Snapshots*, a gorgeous London-based operator, more on the lines of Pamella Bordes. None of the other characters resembled the women at the lunch party".[5] This protagonist has some sort of enmity and envy for every character of the novel due to some malicious reason of his own. This makes not only the party nightmarish, but also establishes the futility of western, selfish and materialistic life-style and view of life, which leads us far away from humanity and life loses its sense of purpose. It can be obviously understood by the comment of the heroine, who is already fed-up with the materialistic world and wants something new to make a film for the western viewers. "I don't know what I was looking for, but let me tell you I didn't find it. It was a colossal waste of time. Energy. Money. Everything. Besides, the lot of you turned out to be such bloody bores. You can have the bloody taps".[6]

There are six female characters in the novel: Swati, Aparna, Reema, Surekha, Rashmi and Noor, who represent nearly the over-all condition of Indian urban women, how they are living at present. Therefore, we can say that, it's a serious attempt at "discovering India through Indian eyes".[7] In this process, we also get a feminist perspective of the power equation with males.

It's correct to say that literature is "a form of communication, through which experience is described, shared, modified and preserved",[8] which according to Urbashi Barat "is the primary function of the media too".[9] But, there is a difference between media and literature; the media is simply a "means of mass communication"[10] about any latest item or incident of importance; while, literature is about "Writings that are valued as work of art from a particular country or period on a particular subject".[11] Therefore, *Snapshots* is a piece of literature, which portrays a specific picture of life and society, embedded with a critical problem and compels the reader to think it over for some solution and resolution.

In the same way, it is also incorrect to say that this novel is a postcolonial text because it is against patriarchal power structure as Madhumalati Adhikari writes:

> Colonial consciousness/patriarchal power structure creates, encourages and nurtures typical psycho-physical tendencies that construct different perceptions in the colonizer and colonized; [she holds it appropriate for it suits the qualities of colonization which are,] suppression, domination, assumed superiority, exploitation [that have] penetrated deep into the culture and literature of the particular society.[12]

She tries to justify her argument with the help of Elivi Whattakar's comment: "Colonialism is not only about the exploitation of countries with resources, cheap labour and less technological power. It is also about assuming unquestioningly, the right to change these cultures, economically, and more invidiously, textually, in ways entirely foreign to them".[13] However, Madhumalati Adhikari is not correct for two reasons that, Indians get inclined towards the western life style deliberately and completely by their own choice and not by force. Therefore, her conclusion about the novel is only partially true, when she writes that, "*Snapshots* embodies the spirit of postcolonial literature that concretises the adventures of powerful, emancipated new woman".[14] Another reason is the rapid development in the area of science and information technology, which is drastically decreasing the geographical, physical, rational, cultural and lingual distances through frequent conversations and contacts, and in the process gradually but inevitably developing a cosmopolitan culture, encompassing one and all. So, it is certain that, one culture will influence the other and vice-versa. Thus, the only option left for us is that of making a choice, which is sane and concrete.

Madhumalati Adhikari is correct up to some extent when she writes that, "*Snapshots* projects an urban society where women battle for power and supremacy",[15] which according to Darwin is nothing but a natural process of struggle or survival. In fact, Shobhaa De's female characters need upliftment in their social status, economic betterment, equal opportunities in education and jobs, equal freedom in every sphere of life and work including decision making process, co-operation, competition, healthy and creative opposition. But, the paramount message of Shobhaa De's novel, however, is that what womankind as a whole requires from men is their unstinted support, loyalty, love, concern and an abiding respect for them in their heart of hearts—things which are far superior and lasting as compared to material comforts and riches which are at best only transitory and short lived. It is shown and experienced by Swati, the prime character in the fiction, whose entire fictitions life style lost into futile. The western trend, technique eventually proved trouble some to her. Her envy, lure and altering nature not only adulterated her life, mind and body but depraved and dehumanized into a hollow zero; "I don't know what I was looking but, it was a colossal waste". (1013)

The next female character of the novel is Aparna, a young divorcee from Rohit, her husband. She is having an illicit love affair with Prem, her employee and "Kept-man". (877) She pays extra-money and facilities (extra salary, car and bungalow), to him for his job and in return he renders extra marital "service" (877) to her, which according to him is "a fair deal". (877)

Aparna, for this affair of hers with Prem, not only hates him, but "often hated herself too". (878) Though she doesn't love him the least, yet she has been left with no other option except for him, as she needs him "both at work and play". (878) It's so, because, she has a troubled past and an uncertain future to face, which she wants to forget for a while in the company of Prem.

Aparna hates to think of lust as a need, she scrutinises and evaluates herself that women need not stoop low for sex, but they certainly "need love, caring. And ternderness" (879) in their life from men, society and members of the family. While the irony is that like Aparna, every woman grows up with "shame about practically every aspect of her life" (880) emotionally and physically, by the man whom she likes the most due to his "high ideals and lofty ambitions", (880) but unfortunately he leaves her "high and dry" (881) and without any prior indication or warning. It won't matter whether he is a hanger-on or an adulterator or kept-man like Prem or husband like Rohit.

Women like Aparna suffer and undergo humiliation at the hands of men due to chicanery and machinations of the Swati-type women. Even the novelist agrees with this assertion when she writes, "Swati's target hadn't been Aparna's man—it had always been and still was Aparna herself". (999) This view of the novelist is corroborated by Aparna, when she says plainly to Swati, "Rohit was my husband your little affair destroyed my marriage, my life", (1002-3) whom she still loves and longs for, he is "a caring, attentive and sensitive person", who brings out her femininity and makes her feel like a woman.

Seeds of this rivalry, jealousy, and hatred were laid in Swati's mind much earlier during her school days when by common consent, Aparna was selected as the most photogenic and best looking girl. Aparna was still not able to overcome the trauma; it also turned out to be a rude shock to her faith in Swati, so much so that the term 'Husband' become an "awful word" (891) for her, justifying the adage that 'women are women's worst enemy.' Another thing responsible for freaking their relationship is their mutual decision of having "No babies" (889) whether or not they could afford it. Aparna evaluates herself, "Did the marriage end that day, Aparna asked herself, Or did it end the evening she had discovered Rohit and Swati in a suspiciously coy mood?" (889) Aparna finds only herself to blame because of her coy and gentle nature and her tendency even to forgive an erring husband and "as always, she preferred to forgive Rohit even if he'd actually been unfaithful to her". (889) But Rohit as cowardice and pusillanimity took this magnanimity on Aparna's part and he becomes all the more hostile. The novelist here asks womankind neither to be silent sufferers nor to be inactive but to be up and doing as it is always better to have tried and failed than never to have tried at all.

Here, the novelist wants to convey that in reality, "all men are unfailingly faithful—till they discover the unadulterated joys of adultery. The reason men cheat on their wives is because the wives ask for it",[16] as Aparna does wooing due to scarcity of time either for a light-flirtation or for love-making, because of pressure of life in a city like Bombay where "nobody [has] time". (891)

The next character in the novel is Reema, a hostess, married to Ravi, a big broker. She has a fifteen-year-old daughter Sonali. Her tragedy is that Ravi is so engrossed in his moneymaking mania that he is oblivious of the practical needs of his better half. His wife's sex starvation is a great emotional strain for her. Like Aparna, Reema needs "care, share" (890) and "laughter touches a steady, warm, attentive companion" (891) from her husband, but the "cold glint of her solitaries often mocked her loneliness". (886)

Relentless pursuit of Mammon leaves Ravi little time and lesser energy to pay attention to his sex-starved wife, who is forced to lead a solitary and monotonous life of "domesticity and imagined bliss". (919) As tension mounted and strain of single living became unbearable, Reema becomes the first of her batch to decide to marry hoping that a good marriage would bring her all those things a woman craves for, but all her hopes and aspirations remained a chimera, a will-o-the wisp.

Ignorance and lack of guidance combined with curiosity and inquisitiveness about male anatomy, so common among girls with first flush of youth, propel Reema in her school days to pick up fancy for Raju, an adolescent boy still underage, and the friendship eventually results into Reema's pregnancy.

The novelist at this point is quite soar with society and school administration alike which leave adolescent school boys and girls uncared and unlooked after, just at the mercy of fate and chance, and in all cases of sex-aberration, condemnation is hurled on the boy and the girl with little inclination on the part of seniors to own responsibility themselves. The novelist is of the opinion that it is high time that, an atmosphere of healthy sex relationship is created and maintained in all educational institutions and the students are taught to sublimate the sex instinct till proper time to indulge in it for the welfare of individual and society.

A shrewd and domineering figure that Swati is, she turns Reema's helplessness to her advantage with the help of her auntie Dr. Rai, who performs Reema's abortion, successfully. Swati pressurizes Raju to marry Reema but he says, "I'm not even eighteen. We'll get arrested". (936-37) But the fact remains that by helping Reema in the hour of her dire need, Swati obliges her for a whole lifetime.

The novelist, here too, has a piece of advice to offer to all women. She exhorts one and all not to be swayed by lust and passion and safeguard one's honour and dignity. Our educational institutions must share responsibility in this regard. While a balanced and scientific sex education should be imparted to the growing youth of both the sexes, their time must be divided between hard physical work and serious mental pursuits, so much so as to allow them little time for sex interests and indulgence.

Just after six months of her marriage to Ravi Nath, Reema falls into an illegal and incestuous relationship with her brother-in-law. This is the direct outcome of Ravi's impotency. Randhir's amorous advances and her own exhibitionism for promiscuity are also responsible for her downfall. Even her mother-in-law is unable to restrain them from it, which "half-suspected, but said nothing in the interest of maintaining family peace". (946)

The novelist here has a stern warning to offer. Money has come to assume undue importance in modern society. The rich in society are hardly susceptible to human feelings and delicacies. With the force of money, they ride rough shod over feminine sensibilities and emotions. Sex for many of them is just a plaything with hardly any strings attached to it. This unscrupulous and animal living is the bane of society and must be discouraged and weeded out by all those having reflective attitude and sterling character.

Randhir and Reema had taken fancy for each other since the engagement ceremony, which took place at Rangoli. There was no question of love at the first sight; it was mere mutual attraction of two healthy bodies of opposite sexes, but at the core of it is the lurking fear of Ravi's impotency which had practically ruined Reema's conjugal life. Ravi too was not unaware of his unmanliness. As a matter of fact he was candid enough after the function when Randhir touches Reema's arms and says, "I hope, Bhaiya marries you. I'd love to have you in our family". (941) In her first small encounter, Reema also concludes "Randhir would be more sexually exciting than hours of mechanical, predictable love making with Ravi". (940)

Ravi, with business pressure and moneymaking, is away from Reema and this provides ample opportunity to Randhir to interact with Reema and entice her. The novelist here is discreet enough to provide hints to one and all that earning fortunes through honest and legitimate means in the *sine-qua-non* for happy family life, but equally important is maintaining vibrant health and radiant masculinity.

On the first wedding night, Reema discovers that she has been married to a wrong man, who leaves her "cold, physically and emotionally". (941) This stark reality of her conjugal life makes her morose; but after going through Sridevi's love life, she realises that it's the general phenomenon of the elite and upper middle class urban families of the India. "Even ravishing superstars suffered a sexless existence". (942) This feelingless sexual behaviour of Ravi decides the future for Reema, "They'd slipped into duty fucking without having fucked in the first place. That night decided all the nights that followed". (943) Ravi was grossly mistaken in so far as he considered mere copulation as consummation of sex relationship while the cardinal factor of satisfaction in sex eluded his grasp and this forced Reema to develop amorous relationship with her brother-in-law.

The novelist here clearly hints at the paramount importance of sex in life because this is a factor which can neither be overlooked nor compensated by any other thing, real or imaginary. Extra-marital relationship, more often than not, is an outcome of unsatisfied sex-life where either the husband or wife is left chafing and pining for fulfilment. Reema is a glowing example of un-fulfilment in conjugal love having direct bearing upon her adultery. This is a tragedy of Indian women and wives which is rendered more poignant by Swati's remarks who says, "**We marry the person we are told to marry**" (943) and sometimes have to suffer inordinately, for unmarried girls like herself she says, "**I made my choices. And was willing to pay the price**—that's what separates the women from the girls". (943)

There are examples of another class of people such as Randhir who revel in womanising, promiscuity and illicit relationship. They are not to be labelled 'Satyriasic' as such, but such things happen when parents have not done their duty of finding a suitable match for the boy or the girl at the prime of his/her life or the youth has not been brought up into high ideals of life and has not been trained for morally and socially evolved egalitarian callings and bent of mind.

In Randhir's case particularly, we find him receiving many proposals from parents, families of his community even though they knew he has "an American girl friend back in New York". (847) At his each rejection, Reema sends up a prayer to her favourite deity—"Santoshi Mata", (947) which means he is still hers, at least in Bombay. The novelist's suggestion that a man or woman must not lead a life of prolonged bachelorhood or virginity is quite appropriate and her suggestion to allow both men and women to choose their partners at appropriate time is praiseworthy. But this open heartedness is possible only when a girl child is accorded the same welcome in the family as the male one and she is also brought up with dignity and status due to her.

Ravi's extra-marital liaisons, lack of dignity and disregard which Reema faces at his hands and above all his inability to provide Reema sex satisfaction, drive her to become quite indifferent to Ravi's out of house activities and affairs. Like a shrewd and practical wife, she has decided not to bother about her husband's "sex-life outside their bedroom" (947) and "never to break-up the home; have fun quietly somewhere. But don't leave the family". (1007)

Thus, Aparna and Reema are dissatisfied with their husbands and this in turn leads them to adopt a pattern of life not sanctioned by social norms and standards. But, it doesn't reflect either "anti-patriarchal/anti-colonial"[17] view of womankind in any way or "women's lives without hope".[18] Instead, it depicts and demands love, respect, purity, honesty and good behaviour and devotion from one and all-human entities.

Next figure in the novel is Noor, an offspring of loveless and heartless parents engrossed in their own extra-marital affairs. In this family atmosphere, Nani, an elderly maidservant of the house, brings her up but is quite incapable to guide her properly. The maidservant is helpless to protect Noor from the unscrupulous Swati and fails to save her from her incestuous younger brother Nawaz.

These factors turn Noor's life into "a pathetic nothing. A zero. A non-person [not even worthy for] victim". (1009) Her life-spirit fades away and life-blood dries up soon after she meets with an accident, after which her boyfriend leaves her and starts a new life for himself. Emotionally scarred, Noor becomes a physically and mentally handicapped being; even though she is taken and treated by her colleagues like Reema as a "Dangerous woman—quiet and deep [simply because she knows] everybody's secrets [and] the names of all lovers". (969) This is why even her mother despises her, for she is scared of her own secrets, which can be revealed by her daughter before her husband, who will definitely kill her without any delay; therefore, she devises a ruse and tells everybody that her daughter is mad "Just to protect herself". (969)

Noor remains desolate and desperate throughout her life due to her physical and mental humiliation by men and women, familiar and unfamiliar. She finally commits suicide, which is a social crime. The reason is not far off to seek. The social crimes she committed, willingly or unwillingly, rankled in her mind and made her low in her own estimation, driving her to her catastrophic end. Swati, a vicious lady knows about Noor's predicament and, therefore, upon her death she could confidently declare that, "Noor is dead.... She was already dead when she decided to come here this afternoon. I saw it in her eyes, she had death written all over in block letters", (1013) and her next remark about Noor is, "She has taken her time. That kid should have died years ago. Before her accident. Before anything. She was born with a death-wish. Something to do with bad *Karma*". (1013-14)

Here, J.P. Tripathi is correct up to some extent when he raises a genuine question about *Snapshots*, "Does the spectacle of life presented in the book constitute literature with value and use for mankind and will it cross the buffets of time and human taste?"[19] It is contrary to what Hudson says about literature:

> Literature is a vital record of what men have seen in life, what they have experienced of it, what they have thought and felt about those aspects of it which have to most immediate and enduring interest for all of us. It is thus fundamentally an expression of life through the medium of language.[20]

Therefore, a piece of literature should be critically evaluated "from a definite ethical and theological standpoint"[21] with an aim at "elucidation of works of art [and] correction of taste",[22] so that the greatness of literature can be determined. However, J.P. Tripathi fails to appreciate the inner worth of the novel, because he considers this work as a specimen of "yellow literature [and more inappropriately calls it] pulp literature".[23] The critics finds the main theme of the novel "just a get-together to catch up on old times",[24] though which Shobhaa De has presented most of the women as lambs growing into wolves when ill treated by men. But "Swati is a veritable 'tiger' who can 'screw' any man and all men and she can lick her women friends working as wolves".[25] It is not so. As the novel is simply not about scandalous, sexy, feminist and envious life of urban Indian women, it depicts the reality and the westernised way of life, which has transgressed the age old Indian culture and customs and the human values, and driven the modern women of India away from their moorings and brought about artificial and undesirable elements in their lives.

The predicament of the modern Indian women is better realized by Bijay Kumar Das when he remarks that the terms like morality, marriage and husband have lost their importance because now most of us are guided by the word 'enjoyment.' He writes further, "Shobhaa De dives deep into the hearts of liberated, upper-class women in the contemporary society and depicted her characters as they are and not as they should have been. The people are presented in their true colours—what they are rather than what they should have been",[26] which is only partially true. But, his comments on the novelist that "she is not concerned with the traditional concept of morality and purity in love"[27] and about the novel, "The women portrayed in *Snapshots* want to enjoy life and are given to sex-antagonism",[28] are not true. The critic is mistaken in understanding the real message of Shobhaa De, which is to denounce the western culture, and if one is willing to accept it, one must accept it only after critical evaluation. Her main stress is that, the most valuable tenets of western culture can be adapted to India's culture, traditions and mores and Indian culture and traditions too can be re-evaluated, and modified in the light of new advancements and realities of the day. However, the critic misses the undercurrent of De's thinking when he writes:

> Shobhaa De seems to say that sex is a part of life and in order to accept life one has to affirm sensuality. She depicts the lives of young men and women, particularly rich upper class people who no longer consider faithfulness and constancy in love a virtue, the description of union between the lovers or wife and husband becomes too open and vulgar to be enjoyable. It offends our sensibility and distracts our attention. Shobhaa De's novels border on pornography and there is a grain of truth in it.[29]

Thus, in De's novels "life is presented as it is, not as it should be",[30] but it does not mean that her novel is based on "unconventional theme [and an] unusual treatment of sensual opulence in an intimate conversational language"[31] for making it the best seller. It is just the style of the novelist, her particular trend of handling the genre, that she presents life's most glaring reality in the way it deserves but under the thin veneer of her abiding love and high regard for India's culture, its customs and traditions, and beliefs. An unquestioned votary of India and her culture that she is, De revels in calling a spade a spade but her message is unmistakable and that is that she wants to go beyond what appears within the ken of mortal eyes.

Her loneliness weighing heavy upon her, Noor easily keeps track of other people's lives, like Dolly and Surekha, who have lesbian relationship with each other; Dolly is the next-building neighbour of Surekha and has neighbourly ties with her and her family members. Dolly belongs to a Parsee family. She still remains unmarried and solely relies on Surekha for her sexual satisfaction, for which Dolly's family blames Surekha, "for Dolly's being unmarried [and breaking up] all her relationships". (970) Dolly tries to commit suicide by taking insecticide, when she learns about the decision of Surekha's family, much against Surekha's wish, to marry her. Again it is the terrorising impact of Surekha, due to which, Dolly misses her last opportunity to escape from her clutches and "to make a new independent life for herself", (971) by not joining the German band in Singapore.

Dolly "come over for afternoon naps very often" (970) at Surekha's home, but their relationship remains unsuspected even by Surekha's mother-in-law, who has an eagle eye. Dolly has endeared herself to all the members of Surekha's family not only by her behaviour and demeanour but also because she helps the family financially. Nobody in the family has an iota of doubt that both are locked in unexpected sexual relationship.

The relation between Dolly and Surekha resembles conjugal love, as if two persons have joined together, once for all, with marital ties. Dolly, for the sake of Surekha, bears the severest castigations and condemnations by Swati. Surekha, too, is as loyal and loving to Dolly as Dolly is to her. Their relationship continues even after Surekha's marriage just because of Surekha's "dissatisfaction with her sex life". (973) Dolly pursues this unusual relationship because of depression, as Surekha says, "She has found someone new to hate now. Herself". (971)

Although, Surekha mentions lesbian relationship with Dolly as the most intimate and "spiritual" (971) one, and as having some connection with their "past lives", (971) yet such outrageous and abnormal things cannot be accepted socially. Dolly's depression, her expulsion from her parent's home and Reema's ironic comment on it as conveyed to Surekha displays the stigma which society at large attaches to such things:

> Actually, it isn't any of our business. As long as you're happy, what does it matter? People will always talk. Just because Dolly is unmarried they'll label her a lesbian. You have a good camouflage. You can hide behind your marriage. But for Dolly it must be very difficult. Anyway, we seek our happiness whichever way we can. Why criticise? (971)

Thus, the novelist is highly critical of such unnatural practices. Such behaviour can't be condoned by any social norm or law and erotic pleasure can hardly be permitted at the cost of individual's dignity and social weal. It's thus vehemently criticized and condemned by the novelist who is not at all in favour of it. Here, she once again finds parents, guardians, teachers and those feeling concern for society as persons neglecting their duties to the young and growing as it is their failure to bring up the youth in the proper atmosphere and inculcate in them the cardinal virtues of man and womanhood, the absence of which leads them astray. Surekha and Dolly are just two examples of gross negligence of the elders towards the young and growing. On the other hand the novelist praises the sweet and happy family life, through the character of Surekha, who chooses and agrees to marry Harsh Shah, at the age of nineteen, when other girls were pursuing their degrees and enjoying their care free life. Though, she does not become an international figure like Swati, but her life is far more serene and free from scandals. She is a complete housewife always engaged in her domestic responsibilities and like a typical Indian daughter-in-law she is always respectful towards her husband and mother-in-law. Because of her engrossing business engagements, she hasn't have enough time even to take lunch at her own parent's home, though she goes to see them only for two hours once a fortnight. Like Aparna, she neither hates the word 'husband' nor complains against him for not bringing a single sari for some special occasion, because she takes interest in making sacrifices for the betterment of the family and its members. This gives her inner peace and joy though deficiencies are there definitely which concern her family life. If Swati is "perfectly miserable", (928) then she is perfectly comfortable as she says to Swati about her own happy life, "May be I am. Yes, I am. I'm married. I live in a comfortable house. I have a well-behaved daughter. A prosperous husband. What more do I need". (928) Even Swati approves of it, when she says, "If your happiness is defined by that, then you are lucky. You've got what you want". (928)

Thus here once again we find the novelist advocating the age-old ideal of simple living and high thinking. Even the noted Urdu poet Firaq Gorakhpuri has said that, 'a happy home and happy family life epitomises all that is best in an individual's life.' The life of Surekha as depicted by the novelist is also symbolic of a happy family life, based on service, sacrifice and satisfaction.

In the presence of her mother-in-law, Surekha is left with no choice except to follow her commands. Though Surekha wishes for a little bit of liberty and privacy, "I'd love to have a place, just a room to call my own without that woman watching me all the time [because she] can't do anything, anything at all, without her knowing about it", (969) which makes the thing horrible for her; but she feels happy and safe in a joint family. It's clear from her reply to Reema, "He'll never agree. He'd rather leave me", (968) Reema criticizes her for giving too much importance to her mother-in-law and suggests, "Why give her so much importance? That is how you women spoil them, just because you've married her son doesn't mean she owns your life. Surekha, take my advice—tell your husband to either move her out or move your family out". (968) She suggests, "You just have to assert yourself once. Once your husband becomes a hundred per cent dependent on you, he won't look elsewhere. Men like their comforts. And men are spoilt lazy babies. Feed them well. Fuck them regularly and sit tight. That's the way to keep them. Control them". (968)

Here, the novelist indirectly tells about the way, how women can keep their relationship in good condition and keep their husbands in control. It can also be done with penance and self-sacrifice. It's reflected in the undercurrent of Reema's comment that permissive sex:

> for a man doesn't really matter with whom you're doing it [because] it becomes a habit. But I bet he's the only man you've ever known. Right? How boring! Imagine not knowing any other body, any other feeling, any other sensation. Forever. Sounds terrible. Like eating dal-chaval day in and day out. (968-69)

Thus, with Surekha's case in point, the novelist not only criticizes the craving and hankering for sensual pleasures and illicit sensuous affairs, but also tenaciously supports the age-old Indian ideal of fidelity in conjugal life. She also holds women responsible for making the entire womankind frail and susceptible to carnal passions in the eyes of men, society and their own. Half the ills that women create for themselves are due to ignorance, while the other half arise from their egotism. What they adore as modernity is mere semblance, not reality. In fact, modernity and antiquity are not antagonistic because both give importance to men's good.

Rush or Rashmi Singh, is a nymphomaniac, which means, "a woman" who has great hatred for the male folk in the unconscious; but because of the fear that her hatred may not be exposed, she goes on seeking sexual satisfaction with several men from time to time with the sole purpose of controlling and repressing her hatred and conflict against men".[32] The nymphomaniac is a woman who runs after the mirage of sexual satisfaction, which she never finds, like the unreachable mirage. She never experiences orgasm. Klaf and Harwood write:

> The world "nymphomania" was first used by the Greek physician Soranus, who lived prior to Galen, during the reign of Trajan. Two ingredients are necessary before a woman can be classified as a nymphomaniac. First, she must experience hyperactive sexual desire. Secondly, the nymphomaniac is sexually frigid, meaning that she is incapable to achieving orgasm during intercourse. Nymphomania then is a medical syndrome or a combination of symptoms.[33]

This happens to Rashmi due to Pips Sr. (short form of Parminder), a wealthy chap of Punjab, whom she loves dearly, but he walks out of her life "for a tidier new home", (899) after exploiting her physically, emotionally, financially and morally. Their six-month company in the bed and out of bed "was a record for both". (900) Both are intrinsically fond of "sex and good food". (900)

Rashmi's Nymphomania is not reflected only through her sexual relationship with many men like, Pips Sr., Max, Younes, Anupam and Balbir, but also by her very attitude towards life which is one of vengeance. "Basically, I think all men are bastards". (975) She thinks, she is correct. About her son Pips Jr., she asserts before both Reema and Aparna, "My son Pips can fuck anyone. Marry anyone. He is a guy after all". (1006) She doesn't care about different girls he'll use and discard, just because "Did anybody care about me? I was someone's daughter once". (1006) Here, the novelist points out the most critical phase of human life, especially of women's lives which is being misinterpreted by men and media, as Reema says, "Funny, I don't know whether we pick it up from the movies. Or those fellows pick it up from us", (1007) a tragic situation in our real life.

Rashmi hates the term "responsibilities", (897) which she is reminded of by Pips Jr., who makes her agonizingly conscious of her motherly duties. "Why can't you be like other Mummies?" (897) This also expresses the novelist's view that children are not playthings for their parents but are grave responsibilities. It is children who actually repeatedly remind parents about what they owe to society and how they can best discharge it. Simultaneously, her imaginative reply to her son shows revulsion against patriarchal system, society and power, partiality, due to which women and children are suffering a lot in the present urban Indian society. "You, my dear chap, are a bastard. Yes, a real-life bastard. Of course, you do have a father. All bastards do. But he is not my husband. He is someone else's husband. And father. Now do you understand why your mummy can't be like other mummies?" (897) Such a reply from Rashmi to her son, can make it difficult, for any one to lead a balanced life.

Here the novelist tends to show that children like Pips become the most vulnerable victims of illicit sex. They feel more insecure than others Pips asks about Max, "Why did that nice uncle leave?" (904) The reply that Rashmi gives is typical of every woman in such conditions and is full of detestation and venom, "**All men leave, baby. That's the way they are**". (904-5). He assures his mother, "I won't leave you when I become a man. Promise". (905) This is evident of the inviolate bonds of love and concern between the mother and her child. This sense is well reflected in her answer to Swati that, "Pips is not like other kids. I've raised him differently. Kids love their mother—even if they're nymphos. If either of us was to be destroyed, it would've happened when that bastard—his father walked out. I survived". (959) The under-current of the novelist's thinking is that becoming a father or mother is a task requiring immense planning. The tragedy is that a task involving the highest wisdom is consummated with the least regard for the outcome. Bringing a living being into the world, is not just a matter of physical attraction and carnal passions, it is a duty of the utmost importance seeking the highest sense of responsibility. Unless man rises to this consciousness, many of the problems affecting mankind cannot be remedied.

The question raised by the novelist through the case of Pips is perennial in nature. What should the society do in a case where the child is not the progeny of his legitimate father? Society can't afford to discard, neglect or finally abandon such children at the mercy of the elements. Instances galore can be found in the annals of man where even an illegitimate child has risen to phenomenal heights. So long as man does not become sensible enough as not to cohabit with a spouse other than his own, there is no other way except to nurture and bring up such children with the best care possible so as to make them a gift to humanity.

Rashmi had a propensity for sex from early childhood. Gradually she grew fonder of male touch. But she was never sneaky and surreptitious. She openly admitted what she did and said that it was simply for enjoyment and "a sexy evening" (1007-8) that she indulged in sex. She had to fend for herself and for her kid and had to sweat for it and lead an independent life without a protective umbrella. She was in contrast to women like Reema who "extract a price from [her own] husband[s]". (1008) And this contributed to her sense of superiority over women like Reema who had the temerity and "nerve to be judgmental about me". (1008)

Rashmi realizes about her humiliating condition and her only weakness, her honesty, when she meets Champabai, a brothel owner, whose each and every girl is happy and declares herself sound and safe in the hands of Champabai. She works on the principle of "Not for nothing" (902) and when she comes to know that Rashmi is Pips's "woman, not wife", (903) then she guides her:

> Never give yourself to any man for free. You know why? Men don't value anything they get so easily. That's why we are here: to satisfy their lust, not for sex but power. Power over women. Power over us—you and me. If they buy your sex, pay for you, they feel like kings. Give to them with love for nothing and they'll kick you in the gut. (903)

So, men get immense pleasure by wielding power and money and reserving "hitting and beating for [his] wives". (902) This suggests the same thing about power equation, between men and women. "Wherever this balance collapses, there is tension in society and double-dealings and hypocrisy predominate".[34] The novelist hereby indicates that many a man has expressed his opinion about the power equation between man and woman and also his anxiety over the changed power equation. Emphasising the importance of power equation the novelist remarks:

> Eventually, every relationship is a power struggle either on an overt or subliminal level. Control over the situation has been a male prerogative over the centuries. It is time they were made aware of their own potential and power. Shakti needs to be harnessed, directed and explored for the furtherance of over all human development. The very concept of the sexes locked in eternal battle is negative and destructive, when one talks of shakti unleashed, one also remembers the two connotations of shakti—the destructive *avtaar* is as potent as the creative one. It is in maintaining the state of equilibrium between these two opposing forces that can lead to creative and dynamic harmony. Men will have to come to terms with woman power.[35]

Thus, the core issue here is not power, but the achievement of equality and respect by power. R.S. Pathak erred here partially by mentioning that "the cardinal issue thrashed by Shobhaa De in her novels relates to power, the desire to dictate and direct action and thinking of others".[36] What led him to think like this is probably Balbir's question, "Do you fuck because you enjoy fucking? Or is it power-play?" (975)

Rashmi was grossly mistaken in her thinking that having free relationship with stray men and maintaining an independent living were enough to bring her honour and satisfaction in life but the inner vacuum and hollowness tormented her. It was not long after that she found that floating of men "in and out of her life like wispy cotton balls [and her status of] being manless is [a] big fat fucking shame". (907) Side by side, her honest nature and bland frankness did not attract men but drove them away, because men "prefer flirts and flatterers. Even manipulators. They felt more comfortable with them", (907) while she does not "make her men feel needed enough". (906) It was high time she felt that she chose a man for herself and for this she was prepared to make drastic changes in her life style. The man of her choice was just a question of finding him and making him her own. Rashmi plans in her mind, "He is out there some where, grab him before some other bitch does. There is a trick to it. And this time, make sure you chain him down. Seal the exists. Block all escape routes. Hang on to the man. Last chance coming up, baby. Take it". (907)

Eventually, the above decision of Rashmi provides her a way to overcome her nymphomania, by cancelling and discarding all the so called modern trends and fervour of 'ism' and independence, to adaptation of sweet homely life and Indian life-style by marrying a man of her own choice. Rashmi's case is one more instance how the novelist gives vent to her preference for Indian norms and how man or woman's inordinate sex desire must be harnessed to a controlled sex life.

The last but not the least figure in the novel is Swati, who is actually the protagonist of the novel in whose honour the meeting is organized and who in the later part of the novel turns nightmarish. Swati is a peculiar character, which the ingenuity of the novelist has introduced with deftness and finesse. Swati is ambitious, ruthless, unscrupulous and excessively prone towards personal egotism. She is marvellous representative character of today's humdrum of life. Her pursuit for success is relentless. Swati emerges as a winner from her fifth standard, in exams, competitions and plays. She goes to London and joins the School of Drama but she becomes a case of high intentions, self-defeated. This first class first talent is spoiled due to negligence on the part of her own parents, especially her mother, who leaves her home in the care of a mid-wife, while Swati becomes accustomed to treating her liberty as libertine.

Swati, a child of mixed parentage, her father is from Kerala and the mother is a half-Assamese, and half-Bengali. Her father being an engineer spends "most of his time on sites out of town"; (951) while her mother is "a prominent social worker and professor of Anthropology, committed her life to the uplift of the toiling masses and was rarely at home". (951) Thus, Swati is not only devoid of parental love and guidance but also "accustomed to a succession of indifferent *ayahas* [who are] assigned to take care of the baby". (951) Because of these factors, she not only picks up bad habits, but also starts boozing and sex. Her distinguishing feature is her desultory habits and foppish, flippant temperament. She remains a spoilt child through out her life, inspite of many difficulties, due to her firm faith like some westerners that "nothing changes" (987) in this world, because money and material haven't have that power. She is quite candid when she confides in Surekha, "even if I were perfectly miserable, surely I wouldn't burden all of you with my problems. So why don't we settle for happy?" (928)

Owing to her malicious mind, she's unable to justify her own deeds, whether it's "triumph or guilt" (1002) to harm others. She takes revenge on each and every girl. She lures Aparna's husband and destroys her harmonious married life, due to which Aparna lures Perm form Renu, with whom she has no axe to grind. Lack of a homely life makes Aparna feel "uncomfortable about being born a woman" (1003) and it seems to her very "unfair". (1003) It's simply due to Aparna's wining 'the best girl trophy' during her school days. Similarly, Swati is treacherous to Reema and Raju, by revealing their secrets before Reema's parents through anonymous bad written letter, due to which Reema has to marry a man, not of her choice and Raju is murdered. She despises Dolly, who serves her at her will, simply because she admits as having grounded twenty laxatives into Priya's soft drink, ripped two of her elaborate costumes and did eavesdropping on Swati's directions, to stop her form winning the 'Best House' shield of the year. Swati abhors Surekha for the simple reason that she helped her Dolly in her humiliating conditions, thereby hurting her ego immeasurably.

Because of her self-centred and capricious nature, Swati does not help Rashmi 'the all rounder,' because of her being physically superior to her. She tries to humiliate Rashmi by hurling remarks at her that "What are you afraid of? You have not reputation to safe guard. And your bastard son must know he has a whore for a mother".(1011) This calumny draws them to wrestle with each other, quite an ignominious scene. She also subjugates Noor, tries to humiliate and make her feel low to a point which compels her to commit suicide. Noor's only mistake was that she exposes Swati's secret of tapping through electronic bugs planted by her in the room. She developed a domineering attitude towards Noor, after enslaving her brother Nawaz in illicit sexual relationship with her just to wean Nawaz away from Noor. Swati gloats under the idea that she is the cynosure of all eyes and that she is far superior to all women. She criticises others when she talks to Aparna:

> You with your bleak little mediocre lives. Plying safe and yet cheating, sneaking on the side. Tell me, which one of you here is all that pure—as pure as the driven snow you'd love to compare yourselves with? I think I'm far more ethical than the lot of you. Look where I'm and look where you are. Nowhere. (1005)

and again

> Who the hell would want to sleep with You? They with their hypocrisies and petty lies. Bitches all. Betraying everyone, fooling everbody, pretending they are virtuous virgins. Give them half a chance and they'd screw themselves from here to Timbucktoo. And you dare criticize me. (1005)

She directly says that, "I don't have to answer any of you. What is this—an investigation? Are you the Gestapo or something?"(1010)

The novelist has portrayed Swati as an example to all oriental women who have to eschew all ways and means adopted by Swati, if they want to lead a decent and respectable life. In this novel, the protagonist is a competitor to Aparna, for Reema a trophy guest, for Rashmi a snooty bitch, for Noor a classy whore, while for Surekha, she is fickle, selfish and manipulative. But like each and every woman, she too "envies but feels proud of her". (929)

Aping Western life and culture has made Swati think that, "sex is a hobby" (947) and a king of "celebration—the highest form of religion [whose] cock worshipper" (977) she is. She rejoices her sexuality instead of regulating it. She puts her view as, "We don't find it dirty. Sex doesn't threaten us. I feel sorry for all you women hanging on so desperately to outdated ideas of purity, morality, chastity. It's pathetic". (977) She develops this unethical and flamboyant attitude and view of life due to her over-ambitious nature. "She wanted more and more [nearly] everything" (993) that fascinated her. The only way to acquire them she thought is money and materials. Her inordinate desire propels her to make a blue film, which she does stealthily and after that venture to make another one with an oriental title, *Maharani*, which changed her life. In it she presented herself as "the exotic, bejewelled Maharani with an insatiable sexual appetite—Terrific. Gorgeous-plus. Blue-blooded and a nympho too". (993) Later, she takes in marriage Juan Mendonca, a divorcee, sado-masochist and an eccentric multi-millionaire of the Honduras and makes a lot of money.

Swati is recognized as "the Oriental Express", (994) "Dusky Hussy" (898) and "Oriental Eyes" (965) by the western people, society and media. With foreign aplomb, she is quick to get recognition here in India. This is why she says, "Make it there [in the western world] and you were made everywhere. There was no escaping the glamour of a foreign tag. Recognition overseas ensured adulation back home. That's what Swati craved—she wanted the folks she'd left behind to know she'd done it". (965) The novelist is critical of this tendency of Indians. She expresses her views through Aparna, who thinks, "How depressing that it still seemed to matter so much—the all important 'recognition' from the west. But it did. Not only to Swati but to everybody else". (965) The novelist, as already mentioned, is dead against Indians selling their conscience, individuality and national aura for some quick bucks. Men and women like Swati, by becoming reckless for material gains from the West, are inflicting irreparable injury to national honour and prestige.

Swati spends "a great deal of money and time on this little [and the latest] expedition", (1011) just to collect some "fresh material to produce a serial on a contemporary subject dealing with women—Indian women"; (1012) for which she has already received a fabulous offer from Hong Kong because this subject is beyond the scope and understanding of the British script writer. So, she gets an opportunity to prove herself worthy enough to "write, direct and produce a bold, meaty series on the exciting world of the Nineties Indian Urban Women [which may] take her a long way—if she played it right". (1012) She needs different types of voices to web some real story. She gets, what she needs, authentic, familiar and confused "voices that would ring true" (1012) from her old school friends in this get together. She even thinks about a suitable title of the serial "Sisters of the sub-continent", (1012) to get more and more fame and money. Here, the novelist criticises Indians, especially Indian women, like Swati, who sell their souls for their selfish ends. The novelist repeatedly criticises such characters who, for a few bucks and name, do not value their own civilization, nation, culture and prestige. Thus, the novelist warns us against this alarming situation, which degrades us.

Though money is sweeter than honey, but human relationship based on humanity, love, service, and sacrifice is the sweetest of all. Money can't buy everything. This is what Swati lacks and longs for. Inwardly she is far from satisfied with luxuries, lucre, lust and labels. This is clear when she concludes about her goal, "Rohit hadn't been worth the time or effort. But in any case, Swati's target hadn't been Aparna's man—it had always been and still was Aparna herself. The smart, cool, efficient, together Aparna". (999) [Owing to her married and homely life]. "The woman Swati secretly longed to be, but never could become". (999) So she craves for her feminity to feel like a woman.

After the death of Noor, Swati's inner self or woman comes up. Her materialistic outlook, thinking and attitudes vanish away. A sort of transformation takes place, which changes her entire being from an occidental to an oriental and from a materialistic to a spiritual one. After a short period of confusion and hazy thinking, she comes to know about good and "bad karma". (1014) After long last, she comes to realize that material things are ephemeral, while things of abiding interest are those of the spirit, viz. truth, purity, love, sacrifice, et al. This realization dawned upon her virtually after Noor's death. It's well reflected in her comment, "I don't know what I was looking for, but let me tell you I didn't find it. It was a colossal waste of time. Energy. Money. Everything. Besides the lot of you turned out to be such bloody bores. You can have the bloody taps". (1013) She finds human life through Noor's body as "unreal, [which after death, looks like a distorted figure] as if a careless painter had overturned a can of scarlet by mistake". (1014)

Thus the novel ends with a hint for an appropriate way of living where things of the spirit are far more valued than things material, though basic well beings and comforts should not be denied. All these things can be attained only through a balanced human life, full of humanity along with noble ideals and deeds.

It's incorrect to say that, "Marriage is not regarded as essential in the fictional world of Shobhaa De".[37] In this novel, the novelist gives much emphasis on marriage. The importance of marriage has been expressed through many characters. In Indian society, lack of husband makes a woman's life and future "uncertain", (879) because she needs love, care, tenderness and honour and above all a life of sharing which is so essential for fulfilment in life.

According to Aparna's mother, "a woman in our society is nothing without a husband":

> Remember, a woman in our society is nothing without a husband. Study as much as you wish. Win prizes. Get a good job. But don't let all these things affect you, give you a big head. You may be the prime minister of India tomorrow, but when you come home, you automatically become your husband's wife. If you forget that, you are finished. Your marriage is finished. (891-892)

Exactly, the same thing happens with her and she started to hate her own self, after being divorced by Rohit.

Surekha after marriage lives a life of "the complete house wife". (892) This ensures her a sound and safe life, free from scandals. Her "arranged marriage [takes place] at nineteen", (895) when she chose and agreed to marry Harsh Shah. But, it is Reema "the first girl from her batch to get married".(919) [She agrees to marry on her mother's suggestion] "whatever you want to do can be done later—after marriage. These people are broad-minded. They won't stop you". (919) Reema has firm opinion about her daughter's marriage as she tells, "I had an arranged marriage. My husband would like our daughter also to have an arranged marriage—**No love marriage nonsense**". (1006) Swati enters the wedlock many a time, but each time she divorces, because they are unable to arouse a feeling of femininity or womanhood in her, as she wants to be a complete woman like Aparna. Rashmi after having affairs with many persons for many years finally decides to marry, to protect herself and her son from social stigma and hostility. Noor is the solitary example where the helpless lady fails to muster will power and courage and finally commits suicide.

According to the novelist, marriage is essential for peace, harmony, prosperity and culture; more than this "**It's a match made in heaven**".[38] It is the cradle where social virtues are nurtured and come to fruition. A happy family life, therefore, is God's own grace upon earth which can find no parallel, much less an alternative. Raju and Noor die due to lack of it. Rashmi and Pips Jr. are crushed, suffocated and humiliated mainly due to lack of family life. For want of it, Aparna,

Reema, Surekha, Dolly, Swati, Rashmi and Noor are led astray and they adopted a way of life generally not approved by the society. This is why marriage at the proper stage in life with abiding love and concern between the couple has been stressed time and again by the novelist.

There are many male characters in the novel like, Pips Sr., Max, Yonous, Randhir, Raju, Nawaz, Nawab, Ashvani etc. All are more or less male-whores and neglected children of their respective parents. Balbir's sorry plight is a case in point. A privileged son of a Brigadier, Jasjit Singh, and an anorexic mother Amrita, he receives no attention from his parents. Rigid atmosphere of the home and domineering attitude of the father makes him leave his parents home but before it, "by age twelve, he'd been seduced by a chowkidar's young wife. By fifteen, [he] was a man who knew what he was looking for", (979) but not for a life in the army. Being a natural achiever, he gets "what he wanted", (983) success, money, girls, fame etc, but his inadequate and "incomplete education wouldn't get him too far", (983) as he is not recognized by his own parents. Though "his relationships with girls who floated through his busy life remained at a need-based, superficial level. While other men envied him his 'score card' but Balbir remained dissatisfied and alone". (984) These and other instances make it amply clear that, parental love and concern is the most important single factor for a child to attain the fullest development of his personality and becoming a complete human being. Balbir, Pips Sr., Randhir and other were dissatisfied with their lonely and boring life, in varying degrees, and to get love and social recognition they swing from pillar to post.

Although we come across instances of adultery, extra-marital sex, incest and promiscuity in this novel, yet what is important is the fact that the novelist through the fate of such characters disapproves all of them. Positive aspects of the institution of marriage and family have been projected. Sanctity of marriage and family emerge as the foundation of healthy society and harmonious life of the individual. The institution of marriage is considered sacred and essential by almost all religions, even in Islam, which allows polygamy. A Muslim historian has written:

> No nation can exist without a regular married life, for it prevents the uproar of passions abhorred by the cultivated mind, and it removes all those causes which excites the animal to a fury always leading to harm. Considering the life of the animals by pairs, how the one member of the pair helps the other, and how the lust of other animals of the same species is kept aloof from them, you cannot help declaring matrimony to be a necessary institution; whilst disorderly cohabitation or harlotry on the part of man is a shameful proceeding that does not even attain to the standing of the development of animals, which in every other respect stands far bellows him.[39]

NOTES

1. Bijay Kumar Das in his article "The Author and the Text: A Study of Shobhaa De", Dr. B.K. Das, *Critical Essays on Post-Colonial Literature* (New Delhi: Atlantic Publishers & Distributors, 2001), p. 101.
2. *Ibid.*, p. 102.
3. *Ibid.*, p. 101.
4. Shobhaa De, "*Selective Memory: Stories from my Life*" (New Delhi: Penguin Books India (P) Ltd., 1998), pp. 334-35.
5. *Ibid.*, p. 335.
6. Shobhaa De, *The Shobhaa De' Omnibus* (New Delhi: Viking/Penguin Books India (P) Ltd., 1995), p. 1013. All further references to the novel will be incorporated in the text.
7. Sarita Vellani, "Interview with David Davidar", *Seminar*, 384, August, 1991, p. 41.
8. Author Unknown, *Communications* (Harmondsworth: Penguin, 1966), p. 18.
9. Urbashi Barat, "The Medium is the Message: A Study of Snapshots", Jayadipsinh Dodiya, ed., *The Fiction of Shobhaa De*" (New Delhi: Prestige Books, 2000), p. 245.
10. *Oxford Advanced Learner's Dictionary* (Calcutta: Oxford University Press, 1992), p. 773.
11. *Ibid.*, p. 728.

12. Madhumalati Adhikari, "*Snapshots*: A Postcolonial Text", Dodiya's, "*The Fiction of Shobhaa De*" (New Delhi: Prestige Books, 2000) p. 237.
13. Elivi Whattakar, "Towards Feminist Ethic and Methodology", "*The India-Canada Relationship*", ed. J.S. Grewal and Hugh Johnston (New Delhi: Sage, 1994), p. 346.
14. Madhumalati Adhikari, "*Snapshots*: A Postcolonial Text", Dodiya's "*The Fiction of Shobhaa De*" (New Delhi: Prestige Books, 2000), p. 241.
15. Madhumalati Adhikari, "The Equation of Power in *Snapshots*" (Dodiya, ed., *The Fiction of Shobhaa De*), p. 255.
16. Shobhaa De, *Surviving Men* (New Delhi: Penguin Books Indian (P) Ltd., 1997), p. 68.
17. Madhumalati Adhikari, "*Snapshots*: A Postcolonial Text", Dodiy's, *The Fiction of Shobhaa De* (New Delhi: Prestige Books, 2000), p. 240.
18. Urbashi Barat, "The Medium is the Message: A Study of Snapshots", Dodiya's "*The Fiction of Shobhaa De*" (New Delhi: Prestige Books), p. 247.
19. J.P. Tripathi, "Sbobha De's *Snapshots*: The Overwhelming Question", R.S. Pathak, "*Indian Fiction of the Nineties*" (New Delhi: Creative Books, Narraina, 1997), p. 156.
20. William Henry Hudson, "An Introduction to the Study of Literature" (London: George G. Harrap, 1944), p. 10.
21. T.S. Eliot, "Religion and Literature", in John Hayward (ed.), "*T.S. Eliot: Selected Prose*" (Harmondsworth: Penguin Books, 1998), p. 32.
22. *Ibid.*, p. 18.
23. J.P. Tripathi, "Sbobha De's *Snapshots*: The Overwhelming Question", R.S. Pathak, "*Indian Fiction of the Nineties*" (New Delhi: Creative Books, Narraina, 1997), p. 157.
24. Shobhaa De, "*Snapshots*" (New Delhi: Penguin India), p. 222.
25. J.P. Tripathi, "Sbobha De's *Snapshots*: The Overwhelming Question", in *The Fiction of Shobhaa De,* p. 157.
26. Bijay Kumar Das, "The Authour and the Text: A Study of Shobhaa De's *Snapshots*", Prof. R.S. Pathak, *Indian Fiction of the Nineties* (New Delhi: Creative Books, 1997), p. 16.
27. Bijay Kumar Das, "*Critical Essays on Post-colonial Literature*" (New Delhi: Atlantic Publishers and Distributors, 2001), p. 98.
28. *Ibid.*, p. 99.
29. *Ibid.*, pp. 98-99.
30. Bijay Kumar Das, "The Authour and the Text: A Study of Shobhaa De's *Snapshots*", R.S. Pathak, *Indian Fiction of the Nineties* (New Delhi: Creative Books, 1997), p. 170.

31. *Ibid.*
32. S.P. Chaube, *Abnormal Psychology* (Agra, U.P.: Luxmi Narain Agarwal, 1995), p. 422.
33. Franklin S. Klaf, M.D. and Bernhardt J. Harwood, *Nymphomania: A Psychiatrist* View (New York: Lancer Books, Inc., 1964), pp. 17-18.
34. Shobhaa De, "Sex in the Time of Stress", in Khushwant Singh and Shobhaa De, ed., "*Uncertain Liaisons: Sex, Strife and Togetherness in Urban India*" (New Delhi: Viking/Penguin India, 1993), p. 6.
35. Shobhaa De, *Shooting from the Hip: Selected Writings* (New Delhi: UBS, Publication, 1994), pp. 111-113.
36. R.S. Pathak, "Feminist Concerns in Shobhaa De's Work: A Study in Attitudes", an article in Jaydipsinh Dodiya's "*The Fiction of Shobhaa De: Critical Study*" (New Delhi: Prestige Books, 2000), p. 37.
37. R.S. Pathak, "Feminist concern in Shobhaa De's Work: A study in Attitudes", Jayadipsinh Dodiya, "*The Fiction of Shobhaa De: Critical Study*" (New Delhi: Prestige Books, 2000), p. 40.
38. Shobhaa De, "Baby, are you lonesome tonight?" in her Column "*The Sexes*", Published in the weekly magazine "*The Week*" (June 24, 2001), p. 12.
39. Al-Biruni, *India* (Abridged edition of E.C. Sachau's English Translation), ed. Qeyamuddin Ahmad (New Delhi: National Book Trust, 1999), p. 239.

8

Second Thoughts: Love is Life, Not Money

The *Second Thought* (1996), the seventh novel of Shobhaa De, has been misunderstood and variously interpreted by critics because of its psychic-cum-social complexities. According to Alka Saxena, *Second Thoughts* presents "a slice of urban life",[1] and "the agony of Maya, who feels trapped in matrimony, is the central theme of the novel".[2] G.D. Barche evaluates this novel as reproduction of "the myth of fall",[3] while Maya is "another Eve in *Second Thoughts*".[4] Jaydipsinh Dodiya considers it as magnum opus of Shobhaa De as "the novel focuses on the hollowness of Indian marriage",[5] According to Asha Khare, "The story depicts over-bearing female characters and weak male characters. It exposes the male ego, social pretence, and public facades. It is a tale of two cities, Bombay [Mumbai] and Calcutta [Kolkotta], and contains vivid descriptions of the two with details of food and dresses. Sexual overtones, the chief characteristics of Shobhaa De's work are over-riding throughout the novel".[6] Every critic, however, has tended to be oblivious of the real message of the novel and the novelist that 'man is neither gross body nor mere intellect, but a happy combination of the two' meaning thereby that, undue emphasis on one aspect alone will necessarily lead to the neglect of the other and this will inevitably result in disharmony in life. Relentless pursuit of careerism in the cut-threat competition and break-neck speed of the modern life by both husband and wife Maya, and Ranjan is reducing them to just physical entities, present in body, but mentally absent with no innate love and concern for each other. Life has been reduced to mere formalities, while genuine relationship is absent.

It's "a bitter sweet love story [of] the nineties",[7] in which Maya the protagonist is "eager to escape her dull, middle-class home in Kolkatta and plunge into the whirl or Mumbai, where she moves after her marriage".[8] She desires "to be the ideal wife. Instead, she finds herself trapped and stifled by the confines of an arranged marriage to a man who, she discovers, is rigidly conservative and completely indifferent to her desires. She begins to experience the utter loneliness of a stranger in suburban Mumbai".[9] At this critical time "she strikes up a friendship with Nikhil, her charming college-going neighbour, and an explosive tale of love, betrayal and paths not taken"[10] takes place, which raises many questions. Why Nikhil takes advantage of her loneliness? Why does she betray her husband? The answer is simple and clear: her husband neither loves her nor cares about her and her sentiments because he is devoted to money, work office, his mother, and patriarchy. This makes her wife indifferent in her loyalties, and is later on exploited by Nikhil. Although she feels guilty about it, yet she remains loyal, as she never accepts Nikhil completely who forced her for sex.

This novel shows the novelist's insight into human nature and presents her as "as sensitive writer".[11] It sets aside all sorts of allegations against the novelist including 'the ever green Queen of Pornography' label. The family background of this novel is the middle-class society instead of the high-class society, therefore, "*Second Thoughts* evokes no conflict".[12] The story of the novel contradicts R.S. Pathak's observations about Shobhaa De, "Marriage is not regarded as essential in the fictional world of Shobhaa De".[13] Shobhaa De herself writes about this novel:

> Second Thoughts was a much quieter book, devoid of a single raunchy line. The critics, of course, thought otherwise—'What? No sex?' And may be, they were

> disappointed. From 'too much sex' to 'zero sex', I made a joke out of my 'vegetarian' novel, but it was lost on the reviewers who'd forgotten their original grouse against my writing—the overdose of 'masala'. Well, here was a sober, spice-free look at a modern-day marriage.[14]

It is a first person narration novel except the prologue, which is in the third person. This work of the novelist proves that to a woman "Marriage is the destiny traditionally offered by the society".[15]

Maya is "an attractive young lady"[16], her skin colour is "a warm, rich golden brown, like sunlight dancing on the Hooghly with her gleaming jet-black hair and large, dark eyes to advantage". (4) She belongs to an educated family of Kolkotta and has a degree "textile designer" (155) but she dreams of "becoming a journalist and changing the world". (141) At Pradipda's request, Maya and her mother Chitra "come to Mumbai and meet Ranjan Malik and his mother" (3) with the marriage proposal which Maliks accepted. Maya comes to Mumbai for "mere sight seeing" (4) but falls in love with the city and feels, "marrying Ranjan would make her a part of it immediately" (12) and for "forever". (12) Owing to it, her condition is like "a high-spirited, energetic, bouncy young girl ready to meet life's several challenges head-on. Ranjan [is] just one of them".(5)

Maya's first experience in the Mumbai metropolis was not good. It "smelt of desperation and deceit". (1) She recoils in horror when she sees the body of "the first dead person of thirty", (2) lying prone, while nobody pays the least attention to it. She watches it with "utter disbelief". (2) It reflects that in Mumbai, emotions and human sensibilities die before thirty, though body exists even after it due to the workaholic, persuasive and money-minded nature of the city. It also shows the death of humanity. She finds a glimpse of it in Ranjan who seems too "remote and disconnected" (8) and "used to being ignored and preferred it that way" (8) because he has some "lack of common courtesy" (8) and sees "life as a careerist in the fast tract" (10), but not as a social being. The conservative-cum-patriarchal view of Ranjan sabotages the spirit of Maya who is "a trained textile designer". (10) Ranjan restrains her from doing a job: "I am earning well enough to support a wife and family. I believe, it is a woman's duty to run a good home" (10-11) Maya does not like this remark of Ranjan. These hostile experiences make her demoralised when she steps out of the taxi at the entrance of her uncle's house. "Maya alighted with a light step and even lighter heart" (14) because she knows the answer of the Maliks will be a "yes" (14) and she will have to stay in Mumbai as it will be eventually her home after her marriage.

Ranjan is dehumanised, and obsessed with his mother. He is a workaholic, "demonstrative and charming". (25) He is "competitive, brilliant", (28) foreign educated. He is "completely self-absorbed", (42) "a keen sportsman", (43) "too inexperienced too uptight" (48) twenty-eight year old "virgin". (48) He looks at his wife in "an almost brotherly gesture" (49) who feels "a little repulsed" (50) by Maya's nearness. Physically, he is an attractive person, thanks to his "lovely white, even teeth, his thick dark hair and the intense, large eyes". (51) Though he is "short in the legs [yet] his chest and shoulders [are] strong and broad, plus he [doesn't] have belly or a jiggly bottom". (51) He prefers to stick "with men" (52) and avoids women because of "his failures with six girls he'd tried to make love to". (52) He has an 'erratic" (77) power of observation, "innocent and sweet". (95) He works very hard and practises economy. Sometimes he appears "boorish and insensitive" (134) because he has faith in "work hard, play hard philosophy". (15) He lives a life of smug respectability. "Women [aren't] important to Ranjan" (234) due to his "complete lack of experience [which makes him a man who has] "turned out to be a novice in" (239) feminine matters. His sex drive is practically non-existent". (258) He is conservative and critical of his wife's family.

Maya who was very happy before her marriage with the conviction that "I would live in this wondrous city some day. Marrying Ranjan was like marrying Mumbai. I thought I was the luckiest girl in my locality. Certainly, I was the only one who had bagged a foreign-educated, Mumbai based bridegroom" (195). Even her mother-in-law Mrs. Malik who was in the lookout of an educated girl, feels satisfied with her decision in selecting Maya: "I think we have made the right choice in Maya". (117) But, the same Maya within a year feels absolutely rejected and useless because nobody needs her, which is evident from her frustrated utterance: "Nobody needed me, absolutely nobody. My parents no longer thought I belong to them. My husband belonged to his mother. It was unlikely that I would bear children who would belong to me. And I didn't have a single true friend to call my own". (266-67) She craves for a sense of belongingness.

Maya's newly wed life has started with "clumsy-sex honeymoon at a depressing hotel in Mahabaleshwar, a hill resort near Mumbai" (48). Ranjan finds it very difficult "to get into a relationship with any woman" (51), besides he has never felt "comfortable" (50) with them. Maya wants "to run form one end of the city to the other end explore every square inch of Mumbai", (178) since the day she came in the city but she doesn't enjoy liberty in the liberated city. Soon after her marriage, she becomes a captive bird in the four walls of her husband's house and never gets out of the house since her husband has "a certain mental picture of "wife" and [She has] to conform to it—no lapses permitted". (157) This depression brings a kind of "crippling loneliness" (158) in her life. She misses her "environment, and freedom" (192) in anticipation of a life of "adventure" (193) for which she has agreed to marry Ranjan. She wants to become a "Mumbaiwali" (27) and wishes to "belong" (27) to it.

Ranjan further aggravates her misery by many restrictions. He asks her to "stay at home" (27) and not to misuse his hard-earned money in things like the "gajra of mogras". (26) He frights her against Mop salesmen and vendors by mentioning them as "useless ruffians". (29) For this reason, he also asks her not to peep through the windows of the house. He never appreciates her for any work, dress, word or any other thing which belongs to her. His attitude towards Maya is derogatory, "Just accept what I'm saying" (55) because he doesn't like any kind of argument. He develops communication gap with his wife and asks her to "stay away" (54) from women of Mumbai because they have "no morals" (55) and more over they are "lazy, spoilt spend all their time shopping or eating—unconcerned about their domestic life". (55) If she needs company, then he asks her to call his "mother". (56) Instead of listening to Maya's "rubbish" (56) talk for which he has not time, he lectures to her about her role that "a housewife's duty is to stay at home and make sure everything is tip-top. That is where her true happiness lies. You have seen my mother's house—learn from her". (56) He doesn't give her any money and prohibits the use of STD phone, TV, and air-conditioner. For Ranjan, watching T.V. is utter "nonsense". (30)

When Maya complains to him about her loneliness, he gets irritated and says, "How can any intelligent person be lonely? In a city like Mumbai at that? There's music. Television. You can read, clean the house, write to your parents. Do something creative. What's the point of complaining all the time?" (29-30) He feels "tiring to watch" (39) his wife around him, which shows his insensitivity to his wife's sentiments, pains or pleasures. Thus, "the kitchen had become symbolic of [Maya's] refuge". (39) She "never felt wanted or welcomed in the bedroom. That remained Ranjan's room, his domain. The kitchen was an area that belonged exclusively" (40) to her.

The insensitive behaviour of Ranjan towards Maya gives rise to the suspicion and rightly so, that, Ranajan was sexually impotent. However, there is no clear indication in the novel. It is surprising that in the presence of a wife as ravishing and captivating as Maya, Ranjan does not feel sexually roused even once and to hide his impotency, he goes on lecturing Maya upon her every demand or wish. It is also an indirect suggestion by the novelist that a mere foreign degree is no guarantee of success in practical life; success is an elusive game, which favours one who meets every situation in life with aplomb and ingenuity.

Ranjan on no account seems to be satisfied with Maya's marketing, whether it is a matter of Bashmati rice, Little Finger, fishes or Babasuit. He always directs Maya to follow the footsteps of his mother, "If you want to go anywhere, ask my mother to accompany you". (27) "If you've problem understanding things, just ask me. And I'll ask my mother". (56) "My God! Maya—is that the way to serve water? Thank God my mother it not here". (57) "Mummy is a very good housekeeper and home-maker. She's amazing. Maybe you should train with her instead of doodling away your time at a drawing board". (66) "Housewives don't have extra time—there's so much to be done around the home. Take Ma's example. She is busy round the clock. She has never gone to some useless classes". (139) All the time, he refers to his mother and is never out of her shadow. Even the least thought of disrespect to his mother is disturbing to him. He expects Maya to hold his mother in high esteem and not to do anything against her wishes. In Psychological term, Ranjan is Paranoid and is suffering from the 'mother-syndrome'. Although his is foreign educated and mature in age, yet he ignores his responsibilities towards his wife and is preoccupied with his mother. Little wonder that he doesn't want to be "tuned into Maya's wavelength" (234) and is critical of her for having "a very negative attitude". (261)

Ranjan's loveless attitude towards Maya hurts her sensitivity. When Maya desires to take up a job, to keep herself engaged in some meaningful vocation, he taunts her, "Mumbai is like New York. Or London. Tough competitive. You have to be good, great, brilliant, to get a job here. People don't waste time on nobodies" (28) but she tolerates it because of her innate humility. At Maya's request to accompany her on "weakends [to] explore Mumbai" (27) he scolds her: "Sometimes, you talk like such a kid. Life is not a picnic. And you aren't in Mumbai on a holiday. As a married woman, you have to learn to deal with responsibilities". (27) Even "the love making...was always a let-down" (47) for which Maya blames herself that she "was too inhibited, too inexperienced, too uptight [but later discovers and is surprised that] it was Ranjan who was all of that". (48) When she evaluates her own condition with that of her husband, she finds that she had one "kissing boy friend" (48) at the age of twenty-three, and there is Ranjan a "foreign-educated, modern, confident Mumbai boy of twenty-eight who had never known another woman. I'd married a virgin". (48) Ranjan is so naive that he and his mother discuss private matter of Maya's "menses" (48) with their family priest, a complete stranger to Maya, which "embarrassed" (49) her. He is never "ready" (53) to perform his role as a husband to satisfy the physical desires of his wife.

The cardinal question, however, is what to do in situations depicted in the novel. The novelist has not tendered any answer herself and has left the matter to the wisdom of readers themselves. One way is to snap the marital ties and find out a partner who is physically more satisfying and interesting as in the West. But the game is not without its risks because one doesn't know what is in store in the move. The next partner may be found wanting in some other respect, more or equally galling as the former and sometimes even more exasperating and exacting.

Sex is a powerful instinct no doubt; it cannot be suppressed but can definitely be harnessed. Her textile designing apart, Maya once wanted to become an enlightened journalist and had desired to change human outlook with her powerful writings. This is a suitable vocation. After all everyone has to become his or her own saviour, no body else can do it for anyone. Our own thinking process is our best refuge.

Ranjan feels "a little ashamed of"(115) Maya, because she doesn't belong to Mumbai and is different from local girls. He asks her to remain "Secretive"(117) and not to "approach"(119) as people will "misunderstand".(119) Moreover, they cannot be "trusted. (119) He lectures Maya on the virtues of sacrifice; when she gives him a few hundred rupees she has received from her mother. "Please do not encourage your mother to spoil you like this. A good wife has to learn to adjust and sacrifice". (123-24). "Ranjan gives credit to his mother for the artistic blend and decoration in the house"(128-29) which is appreciated by Tom Becher II, his company's boss, which was really a work done by his wife Maya. Regarding food he says, "Every wife is not an expert cook", (134) which makes him "appear boorish and insensitive" (135) in comparison to Tom. He does not permit her to join any "useless classes, learning pottery or whatever that nonsense" (139) because they are in his eyes "recruitment places" (140) "for prostitution" (141) as "Mumbai is the country's biggest recruitment centre", (141) which is controlled by "high-powered pimps who prey on women like" (141) her.

Ranjan criticises the city and family of Maya's parent, which is difficult for a woman to tolerate. He doesn't show "the slightest interest in" (211) Maya's past life. He also does not like to go to her parent's home whenever he goes to Kolkotta. "Lack of time" (211) becomes an excuse. Maya accepts it as a "great Bengali culture [for a Bengali son-in-law] to insult the wife's family". (212) Her mother used to say, "It is a woman's lot to hear these curses. Never mind". (213) She remembers her mother whenever her husband hurts her by insulting her parents or relatives. Her mother-in-law hurts her far more when she belittles Maya and her parents. "If you ask me, it's always wiser to get a girl from a socially inferior background. Grief comes to a man who marries above his station. The husband loses all control over her and she ends up having the upper hand". (231). She says, "Such a marriage can never work which is why we are so careful while selecting the right candidate for Ranjan. I think we have made the right choice in Maya" (231-32). But, Ranjan's scathing comment on Kolkotta as "a dying city (244) "definitely not a city for hard-core professionals" (245) provokes Maya to blurt out "If Kolkotta [is] dying, what about Mumbai? It [is] dead and decomposing, going by the stink and piles of uncleared garbage". (244)

Ranjan, provides Maya "nothing more than financial support, a decent house to live in and four square meals a day". (263) He has no "sex drive" (258) to satisfy his "sex-starved" (257) wife. In bed they have "been brothers. Or sister. Or flatmates [because he] was devoid of any passion". (251) It forces Maya to think that he has married her simply "to satisfy his mother". (251) Ranjan criticises Maya as "nymphomaniac" (259) and compares her with "a cheap woman. A prostitute" (259) because he thinks, "that his contribution to the contract was over on the day he decided to make me (Maya) his wife. That act alone had redeemed him for life. That was his effort. He had chosen me. And that was sufficient", (253) neglecting all further responsibilities of a husband towards his wife.

Maya wants to be "free, alive, reckless and mad" (75) she also wishes to see the beach "to get wet in the waves, to laugh [and her] insides to perform a wild dance" (74) but she rather finds herself "pretty much alone". (222) Her silent solitary suffering is further aggravated by total lack of communication with her relatives. The terse assertion of Mrs. Malik at the time of marriage for instance, "Girls can only be moulded if they stop thinking of their parent's home as their own" (222) was supported by Maya's mother Chitra, who also believes that "A girl has to cut the cord to her family quickly and identify with her in-laws. The sooner she does this, the better". (222) Soon after her marriage, her maternal uncle who lives in Mumbai has "inexplicably disappeared from the scene [with a feeling that he has] discharged his duty and there [is] nothing further to be done". (68-9) This act of his is supported by Chitra though her letter to Maya. She writes:

> You are a married woman now. You belong to your husband's family. In traditional families such, as ours, it is simply not done for the bride's relatives. That prevents the girl from integrating into her husband's family. It may also lead to misunderstandings between the couple you have to get to know your new family and become one of them as quickly as possible. It is for your own good, for your sake that *mamu* is leaving you alone. Don't misunderstand that. Girls who cling on to their own family for too long never succeed in adjusting to their husbands people. (67)

On the other hand, soon after her marriage Maya "was keen on everything—making a new beginning in Mumbai, discovering the city, meeting people, learning to keep a good house", (1991) but Ranjan "refused to share a single subject of his professional [or personal] life with" (205) her, considering her too ignorant to understand.

Here, Ranjan forgets that by denigrating his own wife, he is casting aspersions upon himself and is also committing a blunder which tantamounts to social crime. Maya is not anybody. She is his devoted wife. The novelist is here indirectly pointing to the hollowness behind the craze and fondness for a foreign educated man who is more often than not considered a paragon of virtue. The novelist seems to suggest that knowledge and experience cannot replace good conduct, which cannot be borrowed from others. This has to be developed within oneself and then can be extended to others. Ranjan's ego and false sense of prestige do not allow him to respect even his better half and thus he misses the basic cultured life.

However, Maya does not consider that there is anything wrong with either her husband or with her marriage and she rather blames herself for having "something wrong [with her due to which she feels] so restless and depressed". (192) She gives enough reason for her pathetic condition—"I don't have a single friend I can talk to, I miss my parents, my home, my environment, and mainly my freedom" (192) because she wants to fondle, laugh, talk, sing, walk, see, feel and enjoy her life with someone especially along with her husband. She is unable to understand somebody's comment "married means giving up everything you've known as a carefree young girl. And for what?" (192)

Maya does not accept Ranjan's "house" (227) as her "home" (227) for the lack of his affection, affinity and attachment to his house. She says "The house that was how I always referred to this place, even to myself. It was never a home. My home. Our home. Always 'the house'—impersonal, distant, cold. Home continued to be Kolkotta. My parental home". (227) Sometimes she also thinks that she is "living in a rented flat. A company flat. It [does not] belong to Ranjan, and it certainly [has] nothing to do with me" (227) because he has not turned into her "wavelength". (234) Though, for some affectionate moments he pats her "hair fondly, adopting a manner owners use towards their pets". (235) She enjoys his physical closeness yet she sees "a special irony in the word intercourse" (237) because sex is a great and mysterious force in human life. This turns her life into mere "routine". (251) She wants to "belong to" (261) her husband and his family to get rid of her loneliness. But "nobody" (266) belongs to her whether it is her husband, mother, mother-in-law or any true friend. Children remain a distant dream for her, too rare to be fulfilled even after "ten years" (253) of marriage. It worries her much. Maya receives "instructions" (207) because he does not "trust" (205) her for which she will have to wait at least "ten or fifteen years [their] marriage" (205) till he knows her "better" (205) like his mother. This is why he keeps Maya "in the dark", (205) which compels her to think herself aloof and unrelated to Ranjan and his family. "If he could confide in his mother, why couldn't he confide in me? I wasn't his adversary or rival. Didn't he trust me enough?" (205) Prodipmama consoles her "men–husbands–rarely phone their wives just for a chat. All that lovey-dovey talk only takes place during courtship. After marriage, everything changes. And what is married life all about? Routine". (208) He finally, tries to convince her that "the very fact that he phoned means he's thinking of you". (209)

Surely, soon after marriage everything changes in Maya's life and she is reduced from a free and fluttering being to "a fulltime, domestic servant without pay" (154) even worse than "a resident cook, or a hired caterer", (133) simply for the role of "a good wife [who] has to learn to adjust and sacrifice", (124), to work like "cooking, cleaning or pleasing someone" (189) like an ordinary Indian woman. Maya has only seen "the closed door of [her] house and the iron bars on the windows. [Though she] wanted to flirt with the 'other Mumbai'—the one about in the lively city papers and saw in Hindi films". (87) But, she is not permitted to peep through windows because staring at strange may be dangerous. For, "they could be pimps or thieves on the look-out for an opportunity. They are armed and highly treacherous, or they could be drug dealers". (88) Ranjan warns Maya that "these same men you spend hours staring at could be the ones who knock on the door with chloroform to rape and rob housewives like you. Don't blame me if anything happens to you. Remember I've warned you". (88)

It is irony that India which produced a woman Prime Minister like Indira Gandhi and freedom fighters like Aruna Asaf Ali, Usha Mehta, Kamla Devi Chattopadhyaya and modern crusaders like Medha Pateker, Kiran Bedi, Pratibha Patil and Arundhati Roy has still in her lap a house wife in a metropolitan town who is educated with professional competence, is lectured by her husband that she should not trudge out of the house for the fear of being abducted or simply dodged by cheats and absconders.

Ranjan assures Maya to co-operate with her when he says, "now that you are my wife, no secrets. I want to know everything, and I will tell you everything", (123) but he doesn't keep his words, when she queries about his life before marriage he is annoyed, "Why do women always insist on this silly exercise? What's the point in asking all these silly, meaningless questions? Does it really make the slightest difference? What will you get by finding out my past, or I by digging into yours? Forget it, Maya. Let's begin with a clean slate". (50) Maya who has not "a single other diversion" (121) feels "like a servant. A menial [due to] Ranjan's attitude". (47) Maya feels cheated, when she remembers the beginning of her marriage:

> As I stood there uncertainly, I felt utterly low and miserable. At that moment, just about everything seemed wrong with my life–all the choices I'd ever made. My marriage, my decision to more to Mumbai, my cowardice at not asserting myself vis a vis Ranjan, my giving up a career. (171)

As a result of this, her loneliness is intensified and "first thought [that came to her mind was to purchase] a one-way train ticket to Kolkotta and never come back", (161) because Ranjan is too much obsessed with 'Money' and 'Mother' and remains insensitive to all human emotions and feelings, except 'Puppy-love.' Maya mutely mutters about his money-oriented life, "What did Ranjan do with his money? Why was he so mean with it?" (161) She values human life far more important than money and refers to it indirectly when his mother falls ill,

"What is money when Ma's health is involved. She must have the best possible treatment". (276-7) While serving her mother-in-law for ten days like an "*ayab*" (277) and "*nursemaid*" (279) she convincingly calculated that "my mother-in-law's heart flutter was nothing more than a petulant cry for attention" (277) from her son, but till now she has received only "overwhelming filial devotion", (279) which shows his incentive and inhuman nature. The novelist wants to convey that, 'human life is priceless.' God has bequeathed this limitless treasure trove to all. And as diversification of mind from money and materials is one of the secrets to successful investment, so is it the secret to a joyous and blessed life.

Maya's suffering, subjugation, isolation and deprived condition turned her into a confused person unable to take any decision on anything. She is not strong enough to say 'no' to anybody on any issue.

Nikhil is the only son of Dipankar and Pushpa, after two daughters. Dipankar and Ranjan are colleagues at the bank. Nikhil is not yet out of his teens but his acts are far above it, for instance "at the age of sixteen, [he] was mixed up with Nalini Mehta", (20) a ground floor girl of the building. Dipankar's family is on the fourth floor of the same building. Niikhil is five or six years younger than Maya. He is a typical Mumbai boy with bad reputation "No values. No manners. No culture". (18) He never shows any "proper respect" (18) to his elders because his line "is bad" (22) and has "two habits—liquor and sex". (22) There are many reasons like, lack of belongingness, physical dissatisfaction, flattery by Nikhil Verma, emptiness of her [Maya's] married life and the impact of Mumbai's monotonous life, which force Maya in a ridiculous, disgusting and shameful mood to think of Nikhil, "a newly married woman day-dreaming about a neighbour's young son" (32) who is like other young men of Mumbai "good looking, confident, sporty, cocky, flirtatious, lazy, spoilt and quite irresistible". (32) More than this Nikhil has no tough competition to face, as Maya has only encountered men like "door-to-door salesmen, sweepers, drivers, watchmen, domestics and dhobis". (33) On the other hand, if one has "to have a student as a neighbour why not someone as fascinating and Nikhil?" (33)

In the eyes of Maya, Mumbai is a "dead and decomposing" (244) city, where nobody has time to waste on "flowery speeches" (159) when "abusive...vulgar and offensive" (159) language serves them well. Maya who faces depression due to "crippling loneliness [wants to] talk to turn to" (158) somebody, "but nobody gives a shit. You live. You die. Mumbai ticks on. People make money, people lose money. Who cares? Nobody". (158) It is the city of Mammon where people have no time for anything other than goddess Lakshmi. In this "ferociously competitive city", (155) where "nothing remains a secret" (137) due to "a fog of foul air", (139) which is eventually the result of "the dog-eat-dog atmosphere of Mumbai". (114)

Maya notices one thing that "Mumbai didn't have Mumbai people the way Kolkotta had Kolkotta people". (98) As a result of it, Mumbai's people have "No time. No feeling. Everybody saving his own skin. You fight, you shout, you scream. You die. Others will step over your corpse and carry on" (98) is typical of its life-style. "Nobody to share anything with" (65) anybody. The women of the city "have no morals" (55) and have "a very bad habit of arguing". (55) They "spend all their time shopping or eating-unconcerned about their domestic life". (55) Though Mumbai people are "smug about their city" (234) yet when opportunity comes "everyone in Mumbai [takes] advantage of everyone else". (276)

The same is the case here. Maya is a lonely women and Nikhil takes advantage of it and exploits her. He "noticed [her] melancholia" (78) and the need of a companion. Although Maya knows him and his flippant nature, yet she welcomes him in her house because of two factors: the stark loneliness in her life even in the presence of her husband and secondly and more importantly, she has become so demoralized by her husband that her self-confidence and discretion have deserted her. Nikhil is aware of Maya's weaknesses and as a cunning, smart youth, he wins over her.

Nikhil gets a green signal from Maya to call her by her first name, Maya has already started dreaming about him. He gets further encouragement from her on different occasions. His presence delights her and that is why she tolerates his non-chalant and arrogant manner. Nikhil's image reverberates in Maya's mind, which gives her "a strange realization". (33) She enjoys his secret and silent presence in her mind. She listens the song composed by Nikhil entitled "a lonely, lonely lady" (78) in her "hotter than hell kitchen" (78) which consoles her that "at least there [is] something to look forward to at the end of the weekend. A song. A man. In whichever context. And no matter how cruel the final judgement". (79) In response to Nikhil's cassette, Maya appreciates his labour, "I loved your song" (110). So a "worthless, loafer, Zero. Parasite, Shameless lout" (81) becomes an important person for her. She realises with astonishment that in her "green diary" (61) "far too many the entries concerned Nikhil", (61) who enters in her life, like the evil snake in the life of Eve.

Maya is fascinated by Nikhil through his song which she listens to at least "twenty times in a row" (94) and thinks that "a man – not any man, Nikhil—had been inspired enough by me – to write a song, and present me with a copy of the cassette was more flattering than anything. I have ever experienced". (94) Then he offers her "the world's best *bhelpuri*" (90) which is rejected by Maya due to her fear of her husband. One day on the T.V. screen Maya sees a couple "swimming like playful dolphins" (152) and she imagines herself "the woman in orange bikini, and Nikhil; [her] underwater companion". (152)

When Ranjan left the town for ten days, Maya feels relieved. Instead of missing him, she wonders "While I hated the thought that I'd be alone in our home, I also felt free of pressure, free of approval-seeking, free of being judged, watched, corrected, scolded, nagged, pushed, instructed. Why was I not longing for my husband's return like a loyal, loving wife?" (162-3) She finds out its cause that Ranjan has made her "tense [and] self-conscious" (163) with his "smugness judgemental, supercilious attitude that conveyed superiority over" (163) her.

Nikhil's presence lifts up the spirits of Maya to such an extent that she becomes careless about everything "I didn't care who saw him there or what the consequence would be for me later. I didn't care if at that moment Ranjan had walked into the house [or] my mother-in-law herself chose to arrive right then. I would deal with it". (168) Further, he encourages her to be bold enough to take some decision on her own. He offers her to show some prominent places of the city. "Let's get out of here. Come on. Be daring. Do something spontaneous for once in your life, let's go. I'll show you some interesting places, even buy you lunch". (170) Maya says good-buy to her dispired and uninspiring life without any regret just to know whether she is "still in love with Mumbai, or if even that had died within" (171) her. Nikhil takes her out for sightseeing on his motorbike and finally his motorbike reaches "on the top Malabar Hills". (172) Maya is correct when she guesses that Nikhill has "recognized [her] loneliness and claustrophobia" (176) because, he gives some hints about his evil intentions through questions and suggestion to Maya in "Naaz Cafe" (174) at Malabar hills. "How do you like Mumbai now M– without your husband in it? Is it better or worse?" (176) "I happen to enjoy being with bores. Satisfied?" (177) "Each time I meet you, I actually feel nervous thinking about what could happen to you if you opened up the sluice gat of your heart" (177) he says "I Just cannot imagine you are married to him". (177) It fills Maya's eyes with tears and she protests against it in almost inaudible "Don't". (177) She longs for Nikhil's company simply "for companionship, nothing more"(186), as she felt desperately lonely.

Maya in her letter to Nikhil not only thanks for the unique trip but also makes it clear that there is nothing wrong either with her husband or her marriage. Though she feels as if she has "betrayed" (192) her husband, yet she has accompanied Nikhil because she was "Confused and afraid" (193). She makes it clear to Nikhil that she is not in love with him and she has a loyal husband. She writes "I was helpless and wanted to go out with you desperately. Please don't misunderstand me or misjudge me. I am not a flirt. I've never been cheap. May be God will punish me for this"(195). But, she is not able to hand over the letter to Nikhil to clear his misconception and her own conscience.

One day, when Maya is in an offensive and pathetic mood, thinking over her own life that she is "Useless, absolutely nobody" (266) because now she doesn't belong to her parents, while her husband belongs to his mother, and it does not seem possible that she will become a mother of her children who will belong to her, nor she has any friend in the city. When Ranjan is in the hospital to see his mother, Nikhil enters her flat despite her protests and assaults her chastity. Maya was in a confused state but Nikhil makes her feel "free. Lunatic. Wonderful". (268) Although, she shuts her eyes not out of passion but fear and embarrassment [and to] be free to any responsibility, if a conspiracy [is later] sought to be proved", (269) yet she enjoys it because she thinks it is the only bliss and essence of life. She realizes her error ten days later, when she comes to know about the engagement of Nikhil with Anshu, a Delhi based girl.

Though Maya enjoys her relationship including the sexual one with Nikhil because it eases her loneliness and mental tension, but she remains loyal to her husband. She feels disgusted, shameful and guilty about her friendship with Nikhil since the very beginning. It is due to frustration from her husband, her ignorance, her inexperience and boring life, and Nikhil's persistent and forceful persuasion which force her to face a "highly dangerous" (219) and disgraceful situation in her life. It is, therefore, incorrect to say that she is 'another Eve' as she says: "This was ridiculous—a newly married woman day-dreaming about a neighbour's young son". (32) "I realized that for too many of the entries concerned Nikhil. Was I really that bored? That frustrated?" (61) "I was free to brood on my own. Feeling intensely sorry for myself". (78) She detests Nikhil as is quite evident "I really wanted was for him to get out that instant and leave me alone to wallow in my misery". (165) She protests Nikhil's entry, "I hate your attitude. You really have no manners whatsoever. How can you just land up at my home like this and loll around as if you are in your bedroom?" (167) "Listen, Nikhil, whether it's in Kolkotta or Mumbai, a married woman is not supposed to meet other men. That's all". (169)

When she comes to know of Nikhil's engagement, she stands at her door "motionless and unthinking"(288). She realized the futility of the relationship, much more badly than her "uninspiring life". (171) She has two options: to "be happy with what you have". (229) "In life, one needs certain principles. One has to grow up with certain values. No wastage. No false show". (229) She determines upon rebuilding her relationship with her husband Ranjan, by her own efforts expressed in the last lines of the novel: "The more I stared at the spilled soup, the funnier I found it. I knew I would have to make it again from scratch". (289) "So what? I had all the time in the world now". (289) The message of the novelist for men and women both is that a happy family and home is a priceless possession in the absence of which one is not likely to make satisfactory progress in life. They must, therefore, try their best to keep it in harmony instead of deviating for money, and illicit relationship. The harmonious marital life is most important aspect of life.

The novelist emphasises the need of a rational approach to life, equality of sexes, which is only possible through co-operation and understanding. Honesty, loyalty, forgiveness and self-discipline are keys to it.

The novelist suggests a few things for a happy family and sweet relationship between spouses like; "Raise a child with correct values and you will give the nation a good, law-abiding citizen. Raise anybody the wrong way and you'll get a criminal". (230) "Why be afraid to speak your mind? If you have something to say, put it down on paper. That is the way to self-discipline". (235) "Unless you respect your body, nobody else will". (258) She stresses also on "values, manners, culture [because] elders must be shown proper respect". (18) The novel after portraying realistically the life of a middle class housewife, her infidelity caused by a callous mother-fixated husband, upholds the age-old traditional Indian values that alone can make life a success. "Modernity" is not the solution. Fidelity, understanding and caring alone make a marriage successful and lasting. The novel upholds the traditional value of mutual trust and understanding as mentioned in the following *sloka*:

> सन्तुष्टा भार्यया भर्त्ता भर्त्ता भार्य्या तथैव च।
> यस्मिन्नेवकुलेनित्यं कल्याणं तत्र वै ध्रुवमं।।[17]

(The house in which spouses are mutually satisfied and keep each other happy thrives and prospers).

NOTES

1. Alka Saxena, "Second Thoughts: A Slice of Urban Life" in Dodiya's *The Fiction of Shobhaa De: Critical Study* (New Delhi, Prestige Books, 2000), p. 259.
2. *Ibid.*, p. 260.
3. G.D. Barche, "Maya: Another Eve in Second Thoughts" in *The Fiction of Shobhaa De: Critical Study* edited by Jayadipsinh Dodiya (New Delhi: Prestige Books, 2000), p. 280.
4. *Ibid.*, p. 272.
5. Jayadipsinh Dodiya, "Second Thoughts: A Critique" in *The Fiction of Shobhaa De: Critical Study*, p. 281.
6. Asha Khare, "The Text and Context in Shobhaa De's *Second Thoughts*", Quoted by Jaydipsinh Dodiya in his artical "Second Thoughts: A Critique", Jaydipsinh Dodiya, ed., *The Fiction of Shobha De: Critical Study* (New Delhi: Prestige Books, 2000), p. 283.
7. *Second Thoughts* by Shobhaa De (New Delhi: Penguin Books India (P) Ltd., 1996). Back side of the jacket of the novel.
8. *Ibid.*
9. *Ibid.*
10. *Ibid.*
11. Alka Saxena, "Second Thoughts: A Slice of Urban Life" (*The Fiction of Shobhaa De* ed. by Jaydispinh Dodiya), p. 259.
12. *Ibid.*, p. 2259.
13. R.S. Pathak, "Feminist Concern in Shobhaa De's Work: A Study in Attitudes" (*The Fiction of Shobhaa De*), p. 40.
14. Shobhaa De's *Selective Memory: Stories From My Life* (New Delhi: Penguin Book India Private Limited, 1998), p. 336.
15. Simone De Beauvoir's *The Second Sex,* trans, H.M. Parshley (London: Penguin Books, 1983), p. 445.

16. Shobhaa De's *Second Thoughts* (New Delhi: Penguin Books India (P) Ltd., 1996), p. 4, All Further references to the novel will be incorporated in the text.
17. *Kamakunj*, p. 386.

Conclusion

Our study of Shobhaa De's novels shows that she is not a writer of 'pulp fiction' and different epithets like 'Vamp feminist,' 'Masala' writer 'richbitch,' 'India's answer to Jackie Collines,' 'pornographer,' etc. given to her by journalists and scholars are not justified. The surface meaning of her fiction misleads them. It is true that she gives graphic details of different kinds of human sexuality. We admit that at times, the descriptions are somewhat too candid, though there are more sophisticated descriptions of sexuality in some other novelists. She also uses frequently four-letter words, which are still a taboo in print media, at least in India. But, in day-to-day speech, the upper class English knowing people, use them in our country. In our culture, sex has been given its due importance and it is one of the four objectives of human life, namely *dharma, artha, kāma,* and *moksha*. What is to be noted here is that *dharma* (righteousness) comes first, which means the subsequent two objectives must be pursued according to *dharma*. There are several instances in our scriptures where the importance of *kāma* has been described. Here is one instance:

> मृगयाक्षो दिवास्वप्नः परिवादः स्त्रियो मदः।
> तौर्यत्रिकं वृथाटया च कामजो दसको गणाः।।[1]

(According to Manu, hunting, game of dice, sleeping during day, arguing and intercourse with women, drinking alcohol, music, musical instrument, dance and roaming without purpose are attendants of *kāma*. When they are justified, then it is not wrong to indulge in them. Hence, *kāma* is not irrelevant).

Sex is as important for healthy mind as food for healthy body as mentioned in the following:

शरीरस्थितिहेतुत्वादाहारसधार्माणो हि कामा:[2]

(Being the cause of the body, sex satisfaction is as useful as food. It cannot be denounced. As for sustenance and strength of the body, food is essential, likewise for health sex).

That is why *kāma* has been glorified and deified in our culture:

कामोभूतस्य भव्यस्य सम्राटं एको विराजति

स इदं प्रतिपप्रथे

ऋतुनं उत्स्रजते वशी[3]

Kāma, Love, is the sole emperor ruling over what has been and what will be.

He has ever made this world manifest.
He the controller sends forth the love-evoking seasons.

(*Taittiriya Brahmana*)

Thus, Shobhaa De is not unjustified in taking sex as a major theme of her novels. The foregoing analysis of themes shows that even though on surface they deal with sex, the implied meaning is its proper indulgence. She never approves of adultery, promiscuity or deviant sexual behaviour. Each of her novels describes them, but by the end its clear message is to practise restraint and the prime importance of family, children and harmonious marital life, for all her novels are women-centered.

In *Socialite Evenings*, the heroine Karuna begins as a rebel and unconventional woman demanding 'space' for her. She lives the life of a 'liberated woman,' marries, indulges in extra-marital relationship with Krish, and consequently is divorced by her husband. After undergoing these experiences, she goes back to her parents' house. The 'liberated' Karuna after soul-searching and realizing the reality of life comes to the conclusion that her own individuality is most important. Her return to her parents to take care of them and her invalid sister shows that for the novelist, the so-called 'liberated life' of a woman is not important. What is important is the filial devotion and realization of one's duties. By the end of the novel, she emerges as a confident woman with a clear mind, free from the superficial glamour of life.

In *Starry Nights*, we come across the corrupt world of film and high society of Mumbai. It is the story of exploitation of the heroine by her parents, the sharks of the film industry, her lover and her own sister. Despite all odds she fights, and it in only because of her optimistic nature that she survives, though at one point in the novel, she is on the verge of committing suicide. The novel though portraying the dirty reality of the film world, pornographic films, mental, physical and economical exploitations etc., which ultimately gives the message that for a woman, the most important thing is marriage and children. It is because of Sasha, her daughter, that the heroine finds sustenance in life. She wants to bring her up in a proper manner and see to it that she is not exploited in the film world as she herself had been. This novel also, despite graphic portrayal of sexuality and the making of blue films, lays main stress on the prime value of family and proper care of children that have been emphasized by the novelist.

Sisters, which is the story of two half-sisters, Mikki and Alisha, deals with the problem of an illegitimate child, Alisha, daughter of Seth Hiralal, a prosperous industrialist of Mumbai whose sudden death along with his wife in a plane crash brings Mikki to confront the harsh realities of life. The raw girl studying in the United States becomes a victim to the Finance Manager of the company and the object of hatred and hostility of her half-sister. She braves all the challenges and hostile circumstances and finally wins. She wants to have affectionate relationship with her half-sister who spurns her, but when she makes an unsuccessful suicide attempt, Mikki nurses her in hospital. Later, when Alisha becomes a drug-addict, she helps her to come out of the habit. Through sacrifice and love, she wins over her half-sister and her hostility turns into loving relationship. Through this novel, Shobhaa De projects and upholds the values of compassion, mutual understanding, and unity among sisters, demonstrating that even a half-sister can be won over by love and sacrifice.

Strange Obsession is the story of Minx, a spoilt child of a high police official who for the want of proper care and attention becomes a problem child. She becomes a lesbian and victimises a beautiful girl Amrita. Minx is a liar and over-possessive of Amrita and compels her to live in lesbian relationship with her. The cause of Minx's erratic character is the want of parental care and affection. Her mother is mentally ill and her father is too busy to give any time to her. The larger part of the novel deals with lesbianism but the novelist never approves it. The story ends with Minx's death in a mysterious circumstance, which finally frees Amrita. The importance of marriage and children is once again projected in the novel. A happy family life and children, healthy both physically and mentally, is only possible after their proper care and upbringing.

Sultry Days is the story of a man, Deb, nicknamed God who lives an unconventional life under the influence of Hippi movement. But the real story is about Nisha who is attracted towards Deb for his frankness and lack of hypocrisy. But later he becomes a part of the establishment and acquires all the qualities, which he had attacked in the earlier part of the novel. He becomes like any other man indulging in all kinds of activities, which were once against his grain. Nisha who is first attracted by Deb, later realises the hollowness of his character and gets disillusioned. The novel exposes and condemns the pseudo-western life. It shows the ironic change in the character of Deb and Nisha. Deb believes not in the institution of marriage but in free sex. The real focus of the novel is on Nisha who stands for positive norms of society. Out of love for Deb she nurses him in the hospital. The pathetic death of Deb clearly shows that the novelist does not approve of his character and his hankering after money. The novelist also condemns adultery which in our culture has been denounced. Even gods and mythological persons were destroyed by adultery:

छेवराजष्ठचाहल्यामतिबलष्ठचकीचको द्रौपदीं रावणष्ठच सीतामपरे
चान्येच बहवो दष्टष्ठयन्ते कामवष्ठागा विनज़्टा इत्यर्थचिन्तका:[4]

(Many were destroyed because of lust, Indra for Ahalya, Kichak for Draupadi, and Ravana for Sita; so say the wise).

Money is certainly important in life but it can never be its ultimate goal. Once again, humane qualities like love, cooperation and fellow feeling are emphasized. This novel emphasizes natural life and genuine qualities. Artificial life of any kind is denounced.

Snapshots describes the clash of Indian and western values. In the novel, we come across promiscuity, lesbianism, incest, and adultery. But all those who indulge in them meet tragic end. Swati stands for free sex and lack of Indian values. But, by the end of the novel, she realizes the hollowness of western life-style and accepts Indian values. She gives up the project of making a film on Indian women for which she had come to India. Through different characters Shobhaa De presents different kinds of sexual relationships but in the end she establishes the importance of the traditional values of marriage and family. Through Surekha and Reema, the novelist presents the importance of joint-family system, which despite certain ills has many sterling qualities. The novelist is in favour of the emancipation of women and speaks for their independence, but whosoever she is, in house she is only wife:

> ...husband, husband, husband. Awful word. Aparna blamed her mother—all those years of conditioning and brain–washing. She recalled her voice and words, 'Remember, a woman in our society is nothing without a husband. Study as much as you wish. Win prizes. Get a good job. But don't let all these things affect you, give you a big head. You may be the Prime Minister of India tomorrow, but when you come home, you automatically become your husband's wife. If you forget that, you are finished. Your marriage is finished'. How right her mother was. How depressingly accurate. (891-2)

This implies that ultimately, the woman's goal is that of a homemaker. In this novel also, the novelist first presents the surface reality of upper middle-class urban society and then demolishes the artificial western values and establishes the traditional values like that of marriage and family. And her emphasis on marriage is not mere moralizing. In her real life too, she married the second time only after a short interval and has written that she could not live without marriage even for a day:

> I happen to like being married. I believe in marriage. I enjoy being a wife. I don't want to spend the rest of my life on my own....
> The divorce came through at 11.30 a.m.
> I married Dilip at 1 p.m.
> Touch and go.
> That pretty much sums up the way my life has been.[5]

Her latest novel *Second Thoughts* is the only one that deals with middle class character. Thus, it is wrong to say that Shobhaa De writes only about high society. She calls it her "vegetarian novel". However, it contains explicit description of adulterous relationship between the heroine Maya and her college going neighbour Nikhil. It is the story of a frustrated married woman Maya who because of her unfeeling husband falls into adultery. She reminds us of the heroine of Anita Desai's novel *Cry, the Peacock*. Maya is a professionally educated woman who wants to have some engagement in life, but because of male chauvinist attitude of her husband Ranjan falls into depression. Through this novel, Shobhaa De presents the strongest form of male domination in our society. Ranjan, though educated abroad, has the most ugly form of conservatism. For him, wife means merely a dignified maidservant. All the time he humiliates his wife and never shares or reciprocates her feelings. Ranjan, because of the over influence of his mother, has a kind of 'mother-fixation'. Every now and then he refers to his mother and considers his wife inferior to her in every respect. There is an implied suggestion of his impotence, "Clumsy- sex honey-moon", their "love making was always a let down", and his frequent excuses like "Sinus headache", "gas", "joint pains", muscular cramps", "blurred vision". He himself says that he tried to have relationship with six women but failed. Thus Maya is both physically and emotionally deprived. And this is responsible for her fall into adultery. Her relationship with Nikhil is partly because of her and more because of Nikhil's boldness. He provides her all that is denied to her by her husband, which makes her succumb to his advances. When she comes to know about Nikhil's marriage, she breaks away from him. She is only partly responsible for adultery. The real person responsible for it is her husband. Success of marriage depends on mutual understanding and emotional bondage. It can never be a one-way traffic. Through this novel, Shobhaa De emphasizes the importance of caring and understanding husband. The husband should realize and respect the feelings of his wife, for she too has a personality and identity. Unless such relationship is established, no marriage can succeed. In our culture, this has been mentioned in many places. In Sanskrit, one of the words for wife is *Ardhāngini* meaning half of the body. The *Rigveda* says that a wife truly is the home. Without her, man is incomplete:

> She, the wife, in sooth, is one half of his own self; hence, as long as he does not obtain her, so long he is not regenerated, for so long he is incomplete. But as soon as he obtains her, he is regenerated, for than he is complete. 'Complete I want to go to that supreme goal,' thus thinking he, therefore, invites his wife.[6]
>
> (Shapāth Brahmana)

In the following *sloka*, the importance of woman is described and we find the half male and half-female form of Shiva:

> असारभूते संसारे सारभूता नितम्बिनी ।
> इति सजिंत्य वै शम्भुरर्धांग्रे पार्वती दधौ ।।

(In this unsubstantial world, the only substance is the woman. That is why Lord Shiva made Parvati his half.) The novel upholds the importance of woman and attacks the foolish male attitude. The emphasis is on a harmonious relationship between the spouses for the success of marriage.

Since, Shobhaa De is a woman and writes about women, it is but natural that she is called a feminist. But she clearly denies it and rejects the label. She prefers to call herself humanist, which implies that she does not want gender confinement. She has described different roles of women in her novels. Though she is primarily concerned with women and advocates for their intellectual freedom and economic independence, she does not deny the importance of man. She pleads for women's emancipation through education and mental capability to take decision. As stated earlier, though her novels deal with explicit description of sexuality, yet when we read them closely we find, as this study shows, that the real meaning is beneath the surface. And thus she upholds traditional Indian values. This surface portrayal of sexuality in so many words is actually for its condemnation. The general assumption and critical opinion about her is wrong because it does not go beneath the surface. Beneath the turbulent waves of her novels runs the placid current of age-old traditional values, which can be found only by those who go deep into her novels. Thus, she is neither 'Porn pasha' nor 'Vatsyayani' but a writer with meaningful message.

Shobhaa De started her writing earlier with feminist concerns but with the passage of time and the growth in the vision of the novelist, she becomes feminist-cum-humanist, highlighting the problem of urban women and suggesting them ways to be self-reliant and independent through education and economic independence.

Shobhaa De is not a feminist in the sense that she does not accept this label for her writings. However, since she writes about women, therefore, she can be called a feminist; but the ultimate emphasis, as she has said herself, is on human values and all her novels, as discussed in the body of the thesis, project and uphold the traditional Indian values with a focus on family and homely life. This is why Shobhaaa De has taken the help of a lengthy quotation from the "Hindu Sanskaras" on marriage in her latest book "Spouse: The Truth About Marriage" on page 283 of Penguin Publication, New Delhi:

> Marriage, a permanent and stable union[sic]. Marriage is not temporary contract to serve the momentary physical demand or to enjoy good company for

> sometime and then to lapse at the slightest inconvenience. It is a permanent union which stands various vicissitudes in life only to grow stronger and more stable.
>
> Firm and life long companionship is the objective in view. This aspect of marriage is highly prized and the husband pays to the goddess Sarasvati; to protect it: "Saraswati, promote this' understanding, O gracious one, O Bountiful one, thou who will sing first of all that is; in whom what is has been born: in whom this whole world dewlls- that song I will sing today, which will be the highest glory of woman.

Simply to see a "Superstar India"[7] on this globe, embellish with Indians having virtuous characts of "Duety, dignity, forgiveness, empathy, honesty, purity, patience, knowledge, truth, faith, identity, love and peace though a perfect regulated life and character" as emphasized in the ten characterstics of *dharma* without any attachment with eventuality, but giving full regards to the "mother and motherland, which are even higher than the heaven", to revive the lost golden phase once again.

NOTES

1. Quoted in Vijay Bahadur Singh, *Kamakunj* (Varanasi: Mahashakti Sahitya Mandir, 1933), p. 9.
2. *Ibid.*, p. 46.
3. Quoted in P.K. Agrawala, *The Unknown Kamasutras* (Varanasi: Book Asia, 1983), p. 65.
4. *Kamakunj*, p. 17.
5. *Selective Memory*, p. 475.
6. Quoted in *The Unknown Kamasutras*, p. 149.
7. The title of the book "Superstar India" by Shobhaa De, [New Delhi: Penguin Books India (Pvt.) Ltd., 2008].

Bibliography

PRIMARY SOURCES

Fiction

De, Shobhaa. *Socialite Evenings*, New Delhi: Penguin Book India (P) Ltd., 1988-89.

——. *Starry Nights*. New Delhi: Penguin Books India (P) Ltd., 1991.

——. *Sisters*. New Delhi: Penguin Books India (P) Ltd., 1992.

——. *Strange Obsession*. New Delhi: Penguin Books India (P) Ltd., 1992.

——. *Sultry Days*. Included in *The Shobhaa De' Omnibus*. New Delhi: Viking Penguin Books India (P) Ltd., 1995.

——. *Snapshots*. Included in *The Shobhaa De' Omnibus*. New Delhi: Viking Penguin Books India (P) Ltd., 1995.

——. *Second Thoughts*. New Delhi: Penguin Books India (P) Ltd., 1996.

Non-Fiction

De, Shobhaa and Khuswant Singh. *Uncertain Liaisons*. New Delhi: Viking/Penguin Books India (P) Ltd., 1993.

De, Shobhaa. *Shooting from the Hip*. New Delhi: UBS (Pvt.) Ltd., 1994.

De, Shobhaa. *Small Betrayals*. New Delhi: UBS Publishers Distributors Ltd., 1995, 1997.

——. *Surviving Men*. New Delhi: Penguin Books Ltd., 1997.

——. *Speed Post*. New Delhi: Penguin Books Ltd., 1999.

——. *Superstar India*, New Delhi: Penguin Books (Pvt.) Ltd., 2008.

——. *Selective Memory: Stories from My life*. New Delhi: Penguin Books Ltd., 1998.

——. *The Shobhaa De' Omnibus*. New Delhi: Viking Penguin Books (p) Ltd., 1995.

SECONDARY SOURCES

Books

1997 *Britannica Book of the Year*, Encyclopaedia Britannica Inc., Chicago, USA.

Abrahms, M. H. *The Mirror and the Lamp: Romantic Theory and the Critical Tradition*. New York: W.W. Norton, 1958.

Abrams, M.H. *A Glossary of Literary Terms*. Bangalore: Prism Books Pvt. Ltd., 1993.

Absent Authority: *Issues in Contemporary Indian English Criticism*. New Delhi: Sterling, 1992.

Aitereya Brahamana

Amico, Eleanor B. ed. *Reader's Guide to Women's Studies (A Report)*. London: Fitzroy Dearbon Publishers, 1998.

Amur, G.S. *Forbidden Fruit: Views on Indo-Anglian Fiction*. Calcutta: Writers Workshop, 1992.

Anari M. Shyam. *"New Morality in Modern Indo-English Novel" in Explorations in Modern Indo-English Fiction*. New Delhi: Bahri, 1982.

Ashcroft, Bill, Gareth Griffiths and Helen Tiffin. *The Empire Writes Back*. London. Methen, 1987.

Asnani, M. Shyam. *Critical Response to Indian English Fictions*. Delhi: Mittal Publicaiton, 1985.

Asnani, M. Shyam. *Critical Response to Indian English Fiction*. Delhi: Mittal Publications, 1986.

Atharva-Veda

Atwood, Margaret. *Survival: A Thematic Guide to Canadian Literature*. Toronto: Anansi, 1872.

Auerbach, Nina. *Communities of Women: An Idea in Fiction.* Massachusetts: Harvard University Press, 1978.

Awasthi, Kamal N. *Contemporary Indian Fiction: An Anthology of Essays.* Jalandhar: ABS Publication, 2001.

Bai, K. Meera. *The Novels of Indian Women Writers.* New Delhi: Prestige, 1996.

Barua, Geeta, "Rise and Fall of a Star: A Study of *Starry Nights*" in *Indian Women Novelists.*

Beauvoir, Simone de. *The Second Sex.* London: Penguin Books, 1978.

Bechmer, Elleke. *Colonial and Post-colonial Literature.* New Delhi: Oxford University Press, 1995.

Benson, Eugene and Conolly L.W. eds. *Encyclopaedia of Post-Colonial Literatures in English.* London and New York: Routledge, 1994.

Bharucha, Nilufer E. and Sarang Vilas ed. *Indian English Fiction 1980-1900: A Assessment.* New Delhi: B.R. Publishing Corporation, 1994.

Bhatnagar, M.K. *Comparative English Literature.* New Delhi: Prestige Books, 1998.

Bhatnagar, M.K. ed. *Feminist English Literature.* New Delhi: Atlantic Publishers and Distributors, 1999.

Bhatnagar, Manmohan K. ed. *Commonwealth English Literature.* New Delhi: Atlantic Publishers and Distributors, 1999.

Bhatnagar, Manmohan K. and M. Rajeshwar. ed. *Post-Modernism and English Literature.* New Delhi: Atlantic Publishers and Distributors, 1999.

Bhatt, Indira. "Shobhaa De's *Sultry Days* and Gita Mehta's *A River Sutra*: A study in Orientalism" in *Indian Women Novelists.*

Blain, Virginia and Others. *The Feminist Companion to Literature in English: Women Writers from the Middle Ages to the Present.* New Delhi: Atlantic Publishers and Distributors, 1995.

Bande, Usha. *Victime Consciousness in Indian—English Novel.* Jalandhar: ABS Publication, 2001.

Booth, Wayne C. *The Rhetoric of Fiction.* Chicago: University of Chicago Press, 1961.

Bourdieu, Pierre. *Language and Symbolic Power.* Cambridge: Polity Press, 1994.

Brhadaranyaka-Upanishad

Bridgwater, William and Seymour Kurtz ed. *The Columbia Encyclopedia,* Vol. V., New York: Columbia University Press (USA), 1963, Third Edition.

Burman, Erica. *Feminist and Psychological Practice.* New Delhi: Sage Publication, 1990.

Chakravorty, D.K. *Aspects of Indian Fiction in English.* Calcutta: Sahitya Prakash, 1985.

Chandra, Subhash. "Family and Marriage in Shobhaa De's *Socialite Evening" in Indian Women Novelists*, 1995.

Chaudhary, Bidulata. *Woman and Society in the Novels of Amita Desai.* New Delhi: Creative Books, 1995.

Cowasjee, Saros. *Studies in Indian and Anglo-Indian Fiction.* New Delhi: Harper Collins India, 1993.

Cowie, A.P. ed. *Oxford Advanced Learner's Dictionary.* (Fourth Edition). Calcutta: Oxford University Press, 1992.

Cuddon, J.A. ed. *A Dictionary of Literary Terms and Literary Theory.* Malden Massachusetts, USA: Black Well Publishers, 2000 (Fourth Edition).

Das, Bijay Kumar. *Critical Essays on Post Colonial Literature.* New Delhi. Atlantic Publishers and Distributors, 2001.

——. *Modern Indian English Poetry.* Bareilly: Prakash Book Depot., 1992.

——. *Perspectives on Indian English Poetry Criticism.* Bareilly: Prakash Book Depot, 1993.

——. *Aspects of Commonwealths Literature.* New Delhi: Creative Books., 1995.

——. "Shobhaa De's *Sisters*: An Appraisal" in *Indian Women Novelists.*

——. *Comparative Literature*. New Delhi: Prestige Books, 2000.

Das, Bijay Kumar. "The Author and the Text: A Study of Shobhaa De's Snapshots". The *Indian Fiction of the Nineties* ed. by R.S. Pathak. New Delhi: Creative Books, 1997.

Das, Veena Noble. ed. *Feminism and Literature*. New Delhi: Prestige, 1995.

Das, Veena Noble and R.K. Dhawan. ed. *Fiction of the Nineties*. New Delhi: Prestige Books, 1994.

Dass, Veena Noble. *Feminism and Literature*. Jalandhar: ABS Publication, 2001.

Data, Amaresh et al., ed. *Encyclopaedia of Indian Literature*. New Delhi: Sahitya Akademi. Vol. I, 1987, Vol. II, 1988, Vol. III, 1989, Vol. IV, 1991, Vol. V, 1992, Vol. VI, 1994.

Derrett, M.E. *The Modern Indian Novel in English: A Comparative Approach*. (Brussels: Editions de L' Institute de Sociologic, University Libre de Bruxelles, 1996).

Desai, Neera and Vibhuti Patel. ed. *Indian Women: Change and Challenge in the International Decade 1975-85*. Bombay: Popular Prakashan Pvt. Ltd., 1985.

Desai, Tripta. *Women in India: A Brief Historical Survey*. New Delhi: Munshiram Manoharlal Publishers Pvt., Ltd., 1992.

Deshpande, Shashi. *The Dark Holds No Terror*. New Delhi: Penguin Books (P.) Ltd., 1990.

Deshpande, Shashi. *The Binding Vore*. New Delhi: Penguin Books India (P) Ltd., 1992.

Dhawan, R.K. (ed.) *Commonwealth Fiction*. New Delhi: Classical, 1988.

Dhawan, R. K. ed. *Indian Women Novelists*, Vol.-I, Set-3. New Delhi: Prestige Books, 1995.

Dhawan, R.K. *50 Years of Indian Writing*. New Delhi: Prestige Books, 1998.

Dhawan, R.K. ed. *Explorations in Modern Indo-English Fiction*. New Delhi: Bahri Publications, 1982.

Dinesh, Kamini. ed. *Between Spaces of Silence: Women Creative Writers*. New Delhi: Sterling, 1994.

Dodia, Jaydipsinh. *The Fiction of Shobhaa De: Critical Study*. New Delhi: Prestige Books, 2000.

——. *Contemporary Indian Writing in English*. New Delhi: Prestige Books, 1999.

Dodiya, Jaydipsinh. ed. *Contemporary Indian Writing in English*. New Delhi: Atlantic Publishers and Distributors, 1999.

Dodiya, Jaydipsinh K. and K.V. Surendram. *Indian Women Writers: Critical Perspective*. New Delhi: Prestige Books, 2000.

Eagleton, Mary. ed. *Feminist Theory: A Reader*. New Delhi: Atlantic Publishers and Distributors, 1999.

Fergusson, Rosalind. *The Penguin Dictionary of Proverbs*. London: Bloomsbury Books, 1983.

Finke, Laurie A. *Feminist Theory, Women's Writing*. New Delhi: Atlantic Publishers and Distributors, 2000.

Foucault, Michael. *The History of Sexuality: An Introduction* (Vol.-I, Trans. Robert Hurley). New York: Pantheon Books, 1978.

Fox Ralph. *The Novel and the People*. London: Lawrence and Wishart, reprinted in 1979.

Francis, Anne Cranny, "Feminist Romance" in *The Polity Reader in Cultural Theory*. Cambridge: Polity, 1994.

French, Myril. *Beyond Power: On Women, Men and Morals*. New York: Summit Books, 1985.

Freud, Sigmund. *Civilization and its Discontents* (trans. James Strachey). New York: W. W. Norton, 1962.

Friday, Nancy. *Women on Top*. New York: Simon and Schuster, 1991.

Friedam, Betty. *The Feminine Mystic*. New Delhi: Penguin Books India (P) Ltd., 1965.

Friedman, Emanual. *Meri Students Encyclopaedia*. Vol. 19, New York: MacMillan Educational Company, 1985.

Frye, Northrop. *The Secular Scripture: A Study of the Structure of Romance.* Massachusetts: Harvard University Press, 1976.

Gadgil, Gangadhar. *Indian Literature: Issues and Explorations.* New Delhi: B.R. Publishing Corporation, 1995.

George, K.M. *Masterpieces of Indian Literature.* 3 Vols. New Delhi: National Book Trust, 1997.

Gilbert, Sandra M. and Gubar, Susan. "The Mirror and the Vamp: Reflection Feminist Criticism", *The Future of Literary Theory,* ed. Ralph Coher, New York: Routlege.

Gopal, N.R. *A Critical Study of the Novel of Anita Desai.* New Delhi: Atlantic Publishers and Distributors, 1995.

Gowda, H.H. Anniah. *Encyclopaedia of Commonwealth Literature.* 2 Vols. New Delhi: Cosmo Publications, 1998; 68 articles on British, American, Indian and Commonwealth Literature.

Grimke, Sarah. *Letters on the Equality of the Sexes and the Conditions of Women.* New York: Burt Frankline, 1970.

Gupta, G.S. Balarama, *The Journal of Indian Writing in English.* Vol. 26, S.No. 1, January 1998, Karnatak: Gulbarga University Press.

Gupta, G.S. Balaram. "Indian English Women Writers" in Ratnam, A.S. ed. *Critical Essays on Indian Woman Writing in English.* New Delhi – Harman Publication House, 1999.

Gupta, Kalpana Das. *Women on the Indian Scene: An Annoted Bibliography.* New Delhi: Abhinav Publications, 1976.

Gwinn, Robert P. *The New Encyclopaedia Britannica,* Vol. 12 (Micropaedia). Chicago, USA, 1985.

Hawat, G.M. ed. *Dictionary of World History.* London: Thomas Nelson and Sons Ltd., 1973.

Hawthorn, Jermy. *Studying the Novel: An Introduction.* New Delhi: Universal Books Stall, 1992.

Hayward, John. ed. *T.S. Eliot: Selected Prose.* Harmondhsworth: Penguin Books, 1958.

Hemenway, Stephen Ignatius. *The Novel of India,* Vol. II. Kolkotta: Writers Workshop, 1975.

Hite, Shere. *The Hite Report: A Nationwide Study of Female Sexuality*. New York: Dell, 1987.

Howe, Irving. *Political and the Novel.* New Delhi: Atlantic Publishers and Distributors, 2000.

Iyengar, K.R.S. *Indian Writing in English*. Bombay: Asian Publishing House, 1962.

Iyengar, K.R. Srinivasa. *Indian Writing in English*. New Delhi: Sterling Publishers Private Limited, 2000.

Jaidev, "Feminism and the Contemporary Hindu Novel" in *On Literature*, ed. Jaidev. Shimla: Indian Institute of Advanced Study, 1990.

Jain K. Naresh. *Women in Indo-Anglican Fiction*. New Delhi: Manohar Publishers, 1998.

Jain, Naresh K. ed. *Women in Indo-Anglian Fiction: Tradition and Modernity*. New Delhi: Manohar, 1998.

Jain, Nik. ed. *Women in Indo-Anglican Fiction: Tradition and Modernity*. New Delhi: Atlantic Publishers and Distributors, 1998.

Jones, Elders. *The Writing of Wole Soyinka*. London: Heinemann, 1973.

Joshi, Arun. *The Strange Case of Billy Biswas*. Delhi: Orient Paperbacks, 1971.

Jung, Anees. *Unveiling India*. New Delhi: Penguin, 1988.

Kakar, Sudhir. *The Indian Psyche*. New Delhi: Oxford University Press, 1998.

Kalidas. *Kumara-sambhava*.

Kalinnikova, Elana J. *Indian English Literature: A Survey*. Ghaziabad: Vimal Prakashan, 1982.

Kamal, N. Awasthi. ed. *Contemporary Indian English Fiction: An Anthology of Essays*. Jalandhar: ABS Publications, 1994.

Kaplan, Cora. *See Changes: Culture and Feminism*. London: Verso, 1986.

Kautilya, *Arthasastra.*

Kenyon, Olag. *Women Novelist Today.* Sussex: The Harvester Press, 1990.

Kettle, Arnold. *An Introduction to the English Novel.* London: Hutehinson, 1967. Vol. I.

Khan A.G. *Literature: Some New Respective.* New Delhi: Prestige Books, 1999.

Khan, A.G. "*Liberated or Libidinous*: Women Writing English" in R.K. Dhawan's *Indian Women Novelists*, 1995.

Khan, A.G. "Shobhaa De "Vatsyanani", R.K. Dhawan ed. *Fiction of the Ninneties.* New Delhi: Prestige Books, 1994.

Khan, M.Q. and A.G. Khan ed. *Changing Faces of Women in Indian Writing in English.* New Delhi: Creative Books, 1995.

Khan, M.Q. and A.G. Khan. *Writing in English.* New Delhi: Prestige Books, 1999.

Khan, M.Q. and Khan A.G. *Changing Faces of Woman in Indian Writing in English.* New Delhi: Creative Publishers, 1996.

King, Bruce. *The New English Literature – Cultural Nationalism in Changing World.* New York: St. Martin's, 1980.

King, Bruce. ed. *New National and Post-Colonial Literatures: An Introduction.* New Delhi: Oxford University Press, 1996.

King, Bruce (ed.) *Literature of the World in English.* London Routledge and Kegan Paul, 1974.

Klein, Yiola. *The Feminine Character.* London: Rutledge, 1959.

Klotz, Marvin and Abcarian, Richard. ed. *Literature: The Human Experience.* New Delhi: Atlantic Publishers and Distributors, 2000.

Kripalani, Krishna. *Modern Indian Literature: A Panoramic Glimpse.* 1968.

Kumar, Shiv K. *Contemporary Indian Literature in English*. Shimla: Indian Institute of Advanced Study and New Delhi: Manohar Publications, 1992.

Kumar, Sudhir. "Artist as Vamp: A Feminist Approach to Shobhaa De's Starry Nights", R.K. Dhawan (ed.), *Indian Women Novelists*, Vol. I, Set-3. New Delhi: Prestige Books, 1995.

Kumar, V.N. Narendra. *New Perspectives on Indian Writing*. V.I. New Delhi: Prestige, 1997.

Linear, Marcus. *Zapping the Third World: The Disaster of Development Aid*. London: Pluto Press, 1985.

Lodge, D. *Modern Criticism and Theory: A Reader*. London: Longman, 1989.

Lodge, David. ed. *Modern Criticism and Theory: A Reader*. London: Longman, 1988.

Lodge, David. ed. *20th Century Literary Criticism: A Reader*. London: Longman, 1989.

Londfors, Bernth and Bala Kothandaraman (ed.). *South Asian Responses to Chinua Achebe*. New Delhi: Prestige Books, 1993.

Lytard, Jean-Francois. *The Inhuman: Reflections on Time*, (trans.) Geoffrey Bennington and Rachel Bowlby. Cambridge: Polity Press, 1991.

Machwe, Prabhakar. *Four Decades of Indian Literature: A Critical Evaluation*. New Delhi: Chetna Publications, 1975.

Macnell, Sally, Ginet Ruth Borkar and Nelly Furman. ed. *Women and Language in Literature and Society*. New York: Praeger, 1980.

Madge, V.M. "Shobhaa De's Starry Nights" in Ratnam, A.S. ed. *Critical Essays on Indian Woman Writing in English*. New Delhi – Harman Publication House, 1999.

Mahabharata, the.

Manoni, O., Preopero and Caliban. *The Psychology of Colonization*. New York: Fedrick A. Prager, 1956.

Manusmriti.

Mathur, O.P. *Modern Indian English Fiction.* Delhi: Abhinav Publications, 1993.

McCallm, Dorthey Kaufman. *Politics of Difference: The Women's Movement in France from May 1968 to Mitterand.* (Paris: Winter, 1983).

Miles, Rosalind. "Writers and Women Writers". *Women Writers and the Conquest of the Novel.* New York: Routledge and Kegan Paul, 1987.

Milett, Kate. *Sexual Politics.* Garden City N.Y.: Doubleday, 1970.

Moi, Toril. *Sexual/Textual Politics: Feminist Literary Theory.* London: Methuen, 1985.

Mongia, Padmini. *Contemporary Post-Colonial Theory.* New Delhi: Oxford University Press, 1998.

Morgan, R. *The Anatomy of Freedom: Feminism Physics and Global Politics.* Oxford: Martin Robertson, 1983.

Morgan, Robin. *The Anatomy of Freedom: Feminism, Physics, and Global Politics.* New York: Doubleday, 1982.

Mukherjee, Meenakshi (ed.). *Considerations.* New Delhi: Allied Publishers, 1977.

Nabar, Vindra. *Caste As Woman.* New Delhi: Penguin Books (P.) Ltd., 1995.

Nafzavi, Sheikh. *The Glory of the Perfumed Garden.* London: Granada, 1978.

Nagarajan, M.S., Ekambaram N. and Natarajan A. ed. *Essays in Criticism on Indian Literature in English.* Parbhani: Dnyanopasak Prakashan, 1991.

Nahal, Chaman, "Feminism in English Fiction: Forms and Variations" (*Feminism and Recent Fiction in English*, New Delhi: Prestige Books, 1990).

Naik, M.K. *Aspects of Indian Writing in English.* New Delhi: MacMillan, 1979.

——. *Mulk Raj Anand.* New Delhi: Arnold Heinemann, 1973.

——. *A History of Indian English Literature*. New Delhi: Sahitya Akademi, 1982.

Naik, M.K. and Shyamala A. Narayan. *Indian English Literature 1980-2000: A Critical Survey*. New Delhi: Pencraft International, 2000.

Naik, P.M. and Swain S.P. eds. *Feminism and Indian English Fiction*. Bareilly: Prakash Book Depot, 1997.

Nanavati, U.M. and Kar Prafulla C. *Rethinking Indian English Literature*. New Delhi: Pencraft, 2000.

Narasimhaiah, C.D. and Srinath C.N. eds. *Women in Fiction, Fiction by Women*. Mysore: Dhvanyaloka Publications, 1987.

Narasimhaiah, C.D. *Commonwealth Literature. A Handbook of Selected Reading List*. New Delhi: Oxford University Press, 1976.

Narasimhaiah, C.D. (ed.) *The Awakened Conscience*. New Delhi: Sterling Publishers, 1978.

Narasimhaiah, C.D. *Essays in Commonwealth Literature*. Delhi: Pencraft International, 1995.

Natarajan, Nalini. ed. *Handbook of Twentieth Century Literature of India*. Westport, Connecticut: Greenwood Press, 1996.

Nayak, P.M. ed. *Feminism and Indian English Fiction*. Bareilly: Prakash Book Depot, 1996.

Naylor, Gloria. *The Women of Brewster Place*. London: Sphere Books, 1984.

Palmer, Pauling. *Contemporary Women's Fiction: Narrative Practice and Feminist Theory*. New York: Harvester Wheatsheat, 1989.

Pandey Surya Nath. ed. *Writing in a Post Colonial Space*. New Delhi: Atlantic Publishers and Distributors, 1999.

——. ed. *Contemporary Indian Women Writers in English*. New Delhi: Atlantic Publishers and Distributors, 1999.

Pandey, Mithilesh K. *Recent Indian Literature in English*. New Delhi: Prestige Books, 2000.

Pandey, Mithilesh K. ed. *Contemporary Indian Literature in English: A Cultural Perspective.* New Delhi: Anmol Publications, 1999.

——. ed. *Contemporary Indian Literature in English: A Humanistic Perspective.* Ludhiana and New Delhi: Kalyani Publications, 1999.

Pandey, Prabhat Kumar. "Tender, Beautiful and Erotic: Lesbianism in Shobhaa De's *Starry Nights*" in *Indian Women Novelists.*

Paniker, Ayyappa K. ed. *Indian English Literature Since Independence.* New Delhi: Indian Association for English Studies, 1991.

——. ed. *Contemporary Indian Fiction in English.* Trivandrum: University of Kerala, 1987.

Papaneck, Henna and Gail Minault. *Separate Worlds: Studies of Purdah in South Asia.* New Delhi: Chanakya Publications, 1982.

Parameswaran, Uma. *A Study of Representative Indo-English Novelists.* New Delhi: Vikas Publishing House, 1984.

Paranjape, Makarand. ed. *Nativism: Essay in Criticism.* New Delhi: Sahitya Akademi, 1997.

Pathak, R.S. *Indian Fiction of the Nineties.* New Delhi: Creative Books, 1997.

——. *Recent Indian Fiction.* New Delhi: Prestige Books, 1994.

——. "Shobhaa De: from *Starry Nights* to *Sultry Days*" in *Indian Women Novelists.*

——. *Modern Indian Novel in English.* New Delhi: Creative Books, 1999.

Pathak, R.S. ed. *Indian Fiction of the Nineties.* New Delhi: Creative Books, 1997.

——. ed. *Indian Response to Literary Theories.* New Delhi: Creative Books, 1996.

Pathak, R.S. *Modern Indian Novel in English.* New Delhi: Creative Books, 1999.

Pathak, R.S. ed. *Recent Indian Fiction*. New Delhi: Prestige Books, 1999/2000.

Pathak, R.S. *Modern Indian Novel in English*. New Delhi: Creative Books, 1999.

Pathak, R.S. ed. *Indian Fiction in English: Problems and Promises*. New Delhi: Northern Book Centre, 1990.

——. ed. *Recent Indian Fiction*. New Delhi: Prestige, 1994.

Plane, Jack C. and Roy Otan. *The International Relations Dictionary*. California: Santa Barbara, ABC-CUO, 1988.

Prabhakar, M. *Feminism/Postmodernism: Margaret Atwood's Fiction*. New Delhi: Creative Books, 1999.

Prabhu, Pandharinath H. *Hindu Social Organization: A Study is Social-Psychological and Ideological Foundations*. Bombay: Popular, 1958.

Prakash, Bhagwan. *Indian Themes in English Fiction: A Socio-Literary Study*. New Delhi: Mittal Publications, 1995.

Prasad, Amar Nath. (ed.) *Indian Women Novelist in English*. New Delhi: Atlantic Publishers and Distributors, 2001.

Prasad, Madhusudan. ed. *Indian English Novelist: An Anthology of Critical Essays*. New Delhi: Sterling, 1982.

Pratt, Annis, *Archetypal Patterns in Women's Fiction*. Bloomington: Indiana University Press, 1981.

Pres, Joh, ed. *Commonwealth Literature*. London: Heinemann, 1965.

Radhakrishnan S. Introduction to *Great Women of India*.

Rai, Soudha. *V.S. Naipaul: A Study in Expatriate Sensibility*. Atlantic Highlands, NJ: Humanities Press, 1982.

Rajan, Rajeshwari Sunder. ed. *Signposts: Gender Issues in Post-Independence India*. New Delhi: Kali for Women, 1999.

Rajeshwar, M. and P.M. Rao. ed. *Indian Fiction in English*. New Delhi: Atlantic Publishers and Distributors, 1999.

Rajeshwar, M. *Indian Women Novelist and Psychoanalysis: A Study of Neurotic Character*. New Delhi: Atlantic Publishers and Distributors, 1998.

Ram Atma. *Essays on Indian English Literature*. Aurangabad: Parimal, 1984.

Ramaswamy, S. *Explorations: Essays on Commonwealth Literature*. Bangalore: M.C.C. Publication, 1988.

Ramayana, the.

Ramswamy, S. *Exploration: Essays on Commonwealth Literature*. Bangalore: MCC Publicaitons, 1988.

Ranjan, R.K. ed. *Changing Traditions in Indian English Literature*. New Delhi: Prestige Books, 2000.

Rao, A. Ramakrishna and Sivaramakrishna M. eds. *When East Meets West: Indian Thought in Anglo-Indian and Indo-English Fiction*. New Delhi: Sterling, 1994.

Rao, Bhargavi P. "From Purdah to Popular Culture: Anees Jung's *Unveiling India* and Shobhaa De's *Socialite Evenings*" in R.K. Dhawan ed. *Indian Women Novelists*, New Delhi: Prestige Books 1995, Set III, Vol. I.

Ratnam, A.S. ed. *Critical Essays on Indian Woman Writing in English*. New Delhi – Harman Publication House, 1999.

Ratnam, A.S. *Critical Essays on Indian Women Writing in English*. New Delhi: Prestige Books, 1997.

Ratnam, A.S. ed. *Chiaroscuro: Critical Essays on Indian Writing in English*. Parbhani: Dnyanopasak Prakashan, 1991.

Raymond, Janice G. *A Passion for Friends: Towards a Philosophy of Female Affection*. London: Women's, 1986.

Readford, Jean. ed. *The Progress of Romance: The Politics of the Popular Fiction*. London: Routledge and Kegan Paul, 1986.

Reddy, K. Venkata and P.B. Reddy. ed. The *Indian Novel with a Social Purpose*. New Delhi: Atlantic Publishers and Distributors, 1999.

Rig-Veda

Rowbotham, Sheila. *Woman's Consciousness*, Man's World. England: Penguin Books, 1986.

Roy Anuradha. *Patterns of Feminist Consiousness*, Prestige Books, New Delhi, 1999.

Roy, Anuradha. ed. *Patterns of Feminist Consciousness in Indian Women Writers*. New Delhi: Prestige Books, 2000.

Ruth, Sheila. (Third Edition). *Issues in Feminism: An Introduction to Women's Studies*. New Delhi: Atlantic Publishers and Distributors, 2000.

Ruthven, K.K. *Feminist Literary Studies: An Introduction.* Cambridge: Cambridge University Press, 1984.

Ruthven K.K. *Feminist Literary Studies: An Introduction*, 1994.

Ruthven, K.K. *Feminist Literature Studies: An Introduction.* New Delhi: Atlantic Publishers and Distributors, 2000.

Satara, Chhatrapati Shivaji College. *Commonwealth Literature—Recent Respective.* New Delhi: Creative Books, 1999.

Scannel, Paddy, Philipshlesigner, Colin Spark. ed. *Culture and Power: A Media, Culture and Society Reader*. London: Sage, 1992.

Schneider, Dorathy and Carl J. Schneider. *American Women in the Progressive Era; 1900-1920.* New York: Facts on File, 1923.

Seema, Suneel. *Man-Woman Relationship in Indian Fiction.* New Delhi: Prestige Books, 2000.

Selden, R ed. *The Theory of Criticism: From Plato to the Present: A Reader*. London: Longman, 1988.

Seligman, R.A. *Encyclopaedia of the Social Sciences,* Vol. III, Chicago MacMillan Company, Twelfth print, 1957.

Seshadri, Vijayalakshmi. *The New Woman in Indian English Women Writers Since the 1970s.* New Delhi: B.R. Publishing Corporation, 1995.

Sharma, B.D. and S.K. Sharma. *Contemporary Indian English Novel.* New Delhi: Prestige Books, 2000.

Sharma, K.K. ed. *Feminism and Literature: New Points of View*. Delhi: K.K. Publication, 1996.

Showalter, Elaine. *A Literature of their Own: Women Writers from Bronte to Lessing*. New Jersey: Princeton University, 1977.

Showalter, Elaine. ed. *The New Feminist Criticism*. New Pantheon Books, 1985.

Singh Avadesh K. ed. *Contemporary Indian Fiction in English*. New Delhi: Creative Books, 1993.

Singh R.S. *Indian Novels in English: A Critical Study*. New Delhi: Arnold Heinemann Publication Ltd., 1990.

Singh, A.K. *Contemporary Indian Fiction in English*. New Delhi: Prestige Books, 2000.

Singh, Chaaru Sheel. ed. *Confederate Gestures: Search for Method in Indian Literature Studies*. New Delhi: Associated Publishing House, 1993.

Singh, Dr. R.A. and VLVN Narendra Kumar. ed. *Critical Studies on Indian Fiction in English*. New Delhi: Atlantic Publishers and Distributors, 1999.

Singh, Pramod Kumar. (ed.) *Indian Fiction in English*. New Delhi: Atlantic Publishers and Distributors, 2001.

Singh, Shushila. *Feminism: Theory, Criticism, Analysis*. New Delhi: Prestige Books, 1998.

Singh, Sushila. ed. *Feminism and Recent Fiction in English*. New Delhi: Prestige Books, 1998.

Singh, Vijay Bahadur. *Kamakunj*. Varanasi: Mahashakti Sahitya Mandir, 1933.

Sinha, Anita. *Feminist Visions: Indian English Women Novelists*. New Delhi: Creative Books, 2000.

Spacks, Patricia Meyer. *The Female Imagination*. New York, 1975.

Spivak, Gayatri Chakravorty. *In Other worlds: Essays in Cultural Politics*. New York: Methuen, 1987.

Spivak, Gayatri Chakravorty. "Postmarked Calcutta, India", in *The Post-Colonial Critic*, ed. Sarah Harasym. New York and London: Routledge, 1990.

Srivastava K. Ramesh. *Symbolism in Indian Fiction in English*. Jalandhar City: ABC Publication, 2001.

Srivastava, Sahrad. *The New Woman in Indian English Fiction*. New Delhi: Creative Books, 1996.

Sundaram, P.S. *R.K. Narayan*. New Delhi: Arnold Heinemann, 1974.

Sur, A.K. *Sex and Marriage in India: An Ethno-Historical Sruvey*. Bombay: Allied, 1973.

Swamy, Shantha Krishna. *The Women in Indian Fiction in English*. New Delhi: Ashish Publishing House, 1984.

Tharu, Susie and Lalita K. *Women Writing in India*. Vol. I and II. New Delhi: Oxford University Press, 1993.

Tharu, Susie and K Lalita. ed. *Women Writing in India*. New York: The Feminist Press, Vol. I, 1991, Vol. II, 1993.

The World Book of Encyclopaedia. Vol. 21 (WXYZ). Chicago: Field Enterprises Educational Corporation, USA, 1976.

Tikoo, P.N. *Indian Women*. Delhi: B.R. Publishing Corporation, 1985.

Todd, Janet. *Women's Friendship in Literature*. New York: Columbia University Press, 1980.

Tong, Rosemarie. *Feminist Thought*, London: Routledge, 1993.

Tripathi, J.P. "Shobhaa De's *Snapshots: The Overwhelming Question* in *Indian Fiction of the Nineties* ed. by R.S. Pathak. New Delhi: Creative Books. 1997.

Trivedi, Harish and Meenakshi Mukherjee *Interrogating Post-Colonialism: Theory, Text and Context*. Shimla: Indian Institute of Advanced Study, 1996.

Trivedi, Nisha, "Search for Identity in Shobhaa De's Starry Nights" in *Indian Woman Novelists*.

Uma Alladi. "Is There Anything Beyond?" in Ratnam, A.S. ed. *Critical Essays on Indian Woman Writing in English*. New Delhi: Harman Publication House, 1999.

——. *Woman and Her Family*. New Delhi: Sterling, 1989.

Varma, R.M. *Some Aspects of Indo-English Fiction*. New Delhi: Atlantic Publishers and Distributors, 1998.

Vashista, B.K. ed., *Encyclopaedia of Women in India*. New Delhi: Praveen Encyclopaedia Publications, 1976.

Vassani, M.G. *No New Land*. Toronto: Mehelland and Stewart, 1991.

Wagner, Jane. *The Search for Signs of Intelligent Life in the Universe*. New York: Harper and Row, 1987.

Walker, Alexander. *Woman: Physiologically Considered as to Mind, Morals, Marriage, Matrimonial Slavery, Infidelity and Divorce*. Delhi: Mittal, 1987.

Walker, Nancy. "Feminist Alternatives: Irony and Fantasy" in *the Contemporary Novel by Women*. Jackson: Univ. Press of Mississippi, 1990.

Walker, Nancy A. *Feminist Alternatives: Irony and Fantasy in the Contemporary Novel by Women*. New Delhi: Atlantic Publishers and Distributors, 2000.

Walsh, William. *Indian Literature in English*. London: Longman, 1990. (Longman Literature in English Series).

Walsh, Williams. "A Mainfold Voice." *Studies in Commonwealth Literature*. London: Chatto and Widus, 1970.

Walsh, Williams. *Commonwealth Literature*. Oxford Paperback University Series, London: Oxford University Press, 1973.

Walsh, Williams. (ed.) *Readings in Commonwealth Literature*. Oxford: Claredon Press, 1973.

Walsh, Williams. *Indian Literature in English*. London: Longman, 1990.

Ward A.W., G.W. Prothero and Stanley Leather. *The Cambridge Modern History,* Vol. XII, Cambridge University Press, 1910.

Warhol, Robyn R and Price Herndl, eds. *Feminism: An Anthology of Literary Theory and Criticism,* Brunswick NJ: Rutgers University Press, 1991.

Warhop Robyn R. and Dianna Price Herndle. ed. *Feminism: An Anthology of Literary Theory and Criticism*. N. Brunswick, NJ: Rutgers University Press, 1991.

Who's Who of Indian Writers. 1999. 2 Vols. New Delhi: Sahitya Akademi, 2000.

Williams, Haydn Moore. *Galaxy of Indian Writings in English*. Delhi: Akshat Publications, 1987.

Williams, Patrick and Laura Chrisman (eds.) *Colonial Discourse and Post-colonial Theory: A Reader*. London: Harvester Wheatsheaf, 1993.

Wolf, V. *The Common Reader* (1st Series), London: The Hogarth Press, 1953.

Wolgat, Elizabeth H. *Equality and Rights of Women*. Ithaca: Cornell University Press, 1980.

Wollstonecraft, Mary. *A Vindication of the Rights Woman, Carol H. Poston,* ed. New York: W.W. Norton, 1975.

Woolf, Virginia. *A Room of One's Own*. New York: Harcourt, Breace and World, 1929.

Woolf, Virginia. *The Guineas*. New York: Harcourt, Brace and World, 1963.

Yajur-Veda

Periodical and Journals

Agrawal, Amit. "The Great Race". *India Today*. p. 209, New Delhi, October 15, 1994.

Agrawal, Amit. October 11, 1994, *India Today*, p. 251, New Delhi.

Agrawala, P.K. *The Unknown Kamasutras*. Varanasi: Book Asia, 1983.

Alikhan, Anvar. "The Lakme School of Literature". *Indian Review of Books*, pp. 24-25. New Delhi. (16 Feb. 1995 to 15 March 1995).

Banerjee, Nandini. "Review of Sultry Days," *The Hindustan Times*. New Delhi, 9 April, 1994, p. 4.

Bhattacharya's, Sourish. "Enter, the Supermom." *The Hindustan Times Magazine*. New Delhi: November 21. 1999.

Days and Years of De. *The Times of India*. New Delhi: Saturday 03. 1998.

De, Shobhaa. "The Sexes." *The Week*. June 30. 2002.

De, Shobhaa. "Echoes of Snapshots" in *Indian Review of Books*. New Delhi. 1993.

Employment News Weekly. Vol. XXVI. No. 48. New Delhi: Ministry of I&B, R.K. Puram. 2-8 March 2002.

Equality: A fair and foul deal. The Times of India. New Delhi: March 8. 2001.

Guha, Nandini. "Shobhaa De." *The Saturday Statesman*. Calcutta: August 1. 1998.

Jha, Raj Kamal. "Pulp Fiction". *India Today*. pp. 211-12. New Delhi 28th February, 1995.

Jha, Subhash K. "A New De' Dawns" in *Indian Review of Books*. 16 May 1995 – 15 June 1995.

Katyal, Anita. "Days of bra-burning feminism are over." *The Times of India*. New Delhi: June 8, 2001.

Paranjape, Makarand. "*A Good Time to be A Writer, But.*" Indian Review of Books. pp. 20-24. New Delhi, 1992.

Patil, Vimala. "Abhi door hai manjil." "(The Destination is still far off)." (Hindi Translation) *The Dainik Jagaran*. Varanasi, U.P.: March 8, 2002.

Raghavendra, M.K. "Smut and Sensibility" in *Indian Review of Books*. pp. 24-25. New Delhi. 16 June 1995 – 15 July 1995.

Sanghvi, Malavika. "The Word Factory." *The Times of India*. New Delhi: January 28, 2001.

Sethi, Sunil. *De in De Out*. Seminar No. 384, 1991.

Shaikh, Farida. "Mistress of Reinvention." *The Hindustan Times*. New Delhi: Aug. 25, 2002.

Shukla, Ravindra Nath. "Shobhaa De." (Hindi Translation) *The Dainik Jagaran*. Varanasi, U.P.: May 24. 1997.

Surendran, C.P. "Just Another De," *The Illustrated Weekly of India*. 6 November, 1992.

The Times of India. New Delhi: Saturday October 3, 1998.

The Times of India. New Delhi: November 25, 2001.

Varma, Pavan K. "Empress of the First World." *The Indian Express*. New Delhi: October 4, 1998.

Venkata Raman, Janaki. "One More De". *Indian Review of Books*, p. 25, New Delhi, 16 Apr. 1997 – 15 May 1997.

Walunjkar, Somashukla Sinha. "Shobhaa De Storms Soap Box with *Sukanya*." *The Hindustan Times*. New Delhi: December 26, 2000.

Zutshi, Madhvi. "Groping in A Blind Alley" in *Indian Review of Books*. p. 52, New Delhi. 16 July, 1996 – 15 August, 1996.

Appendix

I

> The status of women in any society, is a true index of its cultural, social, religious and spiritual levels. A problem of paramount importance both in ethics and sociology of a people is the status assigned to women in social life. It is one of the criteria of considerable significance in estimating with precision and proper rank attained by a particular group of people in the comity of civilised nations.[1]

This fact is further proved to be true when Elizabeth Cady Stanton says "Social science affirms that a woman's place in society marks the level of civilization".[2] In India, it seems that women are always adored and appreciated by men and society from *Rig-Vedic* time to the present, as has been reflected by the comments on women either in books or by men of eminence. In the *Rig-Veda* there are wishes for a girl who is going to marry, "Over thy husband's father and thy husband's mother bear full sway".[3] "Over the sister of thy lord, over his brothers rule supreme".[4] "Go to the house to be the household's mistress and speak as lady to thy gathered people".[5] Sometimes, she is above man in her role and character as "Yea many a woman is more firm and better than the man who turns away from gods, and offers not".[6] While in *Atharva-Veda,* she has been admired for her unique-cum-prime role in her family and society "as the mighty river won the supremacy of the streams, so be thou supreme, having gone away to thy husband's home".[7] The same thing has been re-uttered in the *Atharva-Veda's* nuptial hymn "Be though supreme among fathers-in-law, supreme also among brothers-in-law, be thou supreme over sisters-in-law, supreme also over mother-in-law".[8] The *Yajur-Veda* through its hymn ensures granting of fundamental rights to women, when it mentions her as the most honourable being in the society. According to it, a "Woman should always be adored by the husband, brother, father, kinsmen, mother-in-law, husband's younger brother and other relatives with ornaments, clothes and food".[9] A woman enjoys such a prestigious place in her home and society simply because of her education and enlightenment, due to which it seems that she was free enough to choose her life-partner at the end of the *Brahmacharya* stage of her life as hinted in *Atharva-Veda* "By Vedic studentship, a girl wins a young husband".[10]

In the Brahmanic period, she enjoyed equality with men in the field of religion because "a man could not become a spiritual whole unless he was accompanied by his wife".[11] In *Upanishads*, which represent the goal of the Vedas to know *Brahamna* by destroying ignorance, the status a woman was equal to that of a man. An ideal wife is treated as the better half of the husband. It has been beautifully delineated by a very telling simile of the half of a shell.[12] In the Epic age, the status of women was very high because they were considered pivots of domestic life as well as of the entire society, which is clearly evident in the *Ramayana* and the *Mahabharata*. Even a maid was looked after with tender care and affection along with emphasis on her education and she was allowed to perform some important duties too. In this age, 'Virtue was an object of reverence,' therefore, dishonour of a woman is considered to be the most heinous crime, its example can be seen in the warning of Mandodari, the chaste and virtuous wife of Ravana, who alerts her husband of impending danger to his life by praising virtuous qualities of Sita. "O you of wicked understanding, it was for the destruction of your wealth, yourself and your relatives that you suddenly cherished a passion for Sita, who is greater than even Arundhati and Rohini. You have been burnt by the fire of her devotion to her husband".[13] So in the Epic Age, a woman was treated as *sahadharmini* and *pativrata* due to which she was honoured everywhere and every time throughout her life. Moreover, they chose their spouse through *Swayamvar*.

In *Manusmriti*, Manu appositely praises womankind with such remarks: "There is no difference between the housewife and the Goddess of Fortune/Both illumine the home and are to be adored as such".[14] "Where women are honoured, there Gods revel, where they are not honoured, all religious acts become futile"[15] (*Yatra naryastu pujyante remante tatra devatah: / Yatraitastu na pujyante sarvastatraphalah kriyah*). "That home perishes in which the daughter-in-law suffers; home cursed by them come to grief".[16] "No religious rite could be performed without the wife [because] the husband and wife are one".[17] "Men should always honour women for their own prosperity and interest".[18] Manu, thus, has assigned esteemed status to women in the home and society of his time.

Kautilya provides even more freedom to womankind compared to Manu, when he declares "the right of a wife to marry another husband under certain circumstances",[19] which provides them with the options of re-marriage and widow-marriage. While, Kalidas a noted *Sanskrit* scholar of his time observes "*Kanyeyam kula—jivitam*"—the girl is the every life of the family,[20] and the *Mahabharata* declares: "*Niyam nivaste lakshmih kanyakasu pratish pratishthia*. Or, in the person of a girl, resides ever steadily fortune as well as grace.[21]

In the Buddhist period too, the women's condition was fine and they achieved glory in the field of education and culture including spiritual attainments. Their condition is reflected in the famous canonical work "The *Their-Gatha*" (Songs of the Nuns) as:

> And be it woman, be it man, for whom
> Such chariot doth wait, but that same car
> Into *Nibbana's* presence shall they come.

Similarly, Lord Mahavira Vardhamana, the twenty-fourth and last *Tirthankaras* emphasised on *samayia* or equality irrespective of caste or sex, that is why Jaina women enjoyed equal rights with men. But, the evil of *purda* and dowry which entered into Indian sub-continent due to Muslim invasion, deteriorated women's status and condition in India. Though, prophet Mohammed had profound respect for women but his followers don't seems to be so. They treated women as a thing of luxury and opted for *purdah* system, which brought in many of its associated evils, because, it is held that as the *purdah* became stricter, prostitution became more popular, while the Moghul *Harem* had its own charms and interesting episodes. Even though there are a few names which are its exceptions: Raziya Sultan, Gulbadan Begum, Nur Jahan, Jahan Ara Begum, Bibi Fatima Sam, Bibi Salikha, Chand Bibi etc. The Sikhs consider gold and woman as two deadly temptations in life, but Guru Gobind Singh changed their views and attitudes towards woman and inspired them to grant women the status of equality.

The British Government in India tried its best to abolish, *Sati* system, *Purdah* system and up to some extent, child-marriages with the help of persistent moral support from people like Raja Ram Mohan Roy. They introduced and encouraged female education so that literacy came to be recognised as a desirable accomplishment, simultaneously they recognised prostitution as a social evil. On the other hand, the Christian missionaries did yeomen service to India by promoting literacy, raising the status of women, building hospitals, encouraging cottage industries and promoting various social services programmes for the uplift of the poor, without any distinction of caste or creed. On the other hand, the Arya Samaj and the Brahma Samaj also worked for the betterment of entire womankind in India. A few pioneering names who contributed towards the upliftment of women including social reforms are: Maharshi Debendranath Tagore, Ishwar Chandra Vidyasagar, Keshab Chandra Sen, M.G. Ranade, Swami Dayananda Saraswathi, Lokamanya Tilak, Sri Aurobindo, Lala Lajpat Rai, Bipinchandra Pal, G.G. Deodher, D.K. Karve, Maharaja Savaji Rao Gaekwad, Mahatma Gandhi, Indira Gandhi and Mother Teresa etc.

There are many eminent women who are not only in themselves embodiment of freedom, for women's emancipation, enlightment, empowerment but who also worked to elevate the status of womankind to new height. Some of the names which we can mention here are from the *Rig-Vedic* period to the present age, they are as: Gargi, Maitreyi, Katyayani, Ghosa, Lopamudra, Sasvati, Apala, Indrani, Leelawati, Sita, Kausalya, Kaikeyi, Sumitra, Uma, Andal, Savitri, Mandodari, Arundhati, Rohini, Anasuya, Shabari, Swayamprabha, Ahalya, Sarama, Trjata, Tara, Gandhari, Kunti, Draupadi, Damayanti, Sakuntala, Satyabhama, Radha, Rukamani, Dhammadinna, Sukka, Princess Sumana, Princess Chandi (Buddhist Nuns), Paumavi, Nur Jahan Begum, Jahan Ara, Bibi Fatima, Bibi Zalikha, Chand Bibi, Smt. M.S. Subbulakshmi, Smt. Rukmini Devi, Smt. Balasaraswati, Smt. Gauri Devi, Vaijayantimala, Padmini, Hemamalini, Saronini Naidu, Putli Bai, Laxmi Bai, Lata Mangeskar, Margaret Alva, Indira Gandhi, Sucheta Kripalani, Vijaya Lakshmi Pandit, Kalpana Chawala, Mother Teresa, Mata Anandmayee, Pratibha Patil, etc. Simultaneously, there are many who worked for the education, enlightenment empowerment and emancipation of entire womankind. Swami Vivekanand went to "the extent that the mother first and the mother last" and salutes them for the future of humanity as:

> Salutations again and again to the Devi [Mother]
> Who abides in all beings in the form of Mother.

While Sri Aurobindo says:

> The Mother is the consciousness and force of the Divine or it may be said, She is the Divine in its consciousness—forces. The Ishwara as Lord of the cosmos comes out of the Mother who takes Her place besides Him as the cosmic Shakti, the cosmic Ishwara is one aspect of the Divine.

Thus, there is some essence when Prof. Rangaswamy Aiyangar gives his views on the status and condition of women in Indian society in general at the time of Manu:

> The idea of the perpetual tutelage of the Indian woman is a myth. It is contradicted by the large freedom enjoyed by the wife in the management of the household, in the wife's concurrence being necessary for all gifts by the

husband, in their enjoying rights of separate property and by the rule that family estate should not be partitioned between the sons during the life-time of the widowed mother.[22]

On the basis of our above discussion, it is apparent that women in the Ancient Indian society, mythology, history, literature and art enjoyed sufficient freedom (and still do), which shows the presence of Feminist values in the Indian Myth, History and literature, even though, there was no work like 'Feminism' or any such term.

II

Since time immemorial, women have protested against the limitations imposed on their lives by men through social, political and religious institutions, irrespective of continents and countries. Even in Europe, its fervour and example can be found in the fifth century A.D., when Hypatia, an influential Roman scholar, sought a reawakening of female dignity and power, while in the fifteenth century A.D. Christine de Pisan chronicled the achievements of women of that time and promoted a kind of feminist debate across Europe on women's equality; and in the seventeenth century, Anna van Schuman, a Dutch woman, wrote books in support of women's education. This feminist approach is further boosted by American and French revolutions for "equality, liberty and fraternity", as well as by the books of the British scholars like Mary Wollstonecraft *A Vindication of the Rights of Woman* (1792), John Stuart Mill's *The Subjection of Women* (1869), and the American Margaret Fuller's *Woman in the Nineteenth Century* (1845). The first wave of modern prototype of feminism started on 19th July 1829 at the Seneca Falls, New York with 100 women and men convention, where Elizabeth Cady Stanton and Lucretia Mott who threw down the gauntlet for women's suffrage, which was later joined by a feminist Susan. B. Anthony. Their dreams turned into actuality long after their deaths, when women won the right to vote in the United States in 1920; But, the term *Feminism* came into existence in the year 1872, thanks to the French dramatist Alexanddr Dumas, who coined it for the first time, later interpreted, re-interpreted and defined by various scholars and books with the passage of time but with one core issue that, women must enjoy and possess the same right, power and opportunity that men have, therefore, "a feminist recognizes the partiality in the phallocentric principles, ideologies and social structure of life and raises a voice of protest against it. While for the woman of the third world, feminism means a rebellion wherein she struggles to achieve a racial, social, economical and spiritual equality with man".[23] We quote below a few definitions of "Feminism" "Women's Lib or Liberation" by eminent authorities on the subject.

According to H.W. Fowler, "Feminism should mean faith in women, advocacy of the rights of women, the prevalence of female influence".[24] In *Oxford Advanced Learner's Dictionary* it has been mentioned as a "belief in the principle that women should have the same rights and opportunities (legal, political, social, economic, etc.) as men"[25] and about Women's Liberation it defines as the "freedom of women to enjoy the same social and economical rights as men"[26] by legislation and by changing people's attitudes towards womankind. *Pears Cyclopaedia* writes about it: "Feminism is an expression which emerged in the mid 19th century. It is an international movement (there was, for example, a feminist congress in Paris in 1890), which aimed at ending female inequality in male-dominated societies".[27] *The Columbia Encyclopaedia* gives a very good account of feminism along with its root cause of origin:

> "Feminism, in general, the movement for the political social, and educational equality of women with men. It had its roots in the humanism of the 18th century and in the Industrial Revolution, both of which contributed to the emergence of society from a feudal aristocracy to an industrial democracy. Women had been regarded as inferior to men physically and intellectually; their minds were assumed to be unfit for much learning. Both law and theology had ordered their subjection. Women could not in their own names posses property, engage in business, or control the disposal of their children or even

> of their own persons" this is why "Little by little, women's demands for higher education, entrance into all trades and professions, married women's property and other rights, and the right to vote were conceded".[28]

The New Encyclopaedia Britannica elucidates feminism or women's liberation as "Women's liberation movement, also called Feminist Movement, social movement that seeks equal rights for women, giving them equal status with men and freedom to decide their own carriers and life patterns",[29] therefore, "the women's liberation movement meets resistance among women and men in various societies".[30] The Merit Students Encyclopaedia expresses the same thing about Feminism and Women's Liberation Movements. "Feminism, the belief that women should have political, social, and economic equality with men. Feminism advocated equality between the sexes in political and legal rights, in social status and mobility, and in opportunities for education and employment".[31] Even if "feminism long achieved practical expression in the United States and Europe in the struggles to secure the vote for women",[32] yet the "origins of Feminism. Demands for equality between women and men have been a continual theme in American and French revolutions fostered demands for equal rights and justified rebellion".[33] It's further stimulated by the increasing numbers of mechanised factory industries in the United States and European countries during the 19th century as it deprived women of all honourable facilities (money, work, freedom, self-esteem) and reduced them to merely maintaining the home as a dependent person on their male counterparts. This is why, this encyclopaedia defines "Women's movements, as organized struggle by women for equality between the sexes inspired by feminism",[34] which is nothing but the belief that:

> Women should have political, social, and economic equality with men. Feminists have sought equal legal rights, voting rights, and access to political office for women. They have demanded that women enjoy an equal social status and have an equal access to public facilities, schools, and private organizations. They have

> fought to give women equal opportunities for jobs, pay, and promotions.[35]

In the eyes of J.A. Cuddon, feminism and feminist criticism is nothing but a retaliatory reaction against men by dissatisfied women for their demand of equality, esteem, economic self-dependency, education, empowerment and freedom, etc., as the following remark brings it out:

> It questions the long-standing, dominant, male, phallocentric ideologies (which add up to a kind of male conspiracy), patriarchal attitudes and male interpretations in literature (and critical evaluation of literature). It attacks male notions of value in literature—by offering critiques of male authors and representations of men in literature and also by privileging women writers. In addition it challenges traditional and accepted male ideas about the nature of women and about how women feel, act and think, or are supposed to feel, act and think, and how in general they respond to life and living. It thus questions numerous prejudices and assumptions about women made by male writers, not least any tendency to cast women in stock character roles.[36]

On the other hand, M.H. Abrams pinpoints the root cause of modern feminism, which started in 1969. It is nothing but male and male dominated society, myths, ideas especially ideas about women, jobs, acts, culture and civilization against which it's existing. With the help of three illustrations, he clears everything about Feminism, Feminist writing and Feminist criticism as given below:

> (1) The Western civilization is pervasively patriarchal (ruled by the father)—that is, it is male-centered and controlled, and is organized and conducted in such a way as to subordinate women to men in all cultural domains: familial, religious, political, economic, social, legal, and artistic. From the Hebrew Bible and Greek Philosophy to the present, the female tends to be defined by negative reference to the male as the human norm, hence, Women themselves are taught,

in the process of their being socialized, to internalise the reigning patriarchal ideology, and so are conditioned to derogate their own sex and to cooperate in their own subordination.

(2) It is widely held that while one's sex is determined by anatomy, the prevailing concepts of gender. As Simone de Beauvoir put it, "One is not born, but rather becomes a woman. It is civilization as a whole that produces this creature which is described as feminine". In this way, the masculine in our culture has come to be identified as active, dominating, adventurous, rational creative; the feminine, by systematic opposition to such traits, has come to be identified as passive, acquiescent, timid, emotional, and conventional.

(3) The patriarchal ideology pervades those writings which have been considered great literature written by men for men, focus on male protagonists—Oedipus, Ulysses, Hamlet, Tom Jones, Captain Ahab, Huck Finn.[37]

Thus, according to M.H. Abrams, 'Feminism' is the product of male prejudices against women to dominate them in every sphere of life, therefore, women adopted "Feminism" and "Feminist Criticism" as a tool to "do justice to female points of views, concerns, and values"[38] by changing men's attitudes and approaches towards women through the technique of "Gynocriticism, a criticism which concerns itself with developing a specifically female framework for dealing with works written by women, in all aspects of their production, motivation, analysis, and interpretation, and in all literary forms, including journals and letters"[39] so that others (men) may understand them (women) better.

Judith Harlan writing about feminism demands "political, economic, and social equality for women"[40] in family and society, and therefore, in her opinion, "the core of feminism seems to envision a world of acceptance and respect for all"[41] irrespective of gender, because, "Feminists envision a world where status is accorded to those females and males who offer something to the world rather being based on a rigid hierarchy of gender, race, religion, or class. Feminists today search for *and* instead of *either/or*".[42] While, Alice Jardine theory is that "Feminism is a movement from the point of view of, by and for women".[43]

There are some Indian writers also who have their perceptions about feminism like T.N. Singh, who believes "Feminism [is] a fictional strategy forged by writers in accordance with the pressures and challenges to which they have been subject, for projecting a feminist view of life and its problems",[44] but Chaman Nahal defines feminism "as a mode of existence in which the woman is free of the dependence syndrome"[45] because she has to rely upon somebody (specially on men such as: husband, father, brother, son, community, religious group, ethnic group etc.), to meet her demands. On the other hand, Sushila Singh considers feminism a holistic, anti-militaristic and life-affirming philosophy embellished with a moral vision. She writes about it as "Feminism is committed to be struggle for equality for women, an effort to make women become *like* men. But, the struggle for equal rights historically and politically emphasizes the *value* of women *as they are*. The very argument rests precisely on the fact that woman is *already* as valuable as men".[46] Further, she assures that "the present-day feminist though seeks to destroy masculinist hierarchy but not sexual dualism, therefore, it is necessarily pro-woman, but this does not mean that it has to be anti-man".[47] So, eventually it may be concluded that, the "feminism emerges as a concept that can encompass both an ideology and movement for socio-political change based on a critical analysis of male privilege and women's subordination within any given society".[48]

M.K. Bhatnagar says, "feminism in the Indian context is a by-product of the Western liberalism in general and feminist thought in particular"[49] and "in literary terms it precipitates in a search for identity and a quest for the definition of the self",[50] but the main issue of its persuasion are the same as

Western: "male chauvinism, sexist bias, psychological and even physical exploitation, hegemonistic inclinations in not merely the male but also the female senctions of society, the utter disregard for the female's psychological, cultural, familial and spiritual quest".[51]

On the basis of the above comments of various scholars, we can conclude that Feminism or Woman's Liberation is a movement started and supported by women and men known as Feminist against men and their patriarchal society, economics, socio-political and administrative systems, norms, traditions, customs, religions, laws and environment which have the least regard for entire womankind, its feeling and honour except as a paltry thing of luxury and exploitation due to their (men's) malignant, malevolent, male chauvinist and prejudiced attitude towards women, to whom they never considered as *Human beings*, for this reason the feminists demand for equality, esteem power and identity with men through education, enlightenment, economical self dependency, socio-political changes in society, unity, and self-realization which will empower them enough to emancipate themselves from their slavish, inhumane and inhuman condition of (present) life, so that they may one day achieve their (women) long cherished golden goal of their fantastic dream world, which will be devoid of any kind of any man's discrimination.

The second phase of feminism started in the late 1960's, particularly in 1969 by middle class women in America and Europe for equality, empowerment liberty, and emancipation of womankind, with a feeling of unity and sisterhood among them. This resurgence was in part stimulated by the American Betty Friedan's *The Feminine Mystique* (1963), A London based woman writer Doris Lessing's *The Golden Notebook* (1962) and the French writer Simone de Beauvoir's *Le Deuxieme Sexe* (1949); *The Second Sex* (1953) which served as a milestone in the field of feminism and raised feminist consciousness worldwide by appealing to the idea that **liberation for women was liberation for men too.** There are many other writers and their writings, which boosted and supported the Feminist Movement. A few of them are as:

Havelock Ellis's *Man and Woman* (1894); Havelock Gilman's *Women and Economics* (1908); Katharine Anthony's *Feminism in Germany and Scandinavia* (1915); Virginia Woolf's *A Room of One's Own* (1929); Mary Beard's *On Understanding Women* (1931); Winifred Holthy's *Women and a Changing World* (1935); Eleanor Flexner's *Century of Struggle: the Women's Rights Movement in the United States* (1959); Jo Freeman's *The Politics of Women's Liberation* (McKay, 1975); Alice S. Rossi's *The Feminist Papers: From Adams to Beauvoir* (Bantam, 1974); Miriam Gurko's *The Ladies of Seneca Falls: The Birth of the Woman's Right Movement* (Macmillan, 1974); Aileen S. Kraditor's *Ideas of the Woman Suffrage Movement, 1890-1920* (Doubleday, 1971); Robin Morgan's *Sisterhood is Powerful: An Anthology of Writings From the Women's Liberation Movement* (Random, 1970); Olivia Coolidge's *Women's Rights: The Suffrage Movement in America, 1848-1920* (Dutton, 1966); Dorothy Richardson's novel *Pilgrimage* in twelve volumes (1915-1967); Mary Ellman's *Thinking About Women* (1968); Kate Millett's *Sexual Politics* (1969); Sandra Gilbert and Susan Gubar's *The Madwoman in the Attic: The Woman Writer and the Nineteenth Century Imagination* (1979); Toril Moi's *Modern Literary Theory* (1982, ed. by Jefferson and Robey); Charlotte Bronte's *Jane Eyre* (1847) in which the protagonist Bertha Rochester in some sense the author's double, an image of her own anxiety and rage. Elaine Showalter's *A Literature of Their Own: British Women Novelists from Bronte to Lessing* (1977), she is also known as the mother of "gynocriticism"; other noteworthy works are Patricia Meyer Spacks's *The Female Imagination* (1975); Ellen Moers's *Literary Women* (1976); Toril Moi's *Sexual/Textual Politics: Feminist Literary Theory* (1985); Juliet Mitchell's *Phychoanalysis and Feminism* (1975); Helen Cixous's *The Laugh of the Medusa* (1976); Judith Fetterly's *The Resisting Reader* (1978); Shulamith Firestone's *The Dialectic of Sex* (1979); Mary Jacobus's *Women Writing and Writing about Women* (1979); Ginet-McConnell, Borker and Furman's *Women and Language in Literature and Society* (1980); Adrienne Rich's *On Lies, Secrets, and Silence: Selected Prose* (1980); Michele Barrett's *Women's Oppression Today:*

Problems in Marxist Feminist Analysis (1980); Ellaine Marks and Isabelle de Courtivron's "*New French Feminisms: An Anthology*" (1981); Elezabeth Able's *Writing and Sexual Difference* (1982); Hester Eisentein's *Contemporary Feminist Thought* (1984); Mary Eagleton's *The New Feminist Criticism: Essays on Women, Literature and Theory: A Reader* (1986); Linda Kauffman's *Gender and Theory: Dialogues in Feminist Criticism* (1989); Judith Harlan's *Feminism: A Reference Handbook* (1998, Calfornia).

There are many Indian novelists who may be treated as Indian feminists because in their works, they have tried their best to raise the issue of feminism symbolically, so that the reader may come to know about women's feelings, demands, desires, dissatisfactions, cause of her anguish, etc. Here are some writers and their works: Jyotsna Bhattacharya's *Shadows in the Sunshine* (1966); Santa and Sita Chatterjee's *Tales of Bengal* (1992), *The Garden Creeper* (translated by Sita Devi in 1931); Sita Chatterjee's *The Knight Errant, The Cage of Gold* (1923); Venu Chitale's *In Transit* (1950) Nargis Dalal's *Minari* (1967); Raj Lakshmi Debi's *The Hindu Wife; or the Enchanted Fruits* (1876); Swarna Kumari Debi (Mrs. Ghoshal's) *An Unfinished Song* (1968); *The Fatal Garland* (1915); Anita Desai's *Cry the Peacock* (1968); *Voices in the City* (1965); *Bye-Bye, Blackbird* (1971); *Journey to Ithaca*; *Where Shall We Go This Summer* (1975); *Fire on the Mountain* (1977); *Clear Light of Day* (1980); *Fasting, Fisting* (1999); Toru Dutt's *Binaca*; or *The Young Spanish Malden* (1878); Sunity Devee's *The Beautiful Mogul Princess* (1988); Attia Hosain's *Phonix Fled, and Other Stories* (1953) *Sunlight on a Broken Column* (1961); Iqbalunnisa Husain's *Purdah and Polygamy: Life in an Indian Muslim Household* (1944); Ruth Prawer Jhabvala's *To Whom She Will* (1955); *The Nature of Passion* (1956); *Esmond in India* (1958); *The Householder* (1960); *Get Ready for Battle* (1962); *Like Birds, Like Fishes* (1963); *A backward Place* (1965); *A Stronger Climate* (1968); *A New Dominion* (1972); *Heat and Dust* (1975); Venna Paintal's *Serenity in Storm* (1966); Pushpa Kapur's *Rajni*; Vimla Kapur's *Life Goes on* (1946); Kamala Markandaya's *Nectar in a Sieve* (1954);

Some Inner Fury (1957); *A Silence of Desire* (1961); *Possession* (1963); *A Handful of Rice* (1966); *The Coffer Dams* (1969); *The Nowhere Man* (1973); *Two Virgins* (1974); *The Golden Honeycomb* (1977); *Pleasure City* (1982); Amrita Pritam's *Doctor Dev* (1968); Nayantara Sahgal's *A Time to be Happy* (1957); *This Time of Morning* (1965); *Storm In Chandigarh* (1969); *The Day in Shadow* (1971); *A Situation in New Delhi* (1977); *Rich Like Us* (1983); Shashi Deshpande's *The Dark has No Terrors* (1980); *Come Up and be Dead* (1983); Rama Mehta's *Inside the Haveli* (1977); Arundhati Roy's *The God of Small Things* (1997); Namita Gokhale's *Paro: Dreams of Passion* (1984); Amita Nair's *The Better* Man, *Mistress*; Manju Kapoor's *Difficult Daughter,* (1998); Deepa Shah's *The Solitude of Surabhi* (1997); *Rebirth,* (1999); Githa Hariharan's *The Thousand Faces* (1992); Belinder Dhanoa's *Waiting for Winter* (1991) and many more like Santha Rama Rau, Geeta Mehta, Bharati Mukherjee, Mahasweta Devi, have left their indelible imprint on the readers of Indian fiction in English and on the Time's sand.

All these Indian women novelists have portrayed different aspects of Indian women in their novels. With changing times, the Indian women have also changed. We notice that she is no more a silent suffering creature, as she was in the past. Now she asserts herself and demands 'space' for her, which is largely because of education and economic independence. These novels present a panorama of the Indian women, in the new India's vista.

NOTES

1. Dr. T.S. Devadoss, "Indian Woman Through the Ages" in the *Encyclopaedia of Women in India* edited by B.K. Vashista (New Delhi: Praveen Encyclopaedia Publications, 1976), p.18.
2. Quoted in the *Employment News Weekly,* Vol. XXVI. No. 48. (New Delhi: Ministry of I&B, R.K. Puram, 2-8 March 2002), p. 1.
3. *Rig-Veda*, X. 85.
4. *Ibid.*, 46.
5. *Ibid.* 26, 27.
6. *Ibid.*, V.61.6.
7. *Atharva-Veda, I* the XIV. 1-43.

8. *Ibid.*, p. 44.
9. *Yajur-Veda*, 1:82.
10. *Atharva-Veda* XIV, 5:18.
11. *Aitereya Brahamana*, I: 25.
12. *Brhadaranyaka-Upanishad*, I, 4: 17.
13. *Ramayana*, VI, 114, 14-17.
14. *Manu*, ix, 26.
15. *Manu*, 3, 56.
16. *Ibid.*, 3. 57, 58.
17. *Manu*, ix, 45.
18. *Manu*, V, 130.
19. *Kautilya, Arthasastra*, pp. 158-159.
20. *Kumara-sambhava*, 6. 63.
21. *Mahabharata*, 13. 11. 14.
22. R. Aiyanger, *Aspects of the Social and Political System of the Manusmriti*, p. 164.
23. Sanjay Kumar, "Two Aspects of Feminism: The expressive and the Explosive in Shobha De", in Jaydipsinh Dodiya's *The Fiction of Shobha De: Critical Study* (New Delhi: Prestige Books, 2000), p. 51.
24. H.W. Fowler's *A Dictionary of Modern English Usage* (New York: Oxford University Press, 1988), p. 196. Second Edition revised by Sir Ernest Gower.
25. A.P. Cowie, ed., *Oxford Advanced Learner's Dictionary* (Calcutta: Oxford University Press), p. 447.
26. *Ibid.*, p. 1470.
27. Dr. Chris Cook, ed., *Pears Cyclopaedia 2001-2002* (London: Penguin Books Ltd., 2001), p. 20.
28. William Bridgwater and Seymourkurtz, ed., *Columbia Encyclopaedia*, (New York: Columbia University. U.S.A., 1963-64), p. 706.
29. Robert P. Gwinn ed., *The New Encyclopaedia Britannica*, Vol. 12 (Micropaedia) (Chicago, USA, 1985), p. 733.
30. *Ibid.*
31. William D. Halsey and Emanuel Friedman ed., *Merit Students Encyclopaedia,* (Vol. VI) (New York: Macmillan Educational Company, U.S.A., 1985), p. 589.
32. *Ibid.*
33. *Ibid.*, Vol. XIX (19), p. 538.
34. *Ibid.*
35. *Ibid.*

36. J.A. Cuddon's, *A Dictionary of Literary Terms and Literary Theory* (Fourth Edition) (Malden Massachusetts: Black Well Publishers, USA, 2000), p. 315.
37. M.H. Abrams, *A Glossary of Literary Terms* (6th edition) (Bangalore: Prism Books Pvt. Ltd., 1993), pp. 234-35.
38. *Ibid.*, p. 235.
39. *Ibid.*, p. 236.
40. Judith Harlan's *Feminism: A Reference Handbook* (California, USA: ABC—CLIO, Inc. Santa Barbara, 1998), p. 73.
41. *Ibid.*, p. 13.
42. *Ibid.*, p. 14.
43. Alice Jardine's *Gynesis: Configurations of Women and Modernity* (Ithaca: Cornell University Press, 1986), p. 15.
44. T.N. Singh, "Feminism and Fiction: Some Reflections" in Prof. Shushila Singh's *Feminism and Recent Fiction in English* (New Delhi: Prestige Books, 1991), p. 11.
45. Chaman Nahal, "Feminism in English Fiction: Forms and Variations" in *Feminism and Recent Fiction in English*, p. 17.
46. Sushila Singh, "Recent Trends in Feminist Thought: A Tour de Hoirizon", in *Feminism and Recent Fiction in English*, p. 23.
47. *Ibid.*, p. 29.
48. Karen Offen, *Defining Feminism: A comparative Historical Approach*, Signs, 14:1 (Autumn 1988), p. 151.
49. M.K. Bhatnagar, "Feminist English Literature—An Introduction" in Manmohan K. Bhatnagar's *Feminist English Literature* (New Delhi: Atlantic Publishers, 1999), p. 1.
50. *Ibid.*, p. 2.
51. *Ibid.*

Epilogue

STATUS OF WOMAN IN INDIA

(According to Hindu scriptures)

(A GLANCE)

One can take the help of two extracts of Jewish Indian poet Nissim Ezekiel. The first one from "Night of Scorpian" to acquaint us with the genuine motherly sentiments of the womankind in our sub-continent. The lines go like this:

> Here it is again
> In colour or in stone,
> Not the whole woman
> But her, 'torso'
> Arms cut off
> Just below the shoulders,
> Legs cut off
> Just below the knees,
> Unperturbed, for art's make
> I hate it,

The above lines reflect that in India, nowdays, a woman is seen as a beautiful pulp and piece of flesh, which is a perfect prey for lustrous eyes of cultured-vultured men, who have cupidity for each and everything by hook or crook. Why women are practically facing such problem? Simply because they have neither the economical base of their own nor have their own identity. So, they need work, economic individualism and identity and independence of their own to get honour in the patriarchal society. This solution is very well given by the poet through symbols in the last two lines of the poem.

The woman plainly needs
Her common arms and legs.

This article aims at the paradoxical condition of Indian (Hindu) women in theory and literature versus practical life. Theoretically, she is applaused as the supreme power of the comos, which highlights the virtuous and vital services for the entire mankind that she plays as a mother, grandmother, sister, wife and daughter-in-law in the family, therefore, she is by men as:

Ya devi sarva bhootesu shaktirupena sanshita.
Namastasyai namastasyai namastasyai namo namah.

We salute several times the greatest Goddess for she is the soul of all creatures and provides them power, energy, wisdom and motivation to commence and complete their respective and regular work. This signifies the higher status of the womankind in the human society; but, it is only in imagination and in hymns. On the contrary there is no honour and esteem for her in the practical field. Goswamy Tulsidas has severly criticized women in his book "Daohavalee". The harsh severities of a waman's life in our society and literature are as:-

Kama kraodha laobhadi mada prabala moah kai dhari.
Tinh mahan ati darun dukhad mayarupee nari..

(Lust, luxury, lure, ego, anger, intoxication, whim and attachment have a strong army; but, a woman is the concrete form of mirage and illusion (MAYA) for she is the root cause of terrific and horrible pain for man. She is so because:

Janampatrika barati kae dekhahu manahin bechari.
Darun baeri mychu ke bycha birajati nari..

(If we consider a man's horoscope and ponder over it, then we will find a woman's place in it between a cruel enemy and death; for, out of twelve blocks of the horoscope the sixth one is for enemy and eighth is for death, while the seventh is for the wife, moreover, in the world many kinds of enmities take place at personal and non-personal level, which finally lead the mankind either to conflict or the worst death, but never to peace, harmony and friendship, except wife / a woman.) Thus, according to Tulsidas a woman has only one shelter for her refuse, and it is in the feet of her husband. He says with much emphasis:

Sahaj apavani nari pati sevat subha gayi lahai.
Jasu gavat shruti chari ajahun tulasika harihi priya...

(A woman is impure since her birth, but by serving her husband, she gets her dignified and divine goal, ultimately and without any effort. For instance, the honour of Pavitra Vrinda is sung by the four Vedas, and still she is revered and worshiped as the beloved of the Lord Hari, in the form of Tulsi.) So, a woman becomes a thing of property, practically against all elevated hymns and hypothesizes.

Now we may come to the ancient Holy Hindu scriptures, which is our main topic of discussion; but let us know what is Hinduism or Sanatan Dharma. According to Manu it is some what;

Satyam brooyaatam priyam brooyaanna bruyaatam satyampriyamam
Priyam cha naanratam bruoyaadesa Dharmah sanaatanah...

(Speak truth, speak politely; but never harsh and unplatable truth, also prohibit from those likeable things which are not true. It is the Sanaatan Dharma.)

In the "Shaantiparva" of *Mahabharat*, Dharma in the perspective of religion has been explained as:

Aasti satyam paro dharmos nanratatam patakum paramum.
Sthitihri satyam dharmasya tasmatam satyam na laopyaetam.

(There is no duty or religion greater than truth and there is no sin greater the falsehood. Duty or religion survives and progresses basically on the basis of truth, therefore, never try to conceal the truth in any condition or circumstances.)

Like this, truth has always been applauded by eminent erudits such as Kabir, Chaankyaa, Tulsidas, etc., as true and main religion of the Hindus, the human. Scholars like manu also support and propound elevated and enlightened theory, such as:

Abhiwadansheelasya nityam bridhaopasewinab.
Chatwari tasya wardhantae sayurwidhya yashao balamam.

(The person who regularly salutes and adores and serves the old aged and elders is always benefited by age, knowledge, fame and power.)

The above mentioned ideals are refined, rational and good but what is the down to earth condition of a woman. It is simply opposite, practically poor, rationally cruel and emotionally harsh. In the case of womankind it is the worst, for, a woman is rarely rewarded, praised either by man (husband/boy), family, society or office for her benign grace, sensitive service and selfless sacrifice; but on the contrary to her esteemed duty, devotion and dextrous work she is ruthlessly exploited by men emotionally, economically, physically, simply due to her innocence, blindfaith, ignorance and dependence (social & economical) in the name of safety, honour, opportunity and identity. They rarely get any type of affection and attention. In childhood they are discriminated by their own parents. Their freedom is choked off. They are chocked a block with heavy domestic duties to continue their education, which is key to everything. Moreover, since birth a girl child becomes an unwanted burden for her parents till they do not get her off by marring her somewhere. In youth, a girl is face to face with some new problems, for instance: (a) her honour is always at the verge of risk. They are many poisonous philanderes who see her body as a temple of their desire to fulfil and play the game of their lust. Their saintly nature is only a matter of chance. (b) There are many eve-teasers who make a girl's life too difficult. After her marriage, a woman or girl becomes trapped creature, even when that increases the fortune of the family by dowry and gifts. She serves her husband's family like an unpaid, bonded labourer for which she is praised by none. (c) In later phase she has to face many tortures by her ownkind: her mother-in-law and sister-in-laws. She is dishonoured, bitten, exploited, butchered and burned savagely in some cases. Why? Just to show superiority. Basically, man is an egoist and possessive in nature, and to fulfil his ego he talks of high ideals simply for shake of pompous conversations and ideals, while in reality he behaves more beastly then the best beast, especially against women and children. Moreover, he gives code of conduct for both forgetting his ownself.

Now, here the question arises, what is the use of impracticable and lofty comments? If men can not keep their own character and conscience within their control. Even more issuing laws for her, as we find in different holy Hindu scriptures.

> *Vaewahikao vidhih streenam sanskarao vaedicah smratah.*
> *Patisewa gurau wasao griharthaosgniparikriyaa.*

(*Manusmrit*: 2/67)

(A married man must do all his works in the company of his wife to get it fruitful; because a woman's matrimonial ceremony is her (Holy sacrament) Vedic ceremony. For her, husband's service is just like getting education and domestic works are her purification (agni ki paricharyaa).

> *Yatra Naryastu pujyante ramante tatra dewatah*
> *Yatraustu na poojayante sarwastraaphalash kriyaah..*

(Manu; 3/56)

(Angles live there where woman are honoured and in reverse case each work is spoiled in futile.) According to Vidur ji; a woman is:

> *Poojaneeyaa mahabhagah punyascha grihadeeptayah.*
> *Striya;skriyao grihasyaoktastasmaadam rashyaa vishestah.*

(*Mahabharat, Udhyoga Parva*; 39/11)

(The woman who maintains her home pure, perfect and pleasant is worthy to be revered, for, this type of woman is said to be the goddess of fortune (*Laxmi*), therefore, she must be (or women like these must be) protected with utmost precations. In the 'Bramah-khanda' of the *Shri Sakandapurna* the religious significance of the married women or woman spouse is well expressed in the sloka (7/64) as:

Bbarya moolam grihasthasya, bharya moolam sukhasya cha.
Bharya dharmaphalayaeva bharya santaanvreahayae..

(Women are the real basis of all worldly and celestial works, therefore, they must be respected. In a family life she is the house wife, which is its main pivot; moreover, she is the epicenter of all kinds of homely bliss. She is the prime person in the family for all kinds of noble deeds and their rewards. Along with it, it is she who increases the numbers of her family members by her selfless love, service and sacrifice.)

Regarding the pure, divinely and motherly power, even Lord Shri Krishna has said in *Bramahwaewarta Puran's* couplet number: (83/123)

Prithivyam yani teerthani sateepadesu tanyapi.
Tejaashcha sarvadewanam muneenam cha satiesu cha.

(All sorts of pilgrims on this surface of the earth are collectively congregated and present in the holy feel of the sanctimonious woman. The glorious and prowess power of all angles/gods and sages are present I sacred figure of a refined woman.) But, in the practical life we find the paradoxical condition. She is not given proper opportunity for her education, inspite of the fact that;

Mata shatruh pita waeri yen balao na pathitah.
Na shaobhate sabhamdhye lansamadhye wakao yatha.

(Chankya is *Chaankya Neeti*, 2/11)

(Those parents are like enemy of their own children who did not educate them (girls), for they will prove unworthy and unfit for the human society just like that of the crane in the mid of the swams and a dumb-fool in the mid of the eminent erudites.) Nearly the same thing has been asserted by the great Indian sage Bharthariji in the sixteenth sloka of his *Nitishatakam*:

Vidhya nam narasya rupamadhikam prachchhannaguptam dhanam
Vidhya bhogakari yashah sudhakary vidhya gurunam guru

Vidhya bandhujanao videshagamans vidhya paraa dewata
Vidhya rajasu poojayate na hi dhanam vidhyawihyanah pashuh.

(The real essence of humanity and all monetary-cum-material properties of any human body and soul are hidden in his education and technological skills, for education is the prime resource for all kind of services, fames and luxuries, therefore, it is Guru's Guru. In abroad, it is like kith and kin, it is accepted and applauded by both crown and crowd, therefore it is the greatest God; but not the money. So, the individual who is illiterate and uneducated is the least better than an animal). Despite above mentioned virtuous of education, which makes anybody virtuoso in the desired field girls are imparted education with jaundiced eyes and the least jocundity. In addition to it their freedom is too curtailed in the name of security, even though, in the matter of education, service, identity and decision making; because there is no provision of freedom for them. Regarding it, Shri Yajawalkya ji says:

Rakshetam kanyam pita winna patih putrastu vardhake.
Abhave jyatayastesam na swatantryam kwachitam striyah.

(Prior to marriage, a girl should be protected by her father, after marriage she should be protected by her husband, in old age by her children and in absence of all by the relatives; because there is no rule and regulation for her liberty, equality and opportunity.) Why it is so? The simplest answer is given by Manu in the *Manusmriti's* couplet no. 9/7 as:

Swam prasootim charitram cha kulamatmanameva cha.
Swam cha dharmam prayatnena jayam rashkanam hi rakhati.

(A husband must protect her wife deliberately so that he may keep himself clean (with character) save his family's honour and can get his true offspring. Thus, he is able to save himself and his own religion). But the irony is that there is no question or limitation on male spouse's role and character as well as about its impact.

Finally, woman has to do nothing for her honour, earnings, identity equality, opportunity, liberty, education, enlightenment and ambitions except to surrender herself to her husband's service physically, mentally, emotionally, deeply and faithfully. As regarding it in *Bramhavaevarty Purana* Lords Krishna says like this:

> *Devpooja vratam danam tapschanashnam japah.*
> *Sanam cha sarvatyrthesu dykcha sarvamakhesu cha.*
> *Pradakshinyam prathivyascha bramhanatithisevanamam.*
> *Sarvani patisevayah kalam narhanti saonashymam.*
>
> (*Bramhavaevarta*. Sri Krishna. 24/34-35)

(Devine worship/worship of gods, fasting, donation, truth, seating near, chanting of names, taking baths in various holy and religious places, experiences and education from various sacrifices, travel and tour of the entire world and service to scholars and guests all in collective way can never equal to the service of husband buy the wife with all her embellished ornamentation.) But, the irony is that men and scholars annotated and interpreted may elevated and noble couplets in their own favour, due to which the entire womankind is deprived from her noble and esteemed human status to a mere puppet for the pleasure of men. Owing to it, Indian women have to opt for the western concept of feminism, which is neither suitable to our Indian context nor in any way better than our ancient Indian concepts which honours a woman much higher than any man's honour, therefore, it was strongly and earnestly resolute in their protection for their vital role as: daughter, sister, mother, mother-in-law, etc. who plays key role in family, neighborhood and indirectly to society and nation for peace, safety and harmony. She also plays the prominent role of man's first Guru; but the same life giving divine mother also plays the role of Shakti like Durga and Kali in the time of need. It shows the importance and power as well as high status of womankind in the Indian society, which is now forgotten by men due to their acute selfishness.

How pertinent and practical is the remark of Shobhaa De that "Indian men are high in high-tec, but low in liberty"; for they can worship the picture or idol or statue of a Devi which stands still and can do nothing; but in any way they are not ready to give any true regard to a woman who serve them a lot. They are ready to sacrifice everything for the stone statue, but nothing for that who sacrifices everything for the stone statue, but nothing for that who sacrifices for them. In *Mahabharat*, it is said that a man must give honour to his wife because:

> *Balitanugrihyta cha stry srih bhawati bharat.*
> *(A woman sho gets honour and love is equal to goddess Laxmi)*

And: *striyastu manmarchanti rm nayal manavah.*
(Women are auspicious and honourable.)

Even saint Kabir has said:

> *Pativrata maelee bhalee Kalee kuchal kurup.*
> *Pativrata ke rup par, waraon kaoti surup.*
> *(A true woman is the best than the rest)*

So, in nut shell, we can say that if men can not worship; let them not; but, they must give proper and due respect to womankind in out door for their vital and virtuous role in the welfare of entire mankind, with which they are ultimately benefited and indebted indeed. Bharat Kokila Sarojani Naidu says convincingly for equality, emancipation, empowerment, education and enlightenment of womankind as:

> Does one man dare to deprive another or his birthright to God's pure air which nourishes his body? How then shall a man dare to deprive a human soul of its immemorial inheritance of liberty and life? And yet, my friends, man has so dared in the case of Indian women. That is why you men of India are today what you are: because your fathers, in depriving your mothers of that immemorial birthright, have robbed you, their sons of your just inheritance. Therefore, I charge you; restore to your women their ancient rights...

On the other hand, women can try to achieve their esteemed status by their Indian ways; service, sacrifice and education; but in no way the western, inhuman and feminist way; violence, reservation, Dharna, Pradarshan, political funda etc., for these are negative things and will further deprive them of ever their present status too. Therefore, the best way is mutual understanding, so-operation peace, harmony and humane humanity. In the words of Nissim Ezekiel, which sympathetically pleads for human balance, "humanly acquired".